ACL-2012 Special Workshop on Rediscovering 50 Years of Discoveries

Held at the 50th Annual Meeting of the Association for Computational Linguistics 2012 (ACL 2012)

Jeju Island, Korea
10 July 2012

ISBN: 978-1-62276-593-5

Printed from e-media with permission by:

Curran Associates, Inc.
57 Morehouse Lane
Red Hook, NY 12571

Some format issues inherent in the e-media version may also appear in this print version.

Printed by Curran Associates, Inc. (2012)

For permission requests, please contact the Association for Computational Linguistics at the address below.

Association for Computational Linguistics
209 N. Eighth Street
Stroudsburg, Pennsylvania 18360

Phone: 1-570-476-8006
Fax: 1-570-476-0860

acl@aclweb.org

Additional copies of this publication are available from:

Curran Associates, Inc.
57 Morehouse Lane
Red Hook, NY 12571 USA
Phone: 845-758-0400
Fax: 845-758-2634
Email: curran@proceedings.com
Web: www.proceedings.com

Preface

Fifty years of Computational Linguistics are nothing when compared to the long history of human language. However, those same fifty years of Computational Linguistics constitute a lot in terms of achievements and advances towards better understanding one of the most natural yet complex human phenomena. Fifty years of Computational Linguistics are, indeed, a lifetime of endeavours, successes and failures, but they just represent the very beginning of an interesting journey over a vast sea of undiscovered knowledge.

In this first 50th anniversary of the Association for Computational Linguistics, we just take this brief pause to review our history and project our future, to ensure that our current legacy will endure the indifference of time and that future generations can step on the shoulders of the many pioneers of this new wonderful discipline, in which language is clearly showing its reluctance to being tamed by mathematics.

Welcome to the ACL-2012 Special Workshop on Rediscovering 50 Years of Discoveries!

Rafael E. Banchs
Jeju, Korea, July 10th, 2012

Workshop Objectives

This workshop is intended to commemorate the 50th anniversary of the Association for Computational Linguistics (ACL) by creating a new space for debating and discussing about specific issues related to preserving, analysing and exploiting the scientific heritage of the ACL, as well as to envisage future trends, applications and research in Computational Linguistics.

The main objective of the workshop has been to gather contributions about the history, the evolution and the future of research in Computational Linguistics. Although the call for papers was open to any kind of technical contribution that was relevant to the main objective of the workshop, we specially encouraged the submission of research work related to the application of natural language processing and text mining techniques to the ACL Anthology Reference Corpus (ACL ARC), which is publicly available from the ACL ARC project website.

In addition to the technical program, the workshop introduces a new contributed task, in the spirit of a crowd-sourcing activity, for augmenting and improving the current status of the ACL Anthology Reference Corpus. The goal of the contributed task is to provide a high quality version of the textual content of the ACL Anthology as a corpus. Besides the more accurate text extraction, the rich text markup can be also an important source of information for corpus-based applications such as summarization, scientific discourse analysis, citation analysis, citation classification, question answering, textual entailment, taxonomy, ontology, information extraction, parsing, coreference resolution, semantic search and many more.

Acknowledgments

This special workshop has been possible thanks to the effort of many people...

Special thanks to the Steering Committee and the Contributed Task Committee for their timely advice and suggestions.

Special thanks also to all Program Committee members for their devoted work and recommendations during the peer reviewing process, as well as to Publicity and Technical Committee members for their invaluable help during the workshop planning and preparation.

Finally, and most important of all; special thanks to all authors and co-authors who had contributed with their work to put together such an interesting technical program.

Workshop Organizer:

Rafael E. Banchs, Institute for Infocomm Research (Singapore)

Steering Committee:

Steven Bird, University of Melbourne (Australia)
Robert Dale, Macquarie University (Australia)
Min Yen Kan, National University of Singapore (Singapore)
Haizhou Li, Institute for Infocomm Research (Singapore)
Dragomir Radev, University of Michigan (USA)
Ulrich Schäfer, German Research Center for Artificial Intelligence (Germany)

Contributed Task Committee:

Jonathon Read, University of Oslo (Norway)
Stephan Oepen, University of Oslo (Norway)
Ulrich Schäfer, German Research Center for Artificial Intelligence (Germany)
Tze Yuang Chong, Nanyang Technological University (Singapore)

Program Committee:

Toni Badia, Barcelona Media Innovation Centre (Spain)
Timothy Baldwin, University of Melbourne (Australia)
Sivaji Bandyopadhyay, Jadavpur University (India)
Emily M. Bender, University of Washington (USA)
Kenneth Church, Johns Hopkins University (USA)
Marta R. Costa-jussa, Barcelona Media Innovation Centre (Spain)
Iryna Gurevych, Technische Universität Darmstadt (Germany)
Carlos Henriquez, Universitat Politecnica de Catalunya (Spain)
Daniel Jurafsky, Stanford University (USA)
Min Yen Kan, National University of Singapore (Singapore)
Kevin Knight, Information Sciences Institute (USA)
Philipp Koehn, University of Edinburgh (UK)
Haizhou Li, Institute for Infocomm Research (Singapore)
Bing Liu, University of Illinois at Chicago (USA)
Yang Liu, National University of Singapore (Singapore)
Yuji Matsumoto, Nara Institute of Science and Technology (Japan)
Kathleen McKeown, Columbia University (USA)
Rada Mihalcea, University of North Texas (USA)
Hwee Tou Ng, National University of Singapore (Singapore)
Joakim Nivre, Uppsala University (Sweden)
Stephan Oepen, University of Oslo (Norway)
Dragomir Radev, University of Michigan (USA)

Jonathon Read, University of Oslo (Norway)
Paolo Rosso, Universidad Politecnica de Valencia (Spain)
Horacio Saggion, Universitat Pompeu Fabra (Spain)
Ulrich Schäfer, German Research Center for Artificial Intelligence (Germany)
Fabrizio Silvestri, Instituto di Scienza e Tecnologie dell'Informazione (Italy)
Eiichiro Sumita, National Institute of Information and Communications Technology (Japan)
Simone Teufel, University of Cambridge (UK)
Junichi Tsujii, Microsoft Research Asia (China)
Anita de Waard, Elsevier Labs (The Netherlands)
Haifeng Wang, Baidu (China)
Magdalena Wolska, Saarland University (Germany)
Deyi Xiong, Institute for Infocomm Research (Singapore)
Min Zhang, Institute for Infocomm Research (Singapore)
Ming Zhou, Microsoft Research Asia (China)

Publicity Committee:

Marta R. Costa-jussa, Barcelona Media Innovation Centre (Spain)
Seokhwan Kim, Institute for Infocomm Research (Singapore)

Technical Committee:

Ming Liu, Institute for Infocomm Research (Singapore)

Table of Contents

Special Workshop Program

Tuesday, July 10th

(11:00-12:30) Session 1: The People (ACL Session 4a)

11:00 *Rediscovering ACL Discoveries Through the Lens of ACL Anthology Network Citing Sentences*
Dragomir Radev and Amjad Abu-Jbara

11:20 *Towards a Computational History of the ACL: 1980-2008*
Ashton Anderson, Dan Jurafsky and Daniel A. McFarland

11:40 *Discovering Factions in the Computational Linguistics Community*
Yanchuan Sim, Noah A. Smith and David A. Smith

12:00 *He Said, She Said: Gender in the ACL Anthology*
Adam Vogel and Dan Jurafsky

(14:00-15:30) Session 2: The Contents (ACL Session 5a)

14:00 *Discourse Structure and Computation: Past, Present and Future*
Bonnie Webber and Aravind Joshi

14:20 *Extracting glossary sentences from scholarly articles: A comparative evaluation of pattern bootstrapping and deep analysis*
Melanie Reiplinger, Ulrich Schäfer and Magdalena Wolska

14:40 *Applying Collocation Segmentation to the ACL Anthology Reference Corpus*
Vidas Daudaravicius

15:00 *Text Reuse with ACL: (Upward) Trends*
Parth Gupta and Paolo Rosso

Tuesday, July 10th (continued)

(16:00-17:30) Session 3: The Anthology (ACL Session 6a)

Rediscovering ACL Discoveries Through the Lens of ACL Anthology Network Citing Sentences

Dragomir Radev
EECS Department
University of Michigan
Ann Arbor, MI, USA
radev@umich.edu

Amjad Abu-Jbara
EECS Department
University of Michigan
Ann Arbor, MI, USA
amjbara@umich.edu

Abstract

The ACL Anthology Network (AAN)[1] is a comprehensive manually curated networked database of citations and collaborations in the field of Computational Linguistics. Each citation edge in AAN is associated with one or more citing sentences. A citing sentence is one that appears in a scientific article and contains an explicit reference to another article. In this paper, we shed the light on the usefulness of AAN citing sentences for understanding research trends and summarizing previous discoveries and contributions. We also propose and motivate several different uses and applications of citing sentences.

1 Introduction

The ACL Anthology[2] is one of the most successful initiatives of the Association for Computational Linguistics (ACL). It was initiated by Steven Bird in 2001 and is now maintained by Min-Yen Kan. It includes all papers published by ACL and related organizations as well as the Computational Linguistics journal over a period of four decades.

The ACL Anthology Network (AAN) is another successful initiative built on top of the ACL Anthology. It was started in 2007 by our group (Radev et al., 2009) at the University of Michigan. AAN provides citation and collaboration networks of the articles included in the ACL Anthology (excluding book reviews). AAN also includes rankings of papers and authors based on their centrality statistics in the citation and collaboration networks. It also includes the citing sentences associated with each citation link. These sentences were extracted automatically using pattern matching and then cleaned manually. Table 1 shows some statistics of the current release of AAN.

The text surrounding citations in scientific publications has been studied and used in previous work. Nanba and Okumura (1999) used the term *citing area* to refer to citing sentences. They define the *citing area* as the succession of sentences that appear around the location of a given reference in a scientific paper and has connection to it. They proposed a rule-based algorithm to identify the *citing area* of a given reference. In (Nanba et al., 2000) they use their citing area identification algorithm to identify the purpose of citation (i.e. the author's reason for citing a given paper.)

Nakov et al. (2004) use the term *citances* to refer to citing sentences. They explored several different uses of *citances* including the creation of training and testing data for semantic analysis, synonym set creation, database curation, summarization, and information retrieval.

Other previous studies have used citing sentences in various applications such as: scientific paper summarization (Elkiss et al., 2008; Qazvinian and Radev, 2008; Mei and Zhai, 2008; Qazvinian et al., 2010; Qazvinian and Radev, 2010; Abu-Jbara and Radev, 2011a), automatic survey generation (Nanba et al., 2000; Mohammad et al., 2009), and citation function classification (Nanba et al., 2000; Teufel et al., 2006; Siddharthan and Teufel, 2007; Teufel, 2007).

[1] http://clair.si.umich.edu/anthology/
[2] http://www.aclweb.org/anthology-new/

Number of papers	18,290
Number of authors	14,799
Number of venues	341
Number of paper citations	84,237
Citation network diameter	22
Collaboration network diameter	15
Number of citing sentences	77,753

Table 1: Statistics of AAN 2011 release

Comparison	Contrast/Comparison in Results, Method, or Goals
Basis	Author uses cited work as basis or starting point
Use	Author uses tools, algorithms, data, or definitions
Description	Neutral description of cited work
Weakness	Limitation or weakness of cited work

Table 2: Annotation scheme for citation purpose

In this paper, we focus on the usefulness of the citing sentences included in AAN. We propose several uses of citing sentences such as analyzing the trends of research, understanding the impact of research and how this impact changes over time, summarizing the contributions of a researcher, summarizing the discoveries in a certain research field, and providing high quality data for Natural Language Processing tasks. In the rest of this paper we present some of these ideas and provide examples from AAN to demonstrate their applicability. Some of these ideas have been explored in previous work, but we believe that they still need further exploration. However, most of the ideas are novel to our knowledge. We present our ideas in the following sections.

2 Temporal Analysis of Citations

The interest in studying citations stems from the fact that bibliometric measures are commonly used to estimate the impact of a researcher's work (Borgman and Furner, 2002; Luukkonen, 1992). Several previous studies have performed temporal analysis of citation links (Amblard et al., 2011; Mazloumian et al., 2011; Redner, 2005) to see how the impact of research and the relations between research topics evolve overtime. These studies focused on observing how the number of incoming citations to a given article or a set of related articles change over time. However, the number of incoming citations is often not the only factor that changes with time. We believe that analyzing the text of citing sentences allows researchers to observe the change in other dimensions such as the purpose of citation, the polarity of citations, and the research trends. The following subsections discuss some of these dimensions.

2.1 Temporal Analysis of Citation Purpose

Teufel et al. (2006) has shown that the purpose of citation can be determined by analyzing the text of citing sentences. We hypothesize that performing a temporal analysis of the purpose for citing a paper gives a better picture about its impact. As a proof of concept, we annotated all the citing sentences in AAN that cite the top 10 cited papers from the 1980's with *citation purpose* labels. The labels we used for annotation are based on Teufel et al.'s annotation scheme and are described in Table 2. We counted the number of times the paper was cited for each *purpose* in each year since its publication date. This analysis revealed interesting observations about the paper impacts. We will discuss these observations in Section 2.3. Figure 1 shows the change in the ratio of each purpose with time for Shieber's (1985) work on parsing.

2.2 Temporal Analysis of Citation Polarity

The bibliometric measures that are used to estimate the impact of research are often computed based on the number of citations it received. This number is taken as a proxy for the relevance and the quality of the published work. It, however, ignores the fact that citations do not necessarily always represent positive feedback. Many of the citations that a publication receives are neutral citations, and citations that represent negative criticism are not uncommon. To validate this intuition, we annotated about 2000 citing sentences from AAN for citation polarity. We found that only 30% of citations are positive, 4.3% are negative, and the rest are neutral. In another published study, Athar (2011) annotated 8736 citations from AAN with their polarity and found that only 10% of citations are positive, 3% are negative and the rest were all neutral. We believe that considering the polarity of citations when conducting temporal analysis of citations gives more insight about

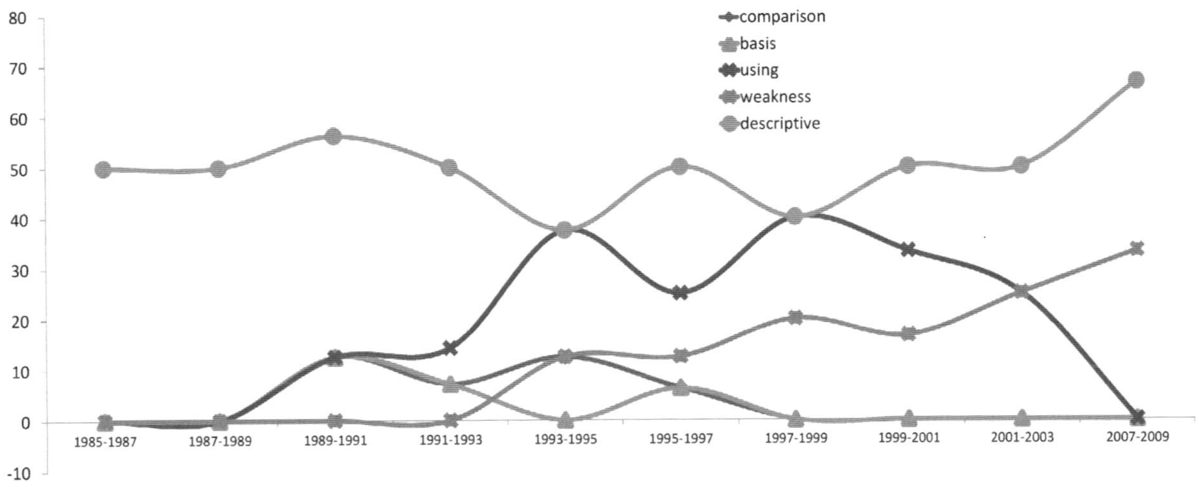

Figure 1: Change in the citation purpose of Shieber (1985) paper

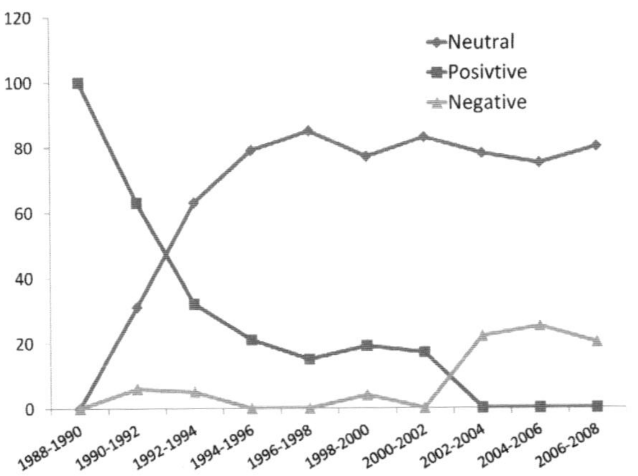

Figure 2: Change in the polarity of the sentences citing Church (1988) paper

how the way a published work is perceived by the research community over time. As a proof of concept, we annotated the polarity of citing sentences for the top 10 cited papers in AAN that were published in the 1980's. We split the year range of citations into two-year slots and counted the number of positive, negative, and neutral citations that each paper received during that time slot. We observed how the ratios of each category changed overtime. Figure 2 shows the result of this analysis when applied to the work of Kenneth Church (1988) on part-of-speech tagging.

2.3 Predict Emergence of New Techniques or Decline of Impact of Old Techniques.

The ideas discussed in Sections 2.1 and 2.2 and the results illustrated in Figures 1 and 2 suggest that studying the change in citation purpose and citation polarity allow us to predict the emergence of new techniques or the decline in impact of old techniques. For example, the analysis illustrated in Figure 2 shows that the work of Ken Church (1988) on part-of-speech tagging received significant positive feedback during the 1990s and until early 2000s before it started to receive more negative feedback. This probably can be explained by the emergence of better statistical models for part-of-speech (POS) tagging (e.g. Conditional Random Fields (Lafferty et al., 2001)) that outperformed Church's approach. However, as indicated by the neutral citation curve, Church's work continued to be cited as a classical pioneering research on the POS tagging task, but not as the state-of-the-art approach. Similar analysis can be applied to the change in citation purpose of Shieber (1985) as illustrated in Figure 1

2.4 Study the Dynamics of Research

In recent research, Gupta and Manning (2011) conducted a study that tries to understand the dynamics of research in computational linguistics (CL). They analyzed the abstracts of CL papers included in the ACL Anthology Reference Corpus. They extracted the contributions, the domain of application, and the

	apply	propose	extend	system
Abstracts	1368	2856	425	5065
Citing Sentences	**2534**	**3902**	**917**	**6633**

Table 3: Comparison of trigger word occurrences in abstracts vs citing sentences.

techniques and tools used in each paper. They combined this information with pre-calculated article-to-community assignments to study the influence of a community on others in terms of techniques borrowed and the maturing of some communities to solve problems from other domains. We hypothesize that conducting such an analysis using the citing sentences of papers instead of (or in combination with) abstracts leads to a more accurate picture of research dynamics and the interaction between different research communities. There are several intuitions that support this hypothesis.

First, previous research (Elkiss et al., 2008) has shown that the citing sentences that cite a paper are more focused and more concise than the paper abstract, and that they consistently contain additional information that does not appear in abstracts. This means that additional characteristics of a paper can be extracted from citing sentences that cannot be extracted from abstracts. To verify this, we compared abstracts vs citing sentences (within AAN) in terms of the number of occurrences of the *trigger words* that Gupta and Manning (2011) deemed to be indicative of paper characteristics (Table 3). All the abstracts and citing sentences included in the 2011 release of AAN were used to get these numbers. The numbers clearly show that the trigger words appear more frequently in the set of citing sentences of papers than they do in the paper abstracts. We also found many papers that none of the *trigger words* appeared in their abstracts, while they do appear in their citing sentences. This suggests that more paper properties (contributions, techniques used, etc.) could be extracted from citations than from abstracts.

Second, while the contributions included in an abstract are the claims of the paper author(s), the contributions highlighted in citing sentences are collectively deemed to be important by peer researchers. This means that the contributions extracted from citations are more important from the viewpoint of the community and are likely to reflect research trends more accurately.

	Rank		
word	1980s	1990s	2000s
grammar	22	71	123
model	75	72	26
rules	77	89	148
statistical	-	69	74
syntax	257	1018	683
summarization	-	880	359

Table 4: Ranks of selected keywords in citing sentences to papers published in 80s, 90s and 2000s

We performed another simple experiment that demonstrates the use of citing sentences to track the changes in the focus of research. We split the set of citing sentences in AAN into three subsets: the set of citing sentences that cite papers from 1980s, the set of citing sentences that cite papers from 1990s, and the set of citing sentences that cite papers from 2000s. We counted the frequencies of words in each of the three sets. Then, we ranked the words in each set by the decreasing order of their frequencies. We selected a number of keywords and compared their ranks in the three year ranges. Some of these keywords are listed in Table 4. This analysis shows, for example, that there was more focus on "grammar" in the computational linguistics research in the 1980s then this focus declined with time as indicated by the lower rank of the keyword "grammar" in the 1990s and 2000s. Similarly, rule based methods were popular in the 1980s and 1990s but their popularity declined significantly in the 2000s.

3 Scientific Literature Summarization Using Citing Sentences

The fact that citing sentences cover different aspects of the cited paper and highlight its most important contributions motivates the idea of using citing sentences to summarize research. The comparison that Elkiss et al. (2008) performed between abstracts and citing sentences suggests that a summary generated from citing sentences will be different and probably more concise and informative than the paper abstract or a summary generated from the full text of the paper. For example, Table 5 shows the abstract of Resnik (1999) and 5 selected sentences that cite it in AAN. We notice that citing sentences contain additional facts that are not in the abstract, not only ones that summarize the paper contributions, but also those that criticize it (e.g., the last citing sentence in the Table).

Previous work has explored this research direction. Qazvinian and Radev (2008) proposed a method for summarizing scientific articles by building a similarity network of the sentences that cite it, and then applying network analysis techniques to find a set of sentences that covers as much of the paper facts as possible. Qazvinian et al. (2010) proposed another summarization method that first extracts a number of important key phrases from the set of citing sentences, and then finds the best subset of sentences that covers as many key phrases as possible.

These works focused on analyzing the citing sentences and selecting a representative subset that covers the different aspects of the summarized article. In recent work, Abu-Jbara and Radev (2011b) raised the issue of coherence and readability in summaries generated from citing sentences. They added a preprocessing and postprocessing steps to the summarization pipeline. In the preprocessing step, they use a supervised classification approach to rule out irrelevant sentences or fragments of sentences. In the postprocessing step, they improve the summary coherence and readability by reordering the sentences, removing extraneous text (e.g. redundant mentions of author names and publication year).

Mohammed et al. (2009) went beyond single paper summarization. They investigated the usefulness of directly summarizing citation texts in the automatic creation of technical surveys. They generated surveys from a set of Question Answering (QA) and Dependency Parsing (DP) papers, their abstracts, and their citation texts. The evaluation of the generated surveys shows that both citation texts and abstracts have unique survey-worthy information. It is worth noting that all the aforementioned research on citation-based summarization used the ACL Anthology Network (AAN) for evaluation.

4 Controversy Identification

Some arguments and claims made by researchers may get disputed by other researchers (Teufel, 1999). The following are examples of citing sentences that dispute previous work.

(1) Even though prior work (Teufel et al., 2006) argues that citation text is unsuitable for summarization, we show that in the framework of multi-document survey creation, citation texts can play a crucial role.

(2) Mining the Web for bilingual text (Resnik, 1999) is not likely to provide sufficient quantities of high quality data.

In many cases, it is useful to know which arguments were confirmed and accepted by the research community and which ones where disputed or even rejected. We believe that analyzing citation text helps identify these contrasting views automatically.

5 Comparison of Different Techniques

Citing sentences that compare different techniques or compare the techniques proposed by the author to previous work are common. The following sentences are examples of such comparisons.

(3) In (Zollmann et al., 2008), an interesting comparison between phrase-based, hierarchical and syntax-augmented models is carried out, concluding that hierarchical and syntax-based models slightly outperform phrase-based models under large data conditions and for sufficiently non-monotonic language pairs.

(4) Brill's results demonstrate that this approach can outperform the Hidden Markov Model approaches that are frequently used for part-of-speech tagging (Jelinek, 1985; Church, 1988; DeRose, 1988; Cutting et al., 1992; Weischedel et al., 1993), as well as showing promise for other applications.

(5) Our highest scores of 90.8% LP and 90.5% LR outperform the scores of the best previously published parser by Charniak (2000) who obtains 90.1% for both LP and LR.

Extracting such comparisons from citations can be of great benefit to researchers. It will allow them to quickly determine which technique works better for their tasks. To verify that citation text could be a good source for extracting comparisons, we created a list of words and phrases that are usually used to express comparisons and counted their frequency in AAN citing sentences. We found, for example, that the word *compare* (at its variations)

Abstract	STRAND (Resnik, 1998) is a language-independent system for automatic discovery of text in parallel translation on the World Wide Web. This paper extends the preliminary STRAND results by adding automatic language identification, scaling up by orders of magnitude, and formally evaluating performance. The most recent end-product is an automatically acquired parallel corpus comprising 2491 English-French document pairs, approximately 1.5 million words per language.
Selected Citing Sentences	Many research ideas have exploited the Web in unsupervised or weakly supervised algorithms for natural language processing (e.g. , Resnik (1999)) Resnik (1999) addressed the issue of language identification for finding Web pages in the languages of interest. In Resnik (1999), the Web is harvested in search of pages that are available in two languages, with the aim of building parallel corpora for any pair of target languages. The STRAND system of (Resnik, 1999), uses structural markup information from the pages, without looking at their content, to attempt to align them. Mining the Web for bilingual text (Resnik, 1999) is not likely to provide sufficient quantities of high quality data.

Table 5: Comparison of the abstract and a selected set of sentences that cite Resnik (1999) work

appears in about 4000 sentences, and that the words *outperform* and *contrast* each appears in about 1000 citing sentences.

6 Ontology Creation

It is useful for researchers to know which tasks and research problems are important, and what techniques and tools are usually used with them. Citation text is a good source of such information. For example, sentence (6) below shows three different techniques (underlined) that were used to extend tools and resources that were created for English so that they work for other languages. For another example, sentence (7) shows different tasks in which re-ranking has been successfully applied. These relations can be easily extracted from citing sentences and can be possibly used to build an ontology of tasks, methods, tools, and the relations between them.

(6) Another strain of research has sought to exploit resources and tools in some languages (especially English) to construct similar resources and tools for other languages, through heuristic projection (Yarowsky and Ngai, 2001; Xi and Hwa, 2005) or constraints in learning (Burkett and Klein, 2008; Smith and Eisner, 2009; Das and Petrov, 2011; McDonald et al., 2011) or inference (Smith and Smith, 2004).

(7) (Re)rankers have been successfully applied to numerous NLP tasks, such as parse selection (Osborne and Baldridge, 2004; Toutanova et al., 2004), parse reranking (Collins and Duffy, 2002; Charniak and Johnson, 2005), question-answering (Ravichandran et al., 2003).

7 Paraphrase Extraction

It is common that multiple citing sentences highlight the same facts about a cited paper. Since these sentences were written by different authors, they often use different wording to describe the cited paper facts. This motivates the idea of using citing sentences to create data sets for paraphrase extraction. For example, sentences (8) and (9) below both cite (Turney, 2002) and highlight the same aspect of Turney's work using slightly different wordings. Therefore, sentences (8) and (9) can be considered paraphrases of each other.

(8) In (Turney, 2002), an unsupervised learning algorithm was proposed to classify reviews as recommended or not recommended by averaging sentiment annotation of phrases in reviews that contain adjectives or adverbs.

(9) For example, Turney (2002) proposes a method to classify reviews as recommended/not recommended, based on the average semantic orientation of the review.

The paraphrase annotation of citing sentences consists of manually labeling which sentence consists of what facts. Then, if two citing sentences consist of the same set of facts, they are labeled as paraphrases of each other. For example, if a paper has 50 sentences citing it, this gives us a paraphrasing data set that consists of 50*49 = 2450 pairs. As a proof of concept, we annotated 25 papers from AAN using the annotation method described above. This data set consisted of 33,683 sentence pairs of which 8,704 are paraphrases.

The idea of using citing sentences to create data sets for paraphrase extraction was initially suggested by Nakov et al. (2004) who proposed an algorithm that extracts paraphrases from citing sentences using rules based on automatic named entity annotation and the dependency paths between them.

8 Scientific Article Classification

Automatic classification of scientific articles is one of the important tasks for creating publication databases. A variety of machine learning algorithms have been proposed for this task. Many of these methods perform the classification based on the title, the abstract, or the full text of the article. Some other methods used citation links in addition to content to make classification decisions. Cao and Gao (2005) proposed a two-phase classification system. The system first applies a content-based statistical classification method which is similar to general text classification. In the second phase, the system uses an iterative method to update the labels of classified instances using citation links. A similar approach is also proposed by Zhang et al. (2006). These approaches use citation links only to improve classification decisions that were made based on content. We hypothesize that using the text of citing sentences in addition to citation structure and content leads to more accurate classification than using the content and citation links only.

9 Terminology Translation

Citing sentences can also be used to improve machine translation systems by using citing sentences from different languages to build parallel corpus of terms and their translations. This can be done by identifying articles written in different languages that cite a common target paper, then extracting the citing sentences from each paper. Word alignment techniques can then be applied to the text surrounding the reference to the common target paper. The aligned words from each source can then be extracted and used as translations of the same term. Sentences (10) and (11) below illustrate how the application of this proposed method can identify that the underlined terms in sentence 10 (Spanish) and sentence 11 (English) are translations of each other.

(10) Spanish: Se comprobó que la agrupación por bloques ofrecía mejores resultados que, la introducción de vocabulario (Hearst, 1997) o ***las cadenas léxicas*** *(Hearst, 1994) y, por tanto, es la que se ha utilizado en la segunda fase del algoritmo.*

(11) English: This can be done either by analyzing the number of overlapping ***lexical chains*** *(Hearst, 1994) or by building a short-range and long-range language model (Beeferman et al., 1999).*

10 Other Uses of Citing Sentences

Nakov et al. (2004) proposed several other uses of citing sentences. First, they suggested using them as a source for unannotated comparable corpora. Such comparable corpora can be used in several applications such as paraphrase extraction as we showed earlier. They also noticed that the scientific literature is rife with abbreviations and synonyms, and hence, citing sentences referring to the same article may allow synonyms to be identified and recorded. They also proposed using citing sentences to build a model of the different ways used to express a relationship between two entities. They hypothesized that this model can help improve both relation extraction and named entity recognition systems. Finally, they proposed improving the indexing and ranking of publications by considering, in addition to the content of the publication, the text of citing sentences that cite it and their contexts.

11 Summarizing 30 years of ACL Discoveries Using Citing Sentences

The ACL Anthology Corpus contains all the proceedings of the Annual Meeting of the Association of Computational Linguistics (ACL) since 1979. All the ACL papers and their citation links and citing sentences are included in the ACL Anthology Network (ACL). In this section, we show how citing sentences can be used to summarize the most important contributions that have been published in the ACL conference since 1979. We selected the most cited papers in each year and then manually picked a citing sentence that cites a top cited and describes it contribution. It should be noted here that the citation counts we used for ranking papers reflect the number of incoming citations the paper received *only* from the venues included in AAN. To create the summary, we used citing sentences that has the reference to the cited paper in the beginning of the sentence. This is

1979	Carbonell (1979) discusses inferring the meaning of new words.
1980	Weischedel and Black (1980) discuss techniques for interacting with the linguist/developer to identify insufficiencies in the grammar.
1981	Moore (1981) observed that determiners rarely have a direct correlation with the existential and universal quantifiers of first-order logic.
1982	Heidorn (1982) provides a good summary of early work in weight-based analysis, as well as a weight-oriented approach to attachment decisions based on syntactic considerations only.
1983	Grosz et al. (1983) proposed the centering model which is concerned with the interactions between the local coherence of discourse and the choices of referring expressions.
1984	Karttunen (1984) provides examples of feature structures in which a negation operator might be useful.
1985	Shieber (1985) proposes a more efficient approach to gaps in the PATR-II formalism, extending Earley's algorithm by using restriction to do top-down filtering.
1986	Kameyama (1986) proposed a fourth transition type, Center Establishment (EST), for utterances E.g., in Bruno was the bully of the neighborhood.
1987	Brennan et al. (1987) propose a default ordering on transitions which correlates with discourse coherence.
1988	Whittaker and Stenton (1988) proposed rules for tracking initiative based on utterance types; for example, statements, proposals, and questions show initiative, while answers and acknowledgements do not.
1989	Church and Hanks (1989) explored tile use of mutual information statistics in ranking co-occurrences within five-word windows.
1990	Hindle (1990) classified nouns on the basis of co-occurring patterns of subjectverb and verb-object pairs.
1991	Gale and Church (1991) extract pairs of anchor words, such as numbers, proper nouns (organization, person, title), dates, and monetary information.
1992	Pereira and Schabes (1992) establish that evaluation according to the bracketing accuracy and evaluation according to perplexity or crossentropy are very different.
1993	Pereira et al. (1993) proposed a soft clustering scheme, in which membership of a word in a class is probabilistic.
1994	Hearst (1994) presented two implemented segmentation algorithms based on term repetition, and compared the boundaries produced to the boundaries marked by at least 3 of 7 subjects, using information retrieval metrics.
1995	Yarowsky (1995) describes a 'semi-unsupervised' approach to the problem of sense disambiguation of words, also using a set of initial seeds, in this case a few high quality sense annotations.
1996	Collins (1996) proposed a statistical parser which is based on probabilities of dependencies between head-words in the parse tree.
1997	Collins (1997)'s parser and its re-implementation and extension by Bikel (2002) have by now been applied to a variety of languages: English (Collins, 1999), Czech (Collins et al. , 1999), German (Dubey and Keller, 2003), Spanish (Cowan and Collins, 2005), French (Arun and Keller, 2005), Chinese (Bikel, 2002) and, according to Dan Bikels web page, Arabic.
1998	Lin (1998) proposed a word similarity measure based on the distributional pattern of words which allows to construct a thesaurus using a parsed corpus.
1999	Rapp (1999) proposed that in any language there is a correlation between the cooccurrences of words which are translations of each other.
2000	Och and Ney (2000) introduce a NULL-alignment capability to HMM alignment models.
2001	Yamada and Knight (2001) used a statistical parser trained using a Treebank in the source language to produce parse trees and proposed a tree to string model for alignment.
2002	BLEU (Papineni et al., 2002) was devised to provide automatic evaluation of MT output.
2003	Och (2003) developed a training procedure that incorporates various MT evaluation criteria in the training procedure of log-linear MT models.
2004	Pang and Lee (2004) applied two different classifiers to perform sentiment annotation in two sequential steps: the first classifier separated subjective (sentiment-laden) texts from objective (neutral) ones and then they used the second classifier to classify the subjective texts into positive and negative.
2005	Chiang (2005) introduces Hiero, a hierarchical phrase-based model for statistical machine translation.
2006	Liu et al. (2006) experimented with tree-to-string translation models that utilize source side parse trees.
2007	Goldwater and Griffiths (2007) employ a Bayesian approach to POS tagging and use sparse Dirichlet priors to minimize model size.
2008	Huang (2008) improves the re-ranking work of Charniak and Johnson (2005) by re-ranking on packed forest, which could potentially incorporate exponential number of k-best list.
2009	Mintz et al. (2009) uses Freebase to provide distant supervision for relation extraction.
2010	Chiang (2010) proposes a method for learning to translate with both source and target syntax in the framework of a hierarchical phrase-based system.

Table 6: A citation-based summary of the important contributions published in ACL conference proceedings since 1979. The top cited paper in each year is found and one citation sentence is manually picked to represent it in the summary.

because such citing sentences are often high-quality, concise summaries of the cited work. Table 6 shows the summary of the ACL conference contributions that we created using citing sentences.

12 Conclusion

We motivated and discussed several different uses of citing sentences, the text surrounding citations. We showed that citing sentences can be used to analyze the dynamics of research and observe how it trends. We also gave examples on how analyzing the text of citing sentences can give a better understanding of the impact of a researcher's work and how this impact changes over time. In addition, we presented several different applications that can benefit from citing sentences such as scientific literature summarization, identifying controversial arguments, and identifying relations between techniques, tools and tasks. We also showed how citing sentences can provide high-quality for NLP tasks such as information extraction, paraphrase extraction, and machine translation. Finally, we used AAN citing sentences to create a citation-based summary of the important contributions included in the ACL conference publication in the past 30 years.

References

Amjad Abu-Jbara and Dragomir Radev. 2011a. Coherent citation-based summarization of scientific papers. In *Proceedings of the 49th Annual Meeting of the Association for Computational Linguistics: Human Language Technologies*, pages 500–509, Portland, Oregon, USA, June. Association for Computational Linguistics.

Amjad Abu-Jbara and Dragomir Radev. 2011b. Coherent citation-based summarization of scientific papers. In *Proceedings of the 49th Annual Meeting of the Association for Computational Linguistics: Human Language Technologies*, pages 500–509, Portland, Oregon, USA, June. Association for Computational Linguistics.

F. Amblard, A. Casteigts, P. Flocchini, W. Quattrociocchi, and N. Santoro. 2011. On the temporal analysis of scientific network evolution. In *Computational Aspects of Social Networks (CASoN), 2011 International Conference on*, pages 169 –174, oct.

Awais Athar. 2011. Sentiment analysis of citations using sentence structure-based features. In *Proceedings of the ACL 2011 Student Session*, pages 81–87, Portland, OR, USA, June. Association for Computational Linguistics.

Christine L. Borgman and Jonathan Furner. 2002. Scholarly communication and bibliometrics. *ANNUAL REVIEW OF INFORMATION SCIENCE AND TECHNOLOGY*, 36(1):2–72.

Susan E. Brennan, Marilyn W. Friedman, and Carl J. Pollard. 1987. A centering approach to pronouns. In *Proceedings of the 25th Annual Meeting of the Association for Computational Linguistics*, pages 155–162, Stanford, California, USA, July. Association for Computational Linguistics.

Minh Duc Cao and Xiaoying Gao. 2005. Combining contents and citations for scientific document classification. In *Proceedings of the 18th Australian Joint conference on Advances in Artificial Intelligence*, AI'05, pages 143–152, Berlin, Heidelberg. Springer-Verlag.

Jaime G. Carbonell. 1979. Towards a self-extending parser. In *Proceedings of the 17th Annual Meeting of the Association for Computational Linguistics*, pages 3–7, La Jolla, California, USA, June. Association for Computational Linguistics.

David Chiang. 2005. A hierarchical phrase-based model for statistical machine translation. In *Proceedings of the 43rd Annual Meeting of the Association for Computational Linguistics (ACL'05)*, pages 263–270, Ann Arbor, Michigan, June. Association for Computational Linguistics.

David Chiang. 2010. Learning to translate with source and target syntax. In *Proceedings of the 48th Annual Meeting of the Association for Computational Linguistics*, pages 1443–1452, Uppsala, Sweden, July. Association for Computational Linguistics.

Kenneth Ward Church and Patrick Hanks. 1989. Word association norms, mutual information, and lexicography. In *Proceedings of the 27th Annual Meeting of the Association for Computational Linguistics*, pages 76–83, Vancouver, British Columbia, Canada, June. Association for Computational Linguistics.

Kenneth Ward Church. 1988. A stochastic parts program and noun phrase parser for unrestricted text. In *Proceedings of the Second Conference on Applied Natural Language Processing*, pages 136–143, Austin, Texas, USA, February. Association for Computational Linguistics.

Michael John Collins. 1996. A new statistical parser based on bigram lexical dependencies. In *Proceedings of the 34th Annual Meeting of the Association for Computational Linguistics*, pages 184–191, Santa Cruz, California, USA, June. Association for Computational Linguistics.

Michael Collins. 1997. Three generative, lexicalised models for statistical parsing. In *Proceedings of the 35th Annual Meeting of the Association for Computational Linguistics*, pages 16–23, Madrid, Spain, July. Association for Computational Linguistics.

Aaron Elkiss, Siwei Shen, Anthony Fader, Güneş Erkan, David States, and Dragomir Radev. 2008. Blind men and elephants: What do citation summaries tell us about a research article? *J. Am. Soc. Inf. Sci. Technol.*, 59(1):51–62.

William A. Gale and Kenneth W. Church. 1991. A program for aligning sentences in bilingual corpora. In *Proceedings of the 29th Annual Meeting of the Association for Computational Linguistics*, pages 177–184, Berkeley, California, USA, June. Association for Computational Linguistics.

Sharon Goldwater and Tom Griffiths. 2007. A fully bayesian approach to unsupervised part-of-speech tagging. In *Proceedings of the 45th Annual Meeting of the Association of Computational Linguistics*, pages 744–751, Prague, Czech Republic, June. Association for Computational Linguistics.

Barbara J. Grosz, Aravind K. Joshi, and Scott Weinstein. 1983. Providing a unified account of definite noun phrases in discourse. In *Proceedings of the 21st Annual Meeting of the Association for Computational Linguistics*, pages 44–50, Cambridge, Massachusetts, USA, June. Association for Computational Linguistics.

Sonal Gupta and Christopher Manning. 2011. Analyzing the dynamics of research by extracting key aspects of scientific papers. In *Proceedings of 5th International Joint Conference on Natural Language Processing*, pages 1–9, Chiang Mai, Thailand, November. Asian Federation of Natural Language Processing.

Marti A. Hearst. 1994. Multi-paragraph segmentation expository text. In *Proceedings of the 32nd Annual Meeting of the Association for Computational Linguistics*, pages 9–16, Las Cruces, New Mexico, USA, June. Association for Computational Linguistics.

George E. Heidorn. 1982. Experience with an easily computed metric for ranking alternative parses. In *Proceedings of the 20th Annual Meeting of the Association for Computational Linguistics*, pages 82–84, Toronto, Ontario, Canada, June. Association for Computational Linguistics.

Donald Hindle. 1990. Noun classification from predicate-argument structures. In *Proceedings of the 28th Annual Meeting of the Association for Computational Linguistics*, pages 268–275, Pittsburgh, Pennsylvania, USA, June. Association for Computational Linguistics.

Liang Huang. 2008. Forest reranking: Discriminative parsing with non-local features. In *Proceedings of ACL-08: HLT*, pages 586–594, Columbus, Ohio, June. Association for Computational Linguistics.

Megumi Kameyama. 1986. A property-sharing constraint in centering. In *Proceedings of the 24th Annual Meeting of the Association for Computational Linguistics*, pages 200–206, New York, New York, USA, July. Association for Computational Linguistics.

Lauri Karttunen. 1984. Features and values. In *Proceedings of the 10th International Conference on Computational Linguistics and 22nd Annual Meeting of the Association for Computational Linguistics*, pages 28–33, Stanford, California, USA, July. Association for Computational Linguistics.

John D. Lafferty, Andrew McCallum, and Fernando C. N. Pereira. 2001. Conditional random fields: Probabilistic models for segmenting and labeling sequence data. In *Proceedings of the Eighteenth International Conference on Machine Learning*, ICML '01, pages 282–289, San Francisco, CA, USA. Morgan Kaufmann Publishers Inc.

Dekang Lin. 1998. Automatic retrieval and clustering of similar words. In *Proceedings of the 36th Annual Meeting of the Association for Computational Linguistics and 17th International Conference on Computational Linguistics, Volume 2*, pages 768–774, Montreal, Quebec, Canada, August. Association for Computational Linguistics.

Yang (1) Liu, Qun Liu, and Shouxun Lin. 2006. Tree-to-string alignment template for statistical machine translation. In *Proceedings of the 21st International Conference on Computational Linguistics and 44th Annual Meeting of the Association for Computational Linguistics*, pages 609–616, Sydney, Australia, July. Association for Computational Linguistics.

Terttu Luukkonen. 1992. Is scientists' publishing behaviour rewardseeking? *Scientometrics*, 24:297–319. 10.1007/BF02017913.

Amin Mazloumian, Young-Ho Eom, Dirk Helbing, Sergi Lozano, and Santo Fortunato. 2011. How citation boosts promote scientific paradigm shifts and nobel prizes. *PLoS ONE*, 6(5):e18975, 05.

Qiaozhu Mei and ChengXiang Zhai. 2008. Generating impact-based summaries for scientific literature. In *Proceedings of ACL-08: HLT*, pages 816–824, Columbus, Ohio, June. Association for Computational Linguistics.

Mike Mintz, Steven Bills, Rion Snow, and Daniel Jurafsky. 2009. Distant supervision for relation extraction without labeled data. In *Proceedings of the Joint Conference of the 47th Annual Meeting of the ACL and the 4th International Joint Conference on Natural Language Processing of the AFNLP*, pages 1003–1011, Suntec, Singapore, August. Association for Computational Linguistics.

Saif Mohammad, Bonnie Dorr, Melissa Egan, Ahmed Hassan, Pradeep Muthukrishan, Vahed Qazvinian, Dragomir Radev, and David Zajic. 2009. Using citations to generate surveys of scientific paradigms. In *Proceedings of Human Language Technologies: The 2009 Annual Conference of the North American Chapter of the Association for Computational Linguistics*, pages 584–592, Boulder, Colorado, June. Association for Computational Linguistics.

Robert C. Moore. 1981. Problems in logical form. In *Proceedings of the 19th Annual Meeting of the Association for Computational Linguistics*, pages 117–124, Stanford, California, USA, June. Association for Computational Linguistics.

Preslav I. Nakov, Ariel S. Schwartz, and Marti A. Hearst. 2004. Citances: Citation sentences for semantic analysis of bioscience text. In *In Proceedings of the SIGIR04 workshop on Search and Discovery in Bioinformatics*.

Hidetsugu Nanba and Manabu Okumura. 1999. Towards multi-paper summarization using reference information. In *IJCAI '99: Proceedings of the Sixteenth International Joint Conference on Artificial Intelligence*, pages 926–931, San Francisco, CA, USA. Morgan Kaufmann Publishers Inc.

Hidetsugu Nanba, Noriko Kando, Manabu Okumura, and Of Information Science. 2000. Classification of research papers using citation links and citation types: Towards automatic review article generation.

Franz Josef Och and Hermann Ney. 2000. Improved statistical alignment models. In *Proceedings of the 38th Annual Meeting of the Association for Computational Linguistics*, pages 440–447, Hong Kong, October. Association for Computational Linguistics.

Franz Josef Och. 2003. Minimum error rate training in statistical machine translation. In *Proceedings of the 41st Annual Meeting of the Association for Computational Linguistics*, pages 160–167, Sapporo, Japan, July. Association for Computational Linguistics.

Bo Pang and Lillian Lee. 2004. A sentimental education: Sentiment analysis using subjectivity summarization based on minimum cuts. In *Proceedings of the 42nd Meeting of the Association for Computational Linguistics (ACL'04), Main Volume*, pages 271–278, Barcelona, Spain, July.

Kishore Papineni, Salim Roukos, Todd Ward, and Wei-Jing Zhu. 2002. Bleu: a method for automatic evaluation of machine translation. In *Proceedings of 40th Annual Meeting of the Association for Computational Linguistics*, pages 311–318, Philadelphia, Pennsylvania, USA, July. Association for Computational Linguistics.

Fernando Pereira and Yves Schabes. 1992. Inside-outside reestimation from partially bracketed corpora. In *Proceedings of the 30th Annual Meeting of the Association for Computational Linguistics*, pages 128–135, Newark, Delaware, USA, June. Association for Computational Linguistics.

Fernando Pereira, Naftali Tishby, and Lillian Lee. 1993. Distributional clustering of english words. In *Proceedings of the 31st Annual Meeting of the Association for Computational Linguistics*, pages 183–190, Columbus, Ohio, USA, June. Association for Computational Linguistics.

Vahed Qazvinian and Dragomir R. Radev. 2008. Scientific paper summarization using citation summary networks. In *Proceedings of the 22nd International Conference on Computational Linguistics (Coling 2008)*, pages 689–696, Manchester, UK, August. Coling 2008 Organizing Committee.

Vahed Qazvinian and Dragomir R. Radev. 2010. Identifying non-explicit citing sentences for citation-based summarization. In *Proceedings of the 48th Annual Meeting of the Association for Computational Linguistics*, pages 555–564, Uppsala, Sweden, July. Association for Computational Linguistics.

Vahed Qazvinian, Dragomir R. Radev, and Arzucan Ozgur. 2010. Citation summarization through keyphrase extraction. In *Proceedings of the 23rd International Conference on Computational Linguistics (Coling 2010)*, pages 895–903, Beijing, China, August. Coling 2010 Organizing Committee.

Dragomir R. Radev, Pradeep Muthukrishnan, and Vahed Qazvinian. 2009. The acl anthology network corpus. In *NLPIR4DL '09: Proceedings of the 2009 Workshop on Text and Citation Analysis for Scholarly Digital Libraries*, pages 54–61, Morristown, NJ, USA. Association for Computational Linguistics.

Reinhard Rapp. 1999. Automatic identification of word translations from unrelated english and german corpora. In *Proceedings of the 37th Annual Meeting of the Association for Computational Linguistics*, pages 519–526, College Park, Maryland, USA, June. Association for Computational Linguistics.

Sidney Redner. 2005. Citation statistics from 110 years of physical review. *Physics Today*, 58(6):49–54.

Philip Resnik. 1999. Mining the web for bilingual text. In *Proceedings of the 37th Annual Meeting of the Association for Computational Linguistics*, pages 527–534, College Park, Maryland, USA, June. Association for Computational Linguistics.

Stuart M. Shieber. 1985. Using restriction to extend parsing algorithms for complex-feature-based formalisms. In *Proceedings of the 23rd Annual Meeting of the Association for Computational Linguistics*, pages 145–152, Chicago, Illinois, USA, July. Association for Computational Linguistics.

Advaith Siddharthan and Simone Teufel. 2007. Whose idea was this, and why does it matter? attributing scientific work to citations. In *In Proceedings of NAACL/HLT-07*.

Simone Teufel, Advaith Siddharthan, and Dan Tidhar. 2006. Automatic classification of citation function. In *In Proc. of EMNLP-06*.

Simone Teufel. 1999. Argumentative zoning: Information extraction from scientific text. Technical report.

Simone Teufel. 2007. Argumentative zoning for improved citation indexing. computing attitude and affect in text. In *Theory and Applications, pages 159170*.

Ralph M. Weischedel and John E. Black. 1980. If the parser fails. In *Proceedings of the 18th Annual Meeting of the Association for Computational Linguistics*, pages 95–95, Philadelphia, Pennsylvania, USA, June. Association for Computational Linguistics.

Steve Whittaker and Phil Stenton. 1988. Cues and control in expert-client dialogues. In *Proceedings of the 26th Annual Meeting of the Association for Computational Linguistics*, pages 123–130, Buffalo, New York, USA, June. Association for Computational Linguistics.

Kenji Yamada and Kevin Knight. 2001. A syntax-based statistical translation model. In *Proceedings of 39th Annual Meeting of the Association for Computational Linguistics*, pages 523–530, Toulouse, France, July. Association for Computational Linguistics.

David Yarowsky. 1995. Unsupervised word sense disambiguation rivaling supervised methods. In *Proceedings of the 33rd Annual Meeting of the Association for Computational Linguistics*, pages 189–196, Cambridge, Massachusetts, USA, June. Association for Computational Linguistics.

M. Zhang, X. Gao, M.D. Cao, and Yuejin Ma. 2006. Neural networks for scientific paper classification. In *Innovative Computing, Information and Control, 2006. ICICIC '06. First International Conference on*, volume 2, pages 51 –54, 30 2006-sept. 1.

Towards a Computational History of the ACL: 1980–2008

Ashton Anderson
Stanford University
ashtona@stanford.edu

Dan McFarland
Stanford University
dmcfarla@stanford.edu

Dan Jurafsky
Stanford University
jurafsky@stanford.edu

Abstract

We develop a people-centered computational history of science that tracks authors over topics and apply it to the history of computational linguistics. We present four findings in this paper. First, we identify the topical subfields authors work on by assigning automatically generated topics to each paper in the ACL Anthology from 1980 to 2008. Next, we identify four distinct research epochs where the pattern of topical overlaps are stable and different from other eras: an early NLP period from 1980 to 1988, the period of US government-sponsored MUC and ATIS evaluations from 1989 to 1994, a transitory period until 2001, and a modern integration period from 2002 onwards. Third, we analyze the flow of authors across topics to discern how some subfields flow into the next, forming different stages of ACL research. We find that the government-sponsored bakeoffs brought new researchers to the field, and bridged early topics to modern probabilistic approaches. Last, we identify steep increases in author retention during the bakeoff era and the modern era, suggesting two points at which the field became more integrated.

1 Introduction

The rise of vast on-line collections of scholarly papers has made it possible to develop a computational history of science. Methods from natural language processing and other areas of computer science can be naturally applied to study the ways a field and its ideas develop and expand (Au Yeung and Jatowt, 2011; Gerrish and Blei, 2010; Tu et al., 2010; Aris et al., 2009). One particular direction in computational history has been the use of topic models (Blei et al., 2003) to analyze the rise and fall of research topics to study the progress of science, both in general (Griffiths and Steyvers, 2004) and more specifically in the ACL Anthology (Hall et al., 2008).

We extend this work with a more people-centered view of computational history. In this framework, we examine the trajectories of individual authors across research topics in the field of computational linguistics. By examining a single author's paper topics over time, we can trace the evolution of her academic efforts; by superimposing these individual traces over each other, we can learn how the entire field progressed over time. One goal is to investigate the use of these techniques for computational history in general. A second goal is to use the ACL Anthology Network Corpus (Radev et al., 2009) and the incorporated ACL Anthology Reference Corpus (Bird et al., 2008) to answer specific questions about the history of computational linguistics. What is the path that the ACL has taken throughout its 50-year history? What roles did various research topics play in the ACL's development? What have been the pivotal turning points?

Our method consists of four steps. We first run topic models over the corpus to classify papers into topics and identify the topics that people author in.

We then use these topics to identify epochs by correlating over time the number of persons that topics share in common. From this, we identify epochs as sustained patterns of topical overlap.

Our third step is to look at the flow of authors between topics over time to detect patterns in how authors move between areas in the different epochs. We group topics into clusters based on when authors move in and out of them, and visualize the flow of people across these clusters to identify how one topic leads to another.

Finally, in order to understand how the field grows and declines, we examine patterns of entry and exit within each epoch, studying how author retention (the extent to which authors keep publishing in the ACL) varies across epochs.

2 Identifying Topics

Our first task is to identify research topics within computational linguistics. We use the ACL Anthology Network Corpus and the incorporated ACL Anthology Reference Corpus, with around 13,000 papers by approximately 11,000 distinct authors from 1965 to 2008. Due to data sparsity in early years, we drop all papers published prior to 1980.

We ran LDA on the corpus to produce 100 generative topics (Blei et al., 2003). Two senior researchers in the field (the third author and Chris Manning) then collaboratively assigned a label to each of the 100 topics, which included marking those topics which were non-substantive (lists of function words or affixes) to be eliminated. They produced a consensus labeling with 73 final topics, shown in Table 1 (27 non-substantive topics were eliminated, e.g. a pronoun topic, a suffix topic, etc.).

Each paper is associated with a probability distribution over the 100 original topics describing how much of the paper is generated from each topic. All of this information is represented by a matrix P, where the entry P_{ij} is simply the loading of topic j on paper i (since each row is a probability distribution, $\sum_j P_{ij} = 1$). For ease of interpretation, we sparsify the matrix P by assigning papers to topics and thus set all entries to either 0 or 1. We do this by choosing a threshold T and setting entries to 1 if they exceed this threshold. If we call the new matrix Q, $Q_{ij} = 1 \iff P_{ij} \geq T$. Throughout all our analyses we use $T = 0.1$. This value is approximately two standard deviations above $\overline{P}$, the mean of the entries in P. Most papers are assigned to 1 or 2 topics; some are assigned to none and some are assigned to more.

This assignment of papers to topics also induces an assignment of authors to topics: an author is assigned to a topic if she authored a paper assigned to that topic. Furthermore, this assignment is naturally *dynamic:* since every paper is published in a particular year, authors' topic memberships change over time. This fact is at the heart of our methodology — by assigning authors to topics in this principled way, we can track the topics that authors move through. Analyzing the flow of authors through topics enables us to learn which topics beget other topics, and which topics are related to others by the people that author across them.

3 Identifying Epochs

What are the major epochs of the ACL's history? In this section, we seek to partition the years spanned by the ACL's history into clear, distinct periods of topical cohesion, which we refer to as *epochs.* If the dominant research topics people are working on suddenly change from one set of topics to another, we view this as a transition between epochs.

To identify epochs that satisfy this definition, we generate a set of matrices (one for each year) describing the number of people that author in every pair of topics during that year. For year y, let N^y be a matrix such that N^y_{ij} is the number of people that author in both topics i and j in year y (where authoring in topic j means being an author on a paper p such that $Q_{pj} = 1$). We don't normalize by the total number of people in each topic, thus proportionally representing bigger topics since they account for more research effort than smaller topics. Each matrix is a signature of which topic pairs have overlapping author sets in that year.

From these matrices, we compute a final matrix C of year-year correlations. C_{ij} is the Pearson correlation coefficient between N^i and N^j. C captures the degree to which years have similar patterns of topic authorship overlap, or the extent to which a consistent pattern of topical research is formed. We visualize C as a thermal in Figure 1.

To identify epochs in ACL's history, we ran hierarchical complete link clustering on C. This resulted in a set of four distinct epochs: 1980–1988, 1989–1994, 1995–2001, and 2002–2008. For three of these periods (all except 1995–2001), years within each of these ranges are much more similar to each other than they are to other years. During the third period (1995–2001), none of the years are highly similar to any other years. This is indicative of a

Number	Name	Topics
1	Big Data NLP	**Statistical Machine Translation (Phrase-Based)**: bleu, statistical, source, target, phrases, smt, reordering **Dependency Parsing**: dependency/ies, head, czech, depen, dependent, treebank **MultiLingual Resources**: languages, spanish, russian, multilingual, lan, hindi, swedish **Relation Extraction**: pattern/s, relation, extraction, instances, pairs, seed **Collocations/Compounds**: compound/s, collocation/s, adjectives, nouns, entailment, expressions, MWEs **Graph Theory + BioNLP**: graph/s, medical, edge/s, patient, clinical, vertex, text, report, disease **Sentiment Analysis**: question/s, answer/s, answering, opinion, sentiment, negative, positive, polarity
2	Probabilistic Methods	**Discriminative Sequence Models**: label/s, conditional, sequence, random, discriminative, inference **Metrics + Human Evaluation**: human, measure/s, metric/s, score/s, quality, reference, automatic, correlation, judges **Statistical Parsing**: parse/s, treebank, trees, Penn, Collins, parsers, Charniak, accuracy, WSJ **ngram Language Models**: n-gram/s, bigram/s, prediction, trigram/s, unigram/s, trigger, show, baseline **Algorithmic Efficiency**: search, length, size, space, cost, algorithms, large, complexity, pruning **Bilingual Word Alignment**: alignment/s, align/ed, pair/s, statistical, source, target, links, Brown **ReRanking**: score/s, candidate/s, list, best, correct, hypothesis, selection, rank/ranking, scoring, top, confidence **Evaluation Metrics**: precision, recall, extraction, threshold, methods, filtering, extract, high, phrases, filter, f-measure **Methods (Experimental/Evaluation)**: experiments, accuracy, experiment, average, size, 100, baseline, better, per, sets **Machine Learning Optimization**: function, value/s, parameter/s, local, weight, optimal, solution, criterion, variables
3	Linguistic Supervision	**Biomedical Named Entity Recognition**: biomedical, gene, term, protein, abstracts, extraction, biological **Word Segmentation**: segment/ation, character/s, segment/s, boundary/ies, token/ization **Document Retrieval**: document/s, retrieval, query/ies, term, relevant/ance, collection, indexing, search **SRL/Framenet**: argument/s, role/s, predicate, frame, FrameNet, predicates, labeling, PropBank **Wordnet/Multilingual Ontologies**: ontology/ies, italian, domain/s, resource/s, i.e, ontological, concepts **WebSearch + Wikipedia**: web, search, page, xml, http, engine, document, wikipedia, content, html, query, Google **Clustering + Distributional Similarity**: similar/ity, cluster/s/ing, vector/s, distance, matrix, measure, pair, cosine, LSA **Word Sense Disambiguation**: WordNet, senses, disambiguation, WSD, nouns, target, synsets, Yarowsky **Machine Learning Classification**: classification, classifier/s, examples, kernel, class, SVM, accuracy, decision **Linguistic Annotation**: annotation/s/ed, agreement, scheme/s, annotators, corpora, tools, guidelines **Tutoring Systems**: student/s, reading, course, computer, tutoring, teaching, writing, essay **Chunking/Memory Based Models**: chunk/s/ing, pos, accuracy, best, memory-based, Daelemans **Named Entity Recognition**: entity/ies, name/s/d, person, proper, recognition, location, organization, mention **Dialog**: dialogue, utterance/s, spoken, dialog/ues, act, interaction, conversation, initiative, meeting, state, agent **Summarization**: topic/s, summarization, summary/ies, document/s, news, articles, content, automatic, stories
4	Discourse	**Multimodal (Mainly Generation)**: object/s, multimodal, image, referring, visual, spatial, gesture, reference, description **Text Categorization**: category/ies, group/s, classification, texts, categorization, style, genre, author **Morphology**: morphological, arabic, morphology, forms, stem, morpheme/s, root, suffix, lexicon **Coherence Relations**: relation, rhetorical, unit/s, coherence, texts, chains **Spell Correction**: error/s, correct/ion, spelling, detection, rate **Anaphora Resolution**: resolution, pronoun, anaphora, antecedent, pronouns, coreference, anaphoric **Question Answering Dialog System**: response/s, you, expert, request, yes, users, query, question, call, database **UI/Natural Language Interface**: users, database, interface, a71, message/s, interactive, access, display **Computational Phonology**: phonological, vowel, syllable, stress, phonetic, phoneme, pronunciation **Neural Networks/Human Cognition**: network/s, memory, acquisition, neural, cognitive, units, activation, layer **Temporal IE/Aspect**: event/s, temporal, tense, aspect, past, reference, before, state **Prosody**: prosody/ic, pitch, boundary/ies, accent, cues, repairs, phrases, spoken, intonation, tone, duration
5	Early Probability	**Lexical Acquisition Of Verb Subcategorization**: class/es, verb/s, paraphrase/s, subcategorization, frames **Probability Theory**: probability/ies, distribution, probabilistic, estimate/tion, entropy, statistical, likelihood, parameters **Collocations Measures**: frequency/ies, corpora, statistical, distribution, association, statistics, mutual, co-occurrences **POS Tagging**: tag/ging, POS, tags, tagger/s, part-of-speech, tagged, accuracy, Brill, corpora, tagset **Machine Translation (Non Statistical + Bitexts)**: target, source, bilingual, translations, transfer, parallel, corpora
6	Automata	**Automata Theory**: string/s, sequence/s, left, right, transformation, match **Tree Adjoining Grammars** : trees, derivation, grammars, TAG, elementary, auxiliary, adjoining **Finite State Models (Automata)**: state/s, finite, finite-state, regular, transition, transducer **Classic Parsing**: grammars, parse, chart, context-free, edge/s, production, CFG, symbol, terminal **Syntactic Trees**: node/s, constraints, trees, path/s, root, constraint, label, arcs, graph, leaf, parent
7	Classic Linguistics	**Planning/BDI**: plan/s/ning, action/s, goal/s, agent/s, explanation, reasoning **Dictionary Lexicons**: dictionary/ies, lexicon, entry/ies, definition/s, LDOCE, **Linguistic Example Sentences**: John, Mary, man, book, examples, Bill, who, dog, boy, coordination, clause **Syntactic Theory**: grammatical, theory, functional, constituent/s, constraints, LFG **Formal Computational Semantics**: semantics, logic/al, scope, interpretation, meaning, representation, predicate **Speech Acts + BDI**: speaker, utterance, act/s, hearer, belief, proposition, focus, utterance **PP Attachment**: ambiguity/ies/ous, disambiguation, attachment, preference, preposition **Natural Language Generation**: generation/ing, generator, choice, generated, realization, content **Lexical Semantics**: meaning/s, semantics, metaphor, interpretation, object, role **Categorial Grammar/Logic**: proof, logic, definition, let, formula, theorem, every, iff, calculus **Syntax**: clause/s, head, subject, phrases, object, verbs, relative, nouns, modifier **Unification Based Grammars**: unification, constraints, structures, value, HPSG, default, head **Concept Ontologies / Knowledge Rep**: concept/s, conceptual, attribute/s, relation, base
8	Government	**MUC-Era Information Extraction**: template/s, message, slot/s, extraction, key, event, MUC, fill/s **Speech Recognition**: recognition, acoustic, error, speaker, rate, adaptation, recognizer, phone, ASR **ATIS dialog**: spoken, atis, flight, darpa, understanding, class, database, workshop, utterances
9	Early NLU	**1970s-80s NLU Work**: 1975-9, 1980-6, computer, understanding, syntax, semantics, ATN, Winograd, Schank, Wilks, lisp **Code Examples**: list/s, program/s, item/s, file/s, code/s, computer, line, output, index, field, data, format **Speech Parsing And Understanding**: frame/s, slot/s, fragment/s, parse, representation, meaning

Table 1: Results of topic clustering, showing some high-probability representative words for each cluster.

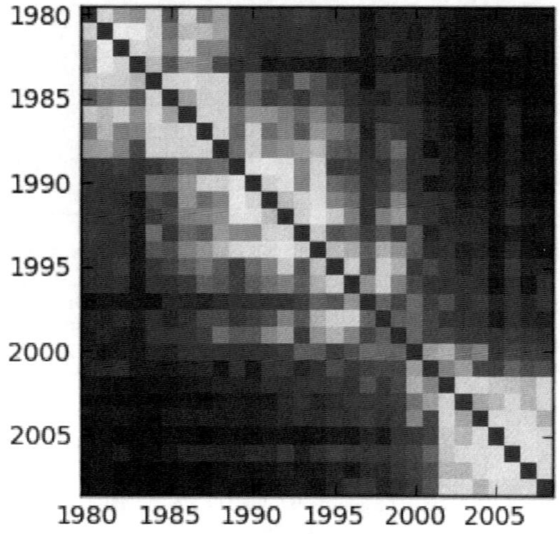

Figure 1: Year-year correlation in topic authoring patterns. Hotter colors indicate high correlation, colder colors denote low correlation.

state of flux in which authors are constantly changing the topics they are in. As such, we refer to this period as a transitory epoch. Thus our analysis has identified four main epochs in the ACL corpus between 1980 and 2008: three focused periods of work, and one transitory phase.

These epochs correspond to natural eras in the ACL's history. During the 1980's, there were coherent communities of research on natural language understanding and parsing, generation, dialog, unification and other grammar formalizations, and lexicons and ontologies.

The 1989–1994 era corresponds to a number of important US government initiatives: MUC, ATIS, and the DARPA workshops. The Message Understanding Conferences (MUC) were an early initiative in information extraction, set up by the United States Naval Oceans Systems Center with the support of DARPA, the Defense Advanced Research Projects Agency. A condition of attending the MUC workshops was participation in a required evaluation (bakeoff) task of filling slots in templates about events, and began (after an exploratory MUC-1 in 1987) with MUC-2 in 1989, followed by MUC-3 (1991), MUC-4 (1992), MUC-5 (1993) and MUC-6 (1995) (Grishman and Sundheim, 1996). The Air Travel Information System (ATIS) was a task for measuring progress in spoken language understanding, sponsored by DARPA (Hemphill et al., 1990; Price, 1990). Subjects talked with a system to answer questions about flight schedules and airline fares from a database; there were evaluations in 1990, 1991, 1992, 1993, and 1994 (Dahl et al., 1994). The ATIS systems were described in papers at the DARPA Speech and Natural Language Workshops, a series of DARPA-sponsored workshsop held from 1989–1994 to which DARPA grantees were strongly encouraged to participate, with the goal of bringing together the speech and natural language processing communities.

After the MUC and ATIS bakeoffs and the DARPA workshops ended, the field largely stopped publishing in the bakeoff topics and transitioned to other topics; participation by researchers in speech recognition also dropped off significantly. From 2002 onward, the field settled into the modern era characterized by broad multilingual work and specific areas like dependency parsing, statistical machine translation, information extraction, and sentiment analysis.

In summary, our methods identify four major epochs in the ACL's history: an early NLP period, the "government" period, a transitory period, and a modern integration period. The first, second, and fourth epochs are periods of sustained topical coherence, whereas the third is a transitory phase during which the field moved from the bakeoff work to modern-day topics.

4 Identifying Participant Flows

In the previous section, we used topic comembership to identify four coherent epochs in the ACL's history. Now we turn our attention to a finer-grained question: How do scientific areas or movements arise? How does one research area develop out of another as authors transition from a previous research topic to a new one? We address this question by tracing the paths of authors through topics over time, in aggregate.

4.1 Topic Clustering

We first group topics into clusters based on how authors move through them. To do this, we group years into 3-year time windows and consider adjacent time periods. We aggregate into 3-year windows because the flow across adjacent single years is noisy and often does not accurately reflect shifts in topical focus. For each adjacent pair of time periods (for example, 1980–1982 and 1983–1985), we construct a matrix S capturing author flow between each topic pair, where the S_{ij} entry is the number of authors who authored in topic i during the first time period and authored in topic j during the second time period. These matrices capture people flow between topics over time.

Next we compute similarity between topics. We represent each topic by its flow profile, which is simply the concatenation of all its in- and out-flows in all of the S matrices. More formally, let F_i be the resulting vector after concatenating the i-th row (transposed into a column) and i-th column of every S matrix. We compute a topic-topic similarity matrix T where T_{ij} is the Pearson correlation coefficient between F_i and F_j. Two topics are then similar if they have similar flow profiles. Note that topics don't need to share authors to be similar — authors just need to move in and out of them at roughly the same times. Through this approach, we identify topics that play similar roles in the ACL's history.

To find a grouping of topics that play similar roles, we perform hierarchical complete link clustering on the T matrix. The goal is to identify clusters of topics that are highly similar to each other but are dissimilar from those in other clusters. Hierarchical clustering begins with every topic forming a singleton cluster, then iteratively merges the two most similar clusters at every step until there is only one cluster of all topics remaining. Every step gives a different clustering solution, so we assess cluster fitness using Krackhard and Stern's E-I index, which measures the sum of external ties minus the sum of internal ties divided by the sum of all ties. Given T as an input, the E-I index optimizes identical profiles as clusters (i.e., topic stages), not discrete groups. The optimal solution we picked using the E-I index entails 9 clusters (shown in Table 1), numbered roughly backwards from the present to the past. We'll discuss the names of the clusters in the next section.

4.2 Flows Between Topic Clusters

Now that we have grouped topics into clusters by how authors flow in and out of them, we can compute the flow between topics or between topic clusters over time. First we define what a flow between topics is. We use the same flow matrix used in the above topic clustering: the flow between topic i in one time period and topic j in the following time period is simply the number of authors present in both at the respective times. Again we avoid normalizing because the volume of people moving between topics is relevant.

Now we can define flow between clusters. Let $\mathbf{A}$ be the set of topics in cluster C_1 and let $\mathbf{B}$ be the set of topics in cluster C_2. We define the flow between C_1 and C_2 to be the average flow between topics in $\mathbf{A}$ and $\mathbf{B}$:

$$f(C_1, C_2) = \frac{\sum_{A \in \mathbf{A}, B \in \mathbf{B}} f(A, B)}{|A| \cdot |B|}$$

(where $f(A, B)$ represents the topic-topic flow defined above). We also tried defining cluster-cluster flow as the maximum over all topic-topic flows between the clusters, and the results were qualitatively the same.

Figure 2 shows the resulting flows between clusters. Figure 2a shows the earliest period in our (post-1980) dataset, where we see reflections of earlier natural language understanding work by Schank, Woods, Winograd, and others, quickly leading into a predominance of what we've called "Classic Linguistic Topics". Research in this period is characterized by a more linguistically-oriented focus, including syntactic topics like unification and categorial grammars, formal syntactic theory, and prepositional phrase attachments, linguistic semantics (both lexical semantics and formal semantics), and BDI dialog models. Separately we see the beginnings of a movement of people into phonology and discourse and also into the cluster we've called "Automata", which at this stage includes (pre-statistical) Parsing and Tree Adjoining Grammars.

In Figure 2b we see the movement of people into the cluster of government-sponsored topics: the ATIS and MUC bakeoffs, and speech.

In Figure 2c bakeoff research is the dominant theme, but people are also beginning to move in and out of two new clusters. One is Early Probabilistic Models, in which people focused on tasks like Part of Speech tagging, Collocations, and Lexical Acqui-

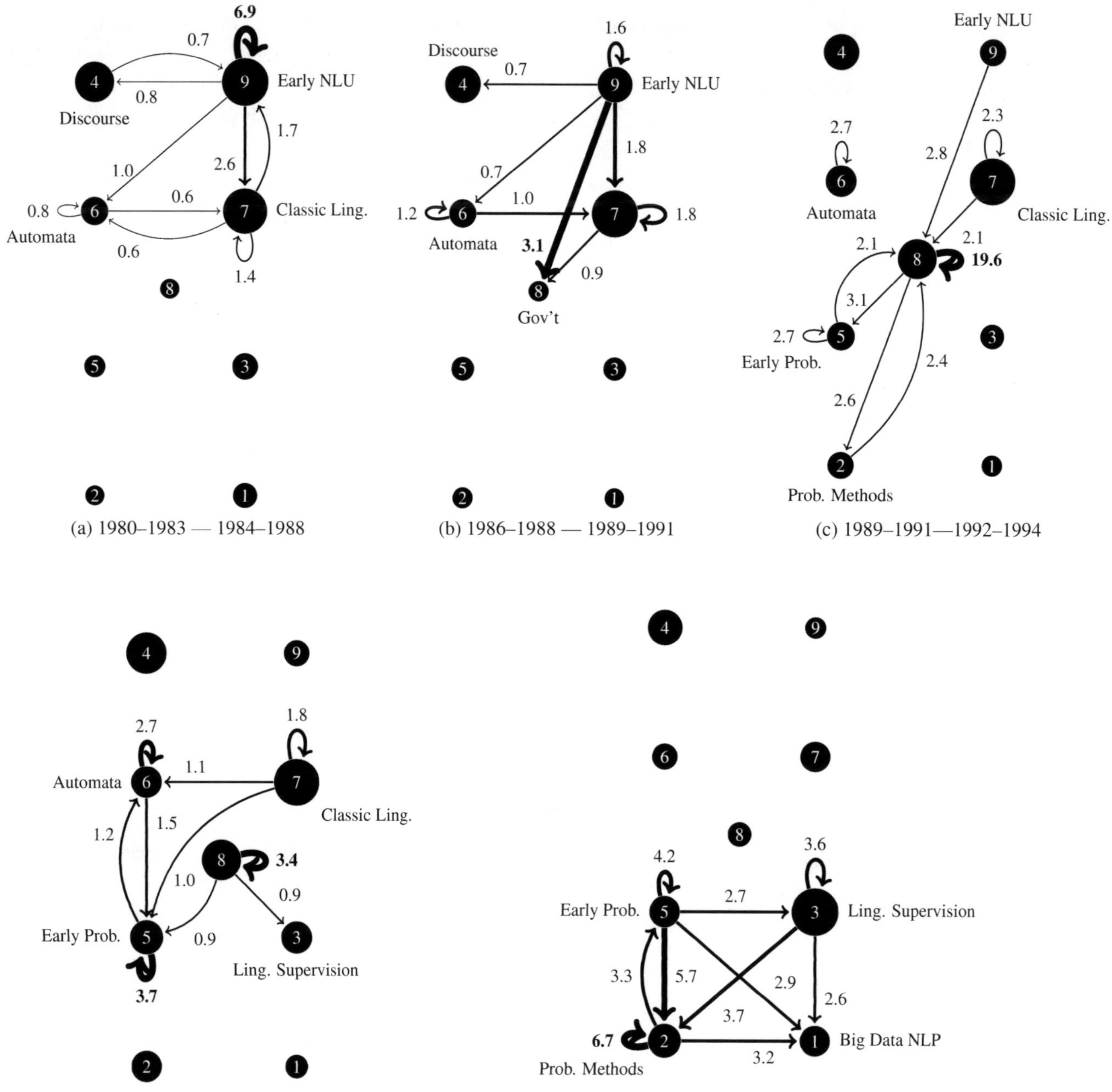

(a) 1980–1983 — 1984–1988

(b) 1986–1988 — 1989–1991

(c) 1989–1991—1992–1994

(d) 1992–1994—1995–1998

(e) 2002–2004—2005–2007

Figure 2: Author flow between topic clusters in five key time periods. Clusters are sized according to how many authors are in those topics in the first time period of each diagram. Edge thickness is proportional to volume of author flow between nodes, relative to biggest flow in that diagram (i.e. edge thicknesses in are not comparable across diagrams).

sition of Verb Subcategorization. People also begin to move specifically from the MUC Bakeoffs into a second cluster we call Probabilistic Methods, which in this very early stage focused on Evaluations Metrics and Experimental/Evaluation Methods. People working in the "Automata" cluster (Tree Adjoining Grammar, Parsing, and by this point Finite State Methods) continue working in these topics.

By Figure 2d, the Early Probability topics are very central, and probabilistic terminology and early tasks (tagging, collocations, and verb subcategorization) are quite popular. People are now moving into a new cluster we call "Linguistic Supervised", a set of tasks that apply supervised machine learning (usually classification) to tasks for which the gold labels are created by linguists. The first task to appear in this area was Named Entity Recognition, populated by authors who had worked on MUC, and the core methods topics of Machine Learning Classification and Linguistic Annotation. Other tasks like Word Sense Disambiguation soon followed.

By Figure 2e, people are leaving Early Probability topics like part of speech tagging, collocations, and non-statistical MT and moving into the Linguistic Supervised (e.g., Semantic Role Labeling) and Probabilistic Methods topics, which are now very central. In Probabilistic Methods, there are large groups of people in Statistical Parsing and N-grams. By the end of this period, Prob Methods is sending authors to new topics in Big Data NLP, the biggest of which are Statistical Machine Translation and Sentiment Analysis.

In sum, the patterns of participant flows reveal how sets of topics assume similar roles in the history of the ACL. In the initial period, authors move mostly between early NLP and classic linguistics topics. This period of exchange is then transformed by the arrival of government bakeoffs that draw authors into supervised linguistics and probabilistic topics. Only in the 2000's did the field mature and begin a new period of cohesive exchange across a variety of topics with shared statistical methods.

5 Member Retention and Field Integration

How does the ACL grow or decline? Do authors come and go, or do they stay for long periods? How much churn is there in the author set? How do these

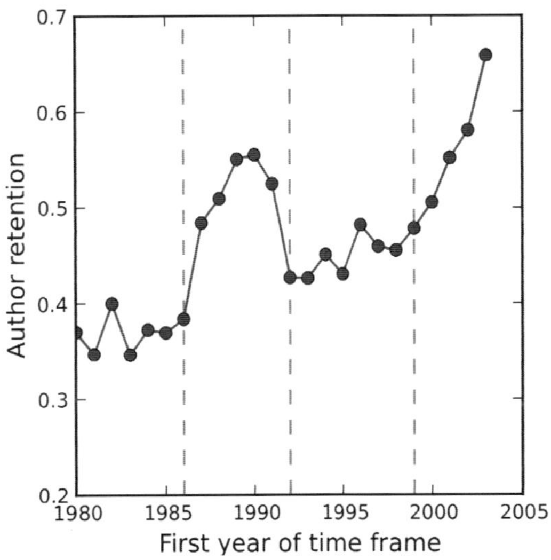

Figure 3: Overlap of authors in successive 3-year time periods over time. The x-axis indicates the first year of the 6-year time window being considered. Vertical dotted lines indicate epoch boundaries, where a year is a boundary if the first time period is entirely in one epoch and the second is entirely in the next.

trends align with the epochs we identified? To address these questions, we examine author retention over time — how many authors stay in the field versus how many enter or exit.

In order to calculate membership churn, we calculate the Jaccard overlap in the sets of people that author in adjacent 3-year time periods. This metric reflects the author retention from the first period to the second, and is inherently normalized by the number of authors (so the growing number of authors over time doesn't bias the trend). We use 3-year time windows since it's not unusual for authors to not publish in some years while still remaining active. We also remove the bulk of one-time authors by restricting the authors under consideration to those who have published at least 10 papers, but the observed trend is similar for any threshold (including no threshold). The first computation is the Jaccard overlap between those who authored in 1980–1982 and those who authored in 1983–1985; the last is between the author sets of the 2003–2005 and 2006–2008 time windows. The trend is shown in Figure 3.

The author retention curve shows a clear alignment with the epochs we identified. In the first epoch, the field is in its infancy: authors are working in a stable set of topics, but author retention is relatively low. Once the bakeoff epoch starts, author retention jumps significantly — people stay in the field as they continue to work on bakeoff papers. As soon as the bakeoffs end, the overlap in authors drops again. The fact that author retention rocketed upwards during the bakeoff epoch is presumably caused by the strong external funding incentive attracting external authors to enter and repeatedly publish in these conferences.

To understand whether this drop in overlap of authors was indeed indicative of authors who entered the field mainly for the bakeoffs, we examined authors who first published in the database in 1989. Of the 50 most prolific such authors (those with more than 8 publications in the database), 25 (exactly half) were speech recognition researchers. Of those 25 speech researchers, 16 exited (never published again in the ACL conferences) after the bakeoffs. But 9 (36%) of them remained, mainly by adapting their (formerly speech-focused) research areas toward natural language processing topics. Together, these facts suggest that the government-sponsored period led to a large influx of speech recognition researchers coming to ACL conferences, and that some fraction of them remained, continuing with natural language processing topics.

Despite the loss of the majority of the speech recognition researchers at the end of the bakeoff period, the author retention curve doesn't descend to pre-bakeoff levels: it stabilizes at a consistently higher value during the transitory epoch. This may partly be due to these new researchers colonizing and remaining in the field. Or it may be due to the increased number of topics and methods that were developed during the government-sponsored period. Whichever it is, the fact that retention didn't return to its previous levels suggests that the government sponsorship that dominated the second epoch had a lasting positive effect on the field.

In the final epoch, author retention monotonically increases to its highest-ever levels; every year the rate of authors publishing continuously rises, as does the total number of members, suggesting that the ACL community is coalescing as a field. It is plausible that this final uptick is due to funding — governmental, industrial, or otherwise — and it is an interesting direction for further research to investigate this possibility.

In sum, we observe two epochs where member retention increases: the era of government bakeoffs (1989–1994) and the more recent era where NLP has received significantly increased industry interest as well as government funding (2002–2008). These eras may thus both be ones where greater external demand increased retention and cohesion.

6 Conclusion

We offer a new people-centric methodology for computational history and apply it to the AAN to produce a number of insights about the field of computational linguistics.

Our major result is to elucidate the many ways in which the government-sponsored bakeoffs and workshops had a transformative effect on the field in the early 1990's. It has long been understood that the government played an important role in the field, from the early support of machine translation to the ALPAC report. Our work extends this understanding, showing that the government-supported bakeoffs and workshops from 1989 to 1994 caused an influx of speech scientists, a large percentage of whom remained after the bakeoffs ended. The bakeoffs and workshops acted as a major bridge from early linguistic topics to modern probabilistic topics, and catalyzed a sharp increase in author retention.

The significant recent increase in author overlap also suggests that computational linguistics is integrating into a mature field. This integration has drawn on modern shared methodologies of statistical methods and their application to large scale corpora, and may have been supported by industry demands as well as by government funding. Future work will be needed to see whether the current era is one much like the bakeoff era with an outflux of persons once funding dries up, or if it has reached a level of maturity reflective of a well-established discipline.

Acknowledgments

This research was generously supported by the Office of the President at Stanford University and the National Science Foundation under award 0835614. Thanks to the anonymous reviewers, and to Steven Bethard for creating the topic models.

References

A. Aris, B. Shneiderman, V. Qazvinian, and D. Radev. 2009. Visual overviews for discovering key papers and influences across research fronts. *Journal of the American Society for Information Science and Technology*, 60(11):2219–2228.

C. Au Yeung and A. Jatowt. 2011. Studying how the past is remembered: towards computational history through large scale text mining. In *Proceedings of the 20th ACM international conference on Information and knowledge management*, pages 1231–1240. ACM.

S. Bird, R. Dale, B.J. Dorr, B. Gibson, M. Joseph, M.Y. Kan, D. Lee, B. Powley, D.R. Radev, and Y.F. Tan. 2008. The acl anthology reference corpus: A reference dataset for bibliographic research in computational linguistics. In *Proc. of the 6th International Conference on Language Resources and Evaluation Conference (LREC'08)*, pages 1755–1759.

D. M. Blei, A. Y. Ng, and M. I. Jordan. 2003. Latent Dirichlet allocation. *Journal of Machine Learning Research*, 3(5):993–1022.

D.A. Dahl, M. Bates, M. Brown, W. Fisher, K. Hunicke-Smith, D. Pallett, C. Pao, A. Rudnicky, and E. Shriberg. 1994. Expanding the scope of the atis task: The atis-3 corpus. In *Proceedings of the workshop on Human Language Technology*, pages 43–48. Association for Computational Linguistics.

S. Gerrish and D.M. Blei. 2010. A language-based approach to measuring scholarly impact. In *Proceedings of the 26th International Conference on Machine Learning*.

T.L. Griffiths and M. Steyvers. 2004. Finding scientific topics. *Proceedings of the National Academy of Sciences of the United States of America*, 101(Suppl 1):5228.

R. Grishman and B. Sundheim. 1996. Message understanding conference-6: A brief history. In *Proceedings of COLING*, volume 96, pages 466–471.

David Hall, Daniel Jurafsky, and Christopher D. Manning. 2008. Studying the history of ideas using topic models. In *Proceedings of EMNLP 2008*.

C.T. Hemphill, J.J. Godfrey, and G.R. Doddington. 1990. The atis spoken language systems pilot corpus. In *Proceedings of the DARPA speech and natural language workshop*, pages 96–101.

P. Price. 1990. Evaluation of spoken language systems: The atis domain. In *Proceedings of the Third DARPA Speech and Natural Language Workshop*, pages 91–95. Morgan Kaufmann.

D.R. Radev, P. Muthukrishnan, and V. Qazvinian. 2009. The acl anthology network corpus. In *Proceedings of the 2009 Workshop on Text and Citation Analysis for Scholarly Digital Libraries*, pages 54–61. Association for Computational Linguistics.

Y. Tu, N. Johri, D. Roth, and J. Hockenmaier. 2010. Citation author topic model in expert search. In *Proceedings of the 23rd International Conference on Computational Linguistics: Posters*, pages 1265–1273. Association for Computational Linguistics.

Discovering Factions in the Computational Linguistics Community

Yanchuan Sim Noah A. Smith
Language Technologies Institute
Carnegie Mellon University
Pittsburgh, PA 15213, USA
{ysim,nasmith}@cs.cmu.edu

David A. Smith
Department of Computer Science
University of Massachusetts
Amherst, MA 01003, USA
dasmith@cs.umass.edu

Abstract

We present a joint probabilistic model of who cites whom in computational linguistics, and also of the words they use to do the citing. The model reveals latent *factions*, or groups of individuals whom we expect to collaborate more closely within their faction, cite within the faction using language distinct from citation outside the faction, and be largely understandable through the language used when cited from without. We conduct an exploratory data analysis on the ACL Anthology. We extend the model to reveal changes in some authors' faction memberships over time.

1 Introduction

The ACL Anthology presents an excellent dataset for studying both the language and the social connections in our evolving research field. Extensive studies using techniques from the field of bibliometrics have been applied to this dataset (Radev et al., 2009a), quantifying the importance and impact factor of both authors and articles in the community. Moreover, recent work has leveraged the availability of digitized publications to study trends and influences within the ACL community (Hall et al., 2008; Gerrish and Blei, 2010; Yogatama et al., 2011) and to analyze academic collaborations (Johri et al., 2011).

To the best of our knowledge, however, existing work has mainly pursued "macroscopic" investigations of the interaction of authors in collaboration, citation networks, or the textual content of whole papers. We seek to complement these results with a "microscopic" investigation of authors' interactions by considering the individual sentences authors use to cite each other.

In this paper, we present a joint model of who cites whom in computational linguistics, and also of *how* they do the citing. Central to this model is the idea of *factions*, or groups of individuals whom we expect to (i) collaborate more closely within their faction, (ii) cite within the faction using language distinct from citation outside the faction, (iii) be largely understandable through the language used when cited from without, and (iv) evolve over time.[1] Factions can be thought of as "communities," which are loosely defined in the literature on networks as subgraphs where internal connections are denser than external ones (Radicchi et al., 2004). The distinction here is that the strength of connections depends on a latent language model estimated from citation contexts.

This paper is an exploratory data analysis using a Bayesian generative model. We aim both to discover meaningful factions in the ACL community and also to illustrate the use of a probabilistic model for such discovery. As such, we do not present any objective evaluation of the model or make any claims that the factions optimally explain the research community. Indeed, we suspect that reaching a broad consensus among community members about factions (i.e., a "gold standard") would be quite difficult, as any social community's factions are likely perceived very

[1]Our factions are computational abstractions—clusters of authors—discovered entirely from the corpus. We do not claim that factions are especially contentious, any more than "subcommunities" in social networks are especially collegial.

subjectively. It is for this reason that a probabilistic generative model, in which all assumptions are made plain, is appropriate for the task. We hope this analysis will prove useful in future empirical research on social communities (including scientific ones) and their use of language.

2 Model

In this paper, our approach is a probabilistic model over (i) coauthorship relations and (ii) the words in sentences containing citations. The words are assumed to be generated by a distribution that depends on the (latent) faction memberships of the citing authors, the cited authors, and whether the authors have coauthored before. To model these different effects on language, we use a sparse additive generative (SAGE) model (Eisenstein et al., 2011). In contrast to the popular Dirichlet-multinomial for topic modeling, which directly models lexical probabilities associated with each (latent) topic, SAGE models the deviation in log frequencies from a background lexical distribution. Imposing a sparsity-inducing prior on the deviation vectors limits the number of terms whose probabilities diverge from the background lexical frequencies, thereby increasing robustness to limited training data. SAGE can be used with or without latent topics; our model does not include topics. Figure 1 shows the plate diagram for our model.

We describe the generative process:

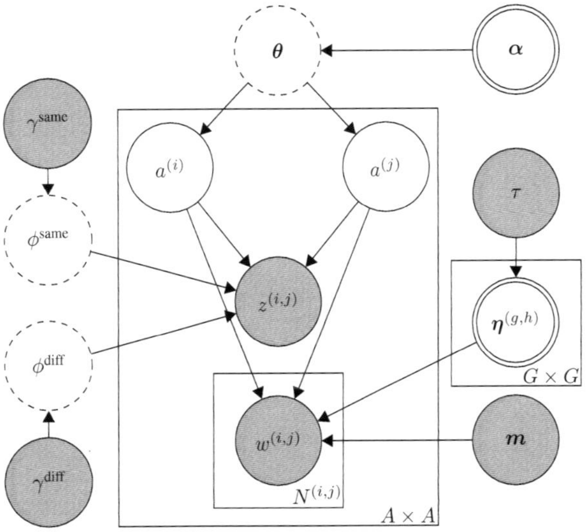

Figure 1: Plate diagram for our graphical model. A and G are the fixed numbers of authors and factions, respectively. $\boldsymbol{m}$ is the background word distribution, $\boldsymbol{\alpha}$, τ, γ are hyperparameters, $\boldsymbol{a}$ are latent author factions, $\boldsymbol{z}$ and $\boldsymbol{w}$ are the observed coauthorship relations and observed words in citation sentences between authors, respectively. Each of the $a^{(i)}$, denoting author i's faction alignment, are sampled once every iteration conditioned on all the other $a^{(j)}$. If i and j are coauthors or i cited j in some publication, $a^{(i)}$ and $a^{(j)}$ will not be conditionally independent due to the v-structure. ϕ^{same} and ϕ^{diff} are binomial distributions over whether two authors have collaborated together before, given that they are assigned to the same/different factions. Dashed variables are collapsed out in the Gibbs sampler, while double bordered variables are optimized in the M-step.

- Generate the multinomial distribution over faction memberships from a Dirichlet distribution: $\boldsymbol{\theta} \sim \text{Dir}(\boldsymbol{\alpha})$.

- Generate the binomial distribution for whether two authors coauthor, given that they are in the same faction, from a Beta distribution: $\phi^{\text{same}} \sim \text{Beta}(\gamma_0^{\text{same}}, \gamma_1^{\text{same}})$. Generate the analogous binomial, given that they are in different factions: $\phi^{\text{diff}} \sim \text{Beta}(\gamma_0^{\text{diff}}, \gamma_1^{\text{diff}})$.

- For each author i, draw a faction indicator $a_i \sim \text{Multinomial}(\boldsymbol{\theta})$.

- For all ordered pairs of factions (g, h), draw a deviation vector $\boldsymbol{\eta}^{(g,h)} \sim \text{Laplace}(0, \tau)$. This vector, which will be sparse, corresponds to the deviations in word log-frequencies when faction g is citing faction h.

- For each word v in the vocabulary, let the unigram probability that an author in faction g uses to cite an author in faction h be

$$\beta_v^{(g,h)} = \frac{\exp(\eta_v^{(g,h)} + m_v)}{\sum_{v'} \exp(\eta_{v'}^{(g,h)} + m_{v'})}$$

.

- For each ordered pair of authors (i, j),
  - For each word that i uses to cite j, draw $w_k^{(i,j)} \sim \text{Multinomial}(\boldsymbol{\beta}^{(a^{(i)}, a^{(j)})})$.
  - If the authors are from the same faction, i.e., $a^{(i)} = a^{(j)}$, draw coauthorship indi-

cator $z^{(i,j)} \sim \text{Binomial}(\phi^{\text{same}})$; else, draw $z^{(i,j)} \sim \text{Binomial}(\phi^{\text{diff}})$.

Thus, our goal is to maximize the conditional likelihood of the observed data

$$p(\boldsymbol{w}, \boldsymbol{z} \mid \boldsymbol{\alpha}, \boldsymbol{\eta}, \tau, \boldsymbol{m}, \gamma) = \int_{\boldsymbol{\theta}} \int_{\boldsymbol{\phi}} \int_{\boldsymbol{a}} p(\boldsymbol{w}, \boldsymbol{z}, \boldsymbol{\theta}, \boldsymbol{\phi}, \boldsymbol{a} \mid \boldsymbol{\alpha}, \boldsymbol{\eta}, \tau, \boldsymbol{m}, \gamma)$$

with respect to $\boldsymbol{\eta}$ and $\boldsymbol{\alpha}$. We fix τ and γ, which are hyperparameters that encode our prior beliefs, and $\boldsymbol{m}$, which we assume to be a fixed background word distribution.

Exact inference in this model is intractable, so we resort to an approximate inference technique based on Markov Chain Monte Carlo simulation. We perform Bayesian inference over the latent author factions while using maximum *a posteriori* estimates of $\boldsymbol{\eta}$ because Bayesian inference of $\boldsymbol{\eta}$ is problematic due to the logistic transformation. We refer the interested reader to Eisenstein et al. (2011). We take an empirical Bayes approach to setting the hyperparameter $\boldsymbol{\alpha}$. Our overall learning procedure is a Monte Carlo Expectation Maximization algorithm (Wei and Tanner, 1990).

3 Learning and Inference

Our learning algorithm is a two-step iterative procedure. During the E-step, we perform collapsed Gibbs sampling to obtain distributions over factions for each author, given the current setting of the hyperparameters. In the M-step, we obtain point estimates for the hyperparameters $\boldsymbol{\eta}$ and $\boldsymbol{\alpha}$ given the current posterior distributions for the author factions.

3.1 E-step

As the Dirichlet and Beta distributions are conjugate priors to the multinomial and binomial respectively, we can integrate out the latent variables $\boldsymbol{\theta}, \phi^{(\text{same})}$ and $\phi^{(\text{diff})}$. For an author i, we sample his faction alignment $a^{(i)}$ conditioned on faction assignments to all other authors and citation words between i and other authors (in both directions). Denoting $\boldsymbol{a}^{-i}$ as the current faction assignments for all the authors except i,

$$\begin{aligned} & p(a^{(i)} = g \mid \boldsymbol{a}^{(-i)}, \boldsymbol{w}, \boldsymbol{\eta}, \boldsymbol{\alpha}, \boldsymbol{\gamma}) \\ & \quad \propto p(a^{(i)} = g, \boldsymbol{a}^{(-i)}, \boldsymbol{w} \mid \boldsymbol{\eta}, \boldsymbol{\alpha}, \boldsymbol{\gamma}) \\ & \quad \propto (N_g + \alpha_g) \prod_j^A \frac{\gamma_z^\epsilon + N_z^\epsilon}{\gamma_0^\epsilon + \gamma_1^\epsilon + N_0^\epsilon + N_1^\epsilon} p(\boldsymbol{w}^{(i)} \mid \eta) \end{aligned}$$

where N_g is the number of authors (except i) who are assigned to faction g, ϵ_{ij} = "same" if $g = a^{(j)}$ and ϵ_{ij} = "diff" otherwise, and $N_1^\epsilon, N_0^\epsilon$ denotes the number of author pairs that have/have not coauthored before respectively, given the status of their factions ϵ. We elide the subscripts of ϵ and superscript of z for notational simplicity and abuse notation to let $\boldsymbol{w}^{(i)}$ refer to all author i's citation words, both incoming and outgoing. Using SAGE, the factor for an author's words is

$$p(\boldsymbol{w}^{(i)} \mid \eta) = \prod_j \prod_v \left(\beta_v^{(g,a^{(j)})}\right)^{w_v^{(i,j)}} \left(\beta_v^{(a^{(j)},g)}\right)^{w_v^{(j,i)}}$$

where $w_v^{(i,j)}$ is the observed count of the number of times word v has been used when author i cites j; j ranges over the A authors.

We sample each author's faction in turn and do so several times during the E-step, collecting samples to estimate our posterior distribution over $\boldsymbol{a}$.

3.2 M-step

In the M-step, we optimize all $\boldsymbol{\eta}^{(g,h)}$ and $\boldsymbol{\alpha}$ given the posterior distribution over author factions.

Optimizing $\boldsymbol{\eta}$. Eisenstein et al. (2011) postulated that the components of $\boldsymbol{\eta}$ are drawn from a compound model $\int \mathcal{N}(\eta; \mu, \sigma)\mathcal{E}(\sigma; \tau)d\sigma$, where $\mathcal{E}(\sigma; \tau)$ indicates the Exponential distribution. They fit a variational distribution $Q(\boldsymbol{\sigma})$ and optimized the log-likelihood of the data by iteratively fitting the parameters $\boldsymbol{\eta}$ using a Newton optimization step and maximizing the variational bound.

The compound model described is equivalent to the Laplace distribution $\mathcal{L}(\eta; \mu, \tau)$ (Lange and Sinsheimer, 1993; Figueiredo, 2003). Moreover, a zero mean Laplace prior has the same effect as placing an L_1 regularizer on $\boldsymbol{\eta}$. Therefore, we can equivalently maximize the regularized likelihood

$$\langle \boldsymbol{c}^{(g,h)} \rangle^T \boldsymbol{\eta}^{(g,h)} - \langle C^{(g,h)} \rangle \log \sum_v \exp(\eta_v^{(g,h)} + m_v) - \lambda \left\| \boldsymbol{\eta}^{(g,h)} \right\|_1$$

with respect to $\eta^{(g,h)}$. $\langle \boldsymbol{c}^{(g,h)} \rangle$ is a vector of expected count of the words that faction g used when citing faction h, $\langle \boldsymbol{c}^{(g,h)} \rangle = \sum_v \langle c_v^{(g,h)} \rangle$ and λ is the regularization constant. The regularization constant and Laplace variance are related by $\lambda = \tau^{-1}$ (Tibshirani, 1996).

We use the gradient-based optimization routine OWL-QN (Andrew and Gao, 2007) to maximize the above objective function with respect to $\boldsymbol{\eta}^{(g,h)}$ for each pair of factions g and h.

Optimizing $\boldsymbol{\alpha}$. As in the empirical Bayes approach, we learn the hyperparameter setting of $\boldsymbol{\alpha}$ from the data by maximizing the log likelihood with respect to $\boldsymbol{\alpha}$. By treating $\boldsymbol{\alpha}$ as the parameter of a Dirichlet-multinomial compound distribution, we can directly use the samples of author factions produced by our Gibbs sampler to estimate $\boldsymbol{\alpha}$. Minka (2009) describes in detail several iterative approaches to estimate $\boldsymbol{\alpha}$; we use the linear-time Newton-Raphson iterative update to estimate the components of $\boldsymbol{\alpha}$.

4 Data Analysis

4.1 Dataset

We used the ACL Anthology Network Corpus (Radev et al., 2009b), which currently contains 18,041 papers written by 12,777 authors. These papers are published in the field of computational linguistics between 1965 and 2011.[2] Furthermore, the corpus provides bibliographic data such as authors of the papers and bibliographic references between each paper in the corpus. We extracted sentences containing citations using regular expressions and linked them between authors with the help of metadata provided in the corpus.

We tokenized the extracted sentences and downcased them. Words that are numeric, appear less than 20 times, or are in a stop word list are discarded. For papers with multiple authors, we divided the word counts by the number of pairings between authors in both papers, assigning each word to each author-pair (i.e., a count of $\frac{1}{nn'}$ if a paper with n authors cites a paper with n' authors).

Due to the large number of authors, we only used the 500 most cited authors (within the corpus) who have published at least 5 papers. Papers with no authors left are removed from the dataset. As a result, we have 8,144 papers containing 80,776 citation sentences (31,659 citation pairs). After text processing, there are 391,711 tokens and 3,037 word types.

In each iteration of the EM algorithm, we run the E-step Gibbs sampler for 300 iterations, discarding the first 100 samples for burn-in and collecting samples at every 3rd iteration to avoid autocorrelation. At the M-step, we update our $\boldsymbol{\eta}$ and $\boldsymbol{\alpha}$ using the samples collected. We run the model for 100 EM iterations.

We fixed $\lambda = 5$, $\gamma^{\text{same}} = (0.5, 1)$ and $\gamma^{\text{diff}} = (1, 0.5)$. Our setting of γ reflects our prior beliefs that coauthors tend to be from the same faction.

4.2 Factions in ACL (1965–2011)

We ran the model with $G = 30$ factions and selected the most probable faction for each author from the posterior distribution of the author-faction alignment obtained in the final E step. Only 26 factions were selected as most probable for some author.[3] Table 1 presents members of selected factions, along with citation words that have the largest positive log frequency deviation from the background distribution.[4] Table 2 shows a list of the top three authors associated with factions not shown in Table 1. Incoming (outgoing) citation words are found by summing the log deviation vectors $\boldsymbol{\eta}$ across citing (cited) factions. The author factions are manually labeled.

We see from Table 1, the model has selected keywords that are arguably significant in certain subfields in computational linguistics. Incoming citations are generally indicative of the subject areas in

[2] For a list of the journals, conferences and workshops archived by the ACL anthology, please visit `http://aclweb.org/anthology-new`.

[3] In future work, nonparametric priors might be employed to automate the selection of G.

[4] We found it quite difficult to make sense of terms with *negative* log frequency deviations. This suggests exploring a model allowing only positive deviations; we leave that for future work.

Formalisms (31)	*Fernando Pereira, Jason M. Eisner, Stuart M. Shieber, Walter Daelemans, Hitoshi Isahara*
Self cites:	parsing
In cites:	parsing, semiring, grammars, tags, grammar, tag, lexicalized, dependency
Out cites:	tagger, regular, dependency, transformationbased, tagging, stochastic, grammars, sense
Evaluation (17)	*Salim Roukos, Eduard Hovy, Marti A. Hearst, Chin-Yew Lin, Dekang Lin*
Self cites:	automatic, bleu, linguistics, evaluation, computational, text, proceedings
In cites:	automatic, bleu, segmentation, method, proceedings, dependency, parses, text
Out cites:	paraphrases, cohesion, agreement, hierarchical, entropy, phrasebased, evaluation, treebank
Semantics (26)	*Martha Palmer, Daniel Jurafsky, Mihai Surdeanu, David Weir, German Rigau*
Self cites:	sense, semantic, wordnet
In cites:	framenet, sense, semantic, task, wordnet, word, project, question
Out cites:	sense, wordnet, moses, preferences, distributional, semantic, focus, supersense
Machine Translation (MT1) (9)	*Kevin Knight, Michel Galley, Jonathan Graehl, Wei Wang, Sanjeev P. Khudanpur*
Self cites:	inference, scalable, model
In cites:	scalable, inference, machine, training, generation, translation, model, syntaxbased
Out cites:	phrasebased, hierarchical, inversion, forest, transduction, translation, ibm, discourse
Word Sense Disambiguation (WSD) (42)	*David Yarowsky, Rada Mihalcea, Eneko Agirre, Ted Pedersen, Yorick Wilks*
Self cites:	sense, word
In cites:	sense, preferences, wordnet, acquired, semcor, word, semantic, calle
Out cites:	sense, subcategorization, acquisition, automatic, corpora, lexical, processing, wordnet
Parsing (20)	*Michael John Collins, Eugene Charniak, Mark Johnson, Stephen Clark, Massimiliano Ciaramita*
Self cites:	parser, parsing, model, perceptron, parsers, dependency
In cites:	parser, perceptron, supersense, parsing, dependency, results, hmm, models
Out cites:	parsing, forest, treebank, model, coreference, stochastic, grammar, task
Discourse (29)	*Daniel Marcu, Aravind K. Joshi, Barbara J. Grosz, Marilyn A. Walker, Bonnie Lynn Webber*
Self cites:	discourse, structure, centering
In cites:	discourse, phrasebased, centering, tag, focus, rhetorical, tags, lexicalized
Out cites:	discourse, rhetorical, framenet, realizer, tags, resolution, grammars, synonyms
Machine Translation (MT2) (9)	*Franz Josef Och, Hermann Ney, Mitchell P. Marcus, David Chiang, Dekai Wu*
Self cites:	training, error
In cites:	error, giza, rate, alignment, training, minimum, translation, phrasebased
Out cites:	forest, subcategorization, arabic, model, translation, machine, models, heuristic

Table 1: Key authors and citation words associated with some factions. For each faction, we show the 5 authors with highest expected incoming citations (i.e $p(\text{faction} \mid \text{author}) \times$ citations). Factions are labeled manually, referring to key sub-fields in computational linguistics. Faction sizes are in parenthesis following the labels. The citation words with the strongest positive weights in the deviation vectors are shown.

which the faction holds recognized expertise. For instance, the faction labeled "semantics" has citation terms commonly associated with propositional semantics: *sense*, *framenet*, *wordnet*. On the other hand, outgoing citations hint at the related work that a faction builds on; discourse might require building on components involving *framenet*, *grammars*, *synonyms*, while word sense disambiguation involves solving problems like *acquisition* and modeling *subcategorization*.

4.3 Sensitivity

Given the same initial parameters, we found our model to be fairly stable across iterations of Monte

Adam Lopez, Paul S. Jacobs (2)
Regina Barzilay, Judith L. Klavans, Robert T. Kasper (3)
Lauri Karttunen, Kemal Oflazer, Kimmo Koskenniemi (3)
John Carroll, Ted Briscoe, Scott Miller (7)
Vincent J. Della Pietra, Stephen A. Della Pietra, Robert L. Mercer (25)
Thorsten Brants, Liang Huang, Anoop Sarkar (9)
Christoph Tillmann, Kenji Yamada, Sharon Goldwater (7)
Alex Waibel, Keh-Jiann Chen, Katrin Kirchhoff (3)
Lynette Hirschman, Claire Cardie, Vincent Ng (26)
Erik F. Tjong Kim Sang, Ido Dagan, Marius Paşca (21)
Yuji Matsumoto, Dragomir R. Radev, Chew Lim Tan (18)
Christopher D. Manning, Owen Rambow, Ellen Riloff (19)
Richard Zens, Hieu Hoang, Nicola Bertoldi (9)
Dan Klein, Jun'ichi Tsujii, Yusuke Miyao (6)
Janyce Wiebe, Mirella Lapata, Kathleen R. McKeown (50)
I. Dan Melamed, Ryan McDonald, Joakim Nivre (10)
Philipp Koehn, Lillian Lee, Chris Callison-Burch (80)
Kenneth Ward Church, Eric Brill, Richard M. Schwartz (19)

Table 2: Top 3 authors of the remaining 18 factions not displayed in Table 1.

Carlo EM. We found that when G was too small (e.g., 10), groups were more mixed and the η vectors could not capture variation among them well. When G was larger, the factions were subjectively cleaner, but fields like translation split into many factions (as is visible in the $G = 30$ case illustrated in Tables 1 and 2. Strengthening the L_1 penalty made η more sparse, of course, but gave less freedom in fitting the data and therefore more grouping of authors into a fewer effective factions.

4.4 Inter-Faction Relationships

By using the most probable *a posteriori* faction for each author, we can compute the number of citations between factions. We define the average inter-faction citations by:

$$\text{IFC}(g, h) = \frac{\Psi(g \to h) + \Psi(h \to g)}{N_g + N_h} \quad (1)$$

where $\Psi(g \to h)$ is the total number of papers written by authors in g that cite papers written by authors in h.

Figure 2 presents a graph of selected factions and how these factions talk about each other. As we would expect, the machine translation faction is quite strongly connected to formalisms and parsing factions, reflecting the heavy use of grammars and parsing algorithms in translation. Moreover, we can observe that "deeper" linguistics research, such as semantics and discourse, are less likely to be cited by the other factions. This is reflected in Figure 3, where the statistical MT and parsing factions in the bottom left exhibit higher citation activity amongst each other. In addition, we note that factions tend to self-cite more often than out of their own factions; this is unsurprising given the prior we selected.

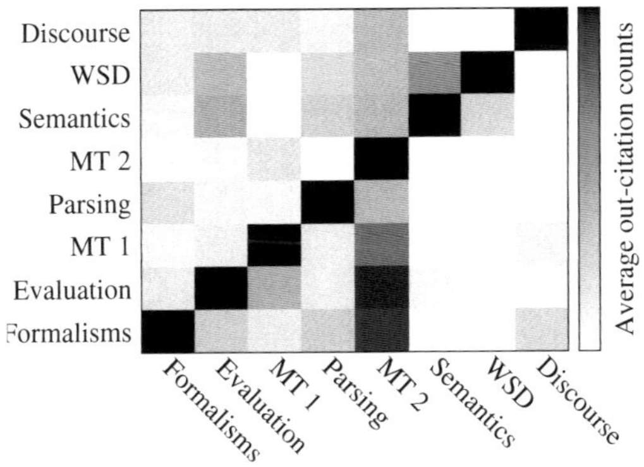

Figure 3: Heat map showing citation rates across selected factions. Factions on the horizontal axis are being cited; factions on the vertical axis are citing. Darker shades denote higher average $\frac{\Psi(g \to h)}{N_g}$.

The IFC between discourse and MT2 (as shown by the edge thickness in figure 2) is higher than expected, given our prior knowledge of the computational linguistics community. Further investigation revealed that, Daniel Marcu, posited by our model to be a member of the discourse faction, has coauthored numerous highly cited papers in MT in recent years (Marcu and Wong, 2002). However, the model split the translation field, which fragmented the counts of MT related citation words. Thus, assigning Daniel Marcu to the discourse faction, which also has a less diverse citation vocabulary, is more probable than assigning him to one of the MT factions. In §4.6, we consider a model of factions over time to mitigate this problem.

4.5 Comparison to Graph Clustering

Work in the field of bibliometrics has largely focused on using the link structure of citation networks to study higher level structures. See Osareh (1996) for a review. Popular methods include bibliographic coupling (Kessler, 1963), and co-citation

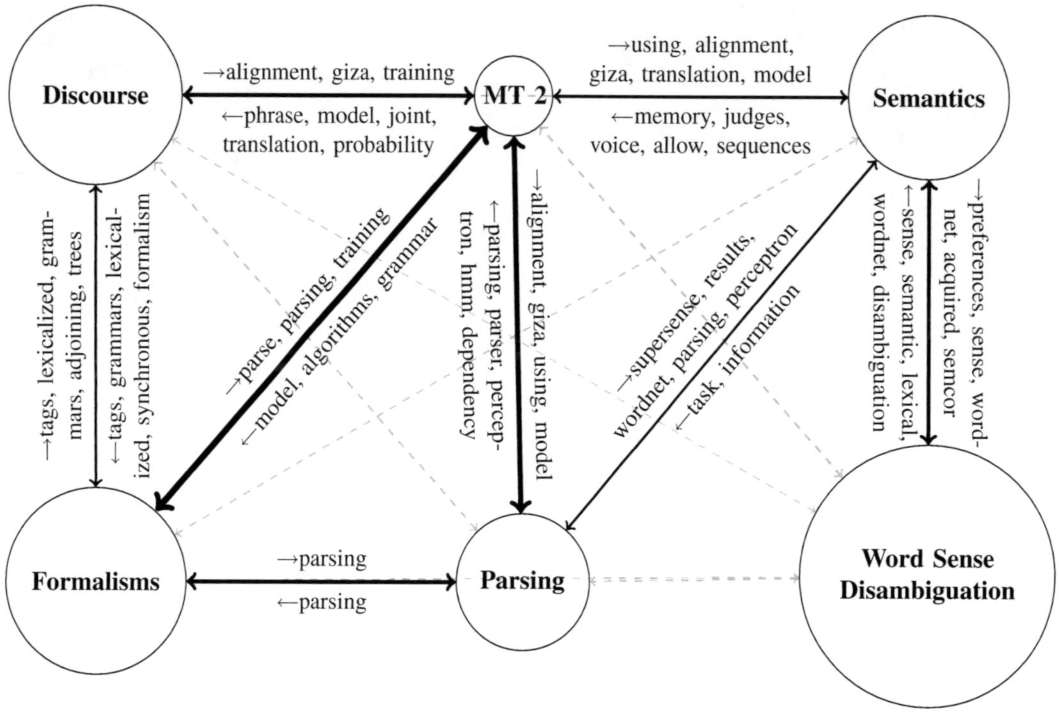

Figure 2: Citations among some factions. The size of a node is relative to the faction size and edge thickness is relative to the average number of inter-faction citations (equation 1). The words on the edges are the highest weighted words from the deviation vectors η, with the arrow denoting the direction of the citation. Edges with below average IFC scores are represented as dashed lines, and their citations words are not shown to preserve readability.

analysis (Small, 1973). By using authors as an unit of analysis in co-citation pairs, author co-citations have been presented as a technique to analyze their subject specialties (White and Griffith, 1981). Using standard graph clustering algorithms on these author co-citation networks, one can obtain a semblance of author factions. Hence, we performed graph clustering on both collaboration and citation graphs[5] of authors in our dataset using Graclus[6], a graph clustering implementation based on normalized cuts and ratio associations (Dhillon et al., 2004).

In Table 3, we compare, for selected authors, how their faction-mates obtained by our model and graph clustering differ. When clustering on the author collaboration network, we obtained some clusters easily identified with research labs (e.g., Daniel Marcu at the Information Sciences Institute). The co-citation graph leads to groupings dominated by heavily co-cited papers in major research areas. While we do not have an objective measurement of quality or usefulness, we believe that the factions identified by our model align somewhat better with familiar technical themes around which sub-communities naturally form than major research problems or institutions.

[5]We converted the directed citation graph into a symmetric graph by performing bibliometric symmetrization described in Satuluri and Parthasarathy (2011, section 3.3).

[6]`http://www.cs.utexas.edu/users/dml/Software/graclus.html`

4.6 Factions over Time

Faction alignments may be dynamic; we expect that, over time, individual researchers may move from one faction to another as their interests evolve. We consider a slightly modified model whereby authors are split into different copies of themselves during a non-overlapping set of discrete time periods. Given a set of disjoint time periods T, we denote each author-faction node by $\{a^{(i,t)} \mid (i,t) \in A \times T\}$. As we treat each "incarnation" of an author as a distinct individual, we can simply use the same inference algorithm described in §2. (In future work we might impose an expectation of gradual changes along a more continuous representation of time.)

Our Model	Collaboration Network	Co-citation Network
Franz Josef Och		
Franz Josef Och, Hermann Ney, Mitchell P. Marcus, David Chiang, Dekai Wu error, giza, rate, alignment, training	Franz Josef Och, Hermann Ney, Richard Zens, Stephan Vogel, Nicola Ueffing giza, mert, popovic, moses, alignments	Franz Josef Och, Hermann Ney, Vincent J. Della Pietra, Daniel Marcu, Robert L. Mercer giza, bleu, phrasebased, alignment, mert
Daniel Marcu		
Daniel Marcu, Aravind K. Joshi, Barbara J. Grosz, Marilyn A. Walker, Bonnie Lynn Webber discourse, phrasebased, centering, tag, focus	Daniel Marcu, Kevin Knight, Daniel Gildea, David Chiang, Liang Huang phrasebased, forest, cube, spmt, hiero	Franz Josef Och, Hermann Ney, Vincent J. Della Pietra, Daniel Marcu, Robert L. Mercer giza, bleu, phrasebased, alignment, mert
Michael John Collins		
Eugene Charniak, Michael John Collins, Mark Johnson, Stephen Clark, Massimiliano Ciaramita parser, perceptron, supersense, parsing, dependency	Michael John Collins, Joakim Nivre, Lluís Márquez, Xavier Carreras, Jan Hajič pseudoprojective, maltparser, perceptron, malt, averaged	Michael John Collins, Christopher D. Manning, Dan Klein, Eugene Charniak, Mark Johnson tnt, prototypedriven, perceptron, coarsetofine, pcfg
Kathleen R. McKeown		
Mirella Lapata, Janyce Wiebe, Kathleen R. McKeown, Dan Roth, Ralph Grishman semantic, work, learning, corpus, model	Kathleen R. McKeown, Regina Barzilay, Owen Rambow, Marilyn A. Walker, Srinivas Bangalore centering, arabic, pyramid, realpro, cue	Kenneth Ward Church, David Yarowsky, Eduard Hovy, Kathleen R. McKeown, Lillian Lee rouge, minipar, nltk, alignment, montreal

Table 3: Comparing selected factions between our model and graph clustering algorithms. Authors with highest incoming citations are shown. For our model, we show the largest weighted words in the SAGE vector of incoming citations for the faction, while for graph clustering, we show words with the highest tf-idf weight.

We split the same data as the earlier sections into four disjoint time periods, 1965–1989, 1990–1999, 2000–2005 and 2006–2011. The split across time is unequal due to the number of papers published in each period: these four periods include 1,917, 3,874, 3,786, and 8,105 papers, respectively. Here we used $G = 20$ factions for faster runtime, leading to diminished interpretability, though the sparsity of the deviation vectors mitigates this problem somewhat. Figure 4 shows graphical plots of selected authors and their faction membership posteriors over time (drawn from the final E-step).

With a simple extension of the original model, we can learn shifts in the subject area the author is publishing about. Consider Eugene Charniak: the model observed a major change in faction alignment around 2000, when one of the popular Charniak parsers (Charniak, 2000) was released; this is somewhat later than Charniak's interests shifted, and the earlier faction's words are not clearly an accurate description of his work at that time. More fine-grained modeling of time and also accounting for the death and birth of factions might ameliorate these inconsistencies with our background knowledge about Charniak. The model finds that Aravind Joshi was associated with the tagging/parsing faction in the 1990s and in recent years moved back towards discourse (Prasad et al., 2008). David Yarowsky, known for his early work on word sense disambiguation, has since focused on applying word sense disambiguation techniques in a multilingual context (Garera et al., 2009; Bergsma et al., 2011). As mentioned in the previous section, we observe that the extended model is able to capture Daniel Marcu's shift from discourse-related work to MT with his work in phrase-based statistical MT (Marcu and Wong, 2002).

5 Related Work

A number of algorithms use topic modeling to analyze the text in the articles. Topic models such as latent Dirichlet allocation (Blei et al., 2003) and its variations have been increasingly used to study trends in scientific literature (McCallum et al., 2006; Dietz et al., 2007; Hall et al., 2008; Gerrish and Blei, 2010), predict citation information (McNee et al.,

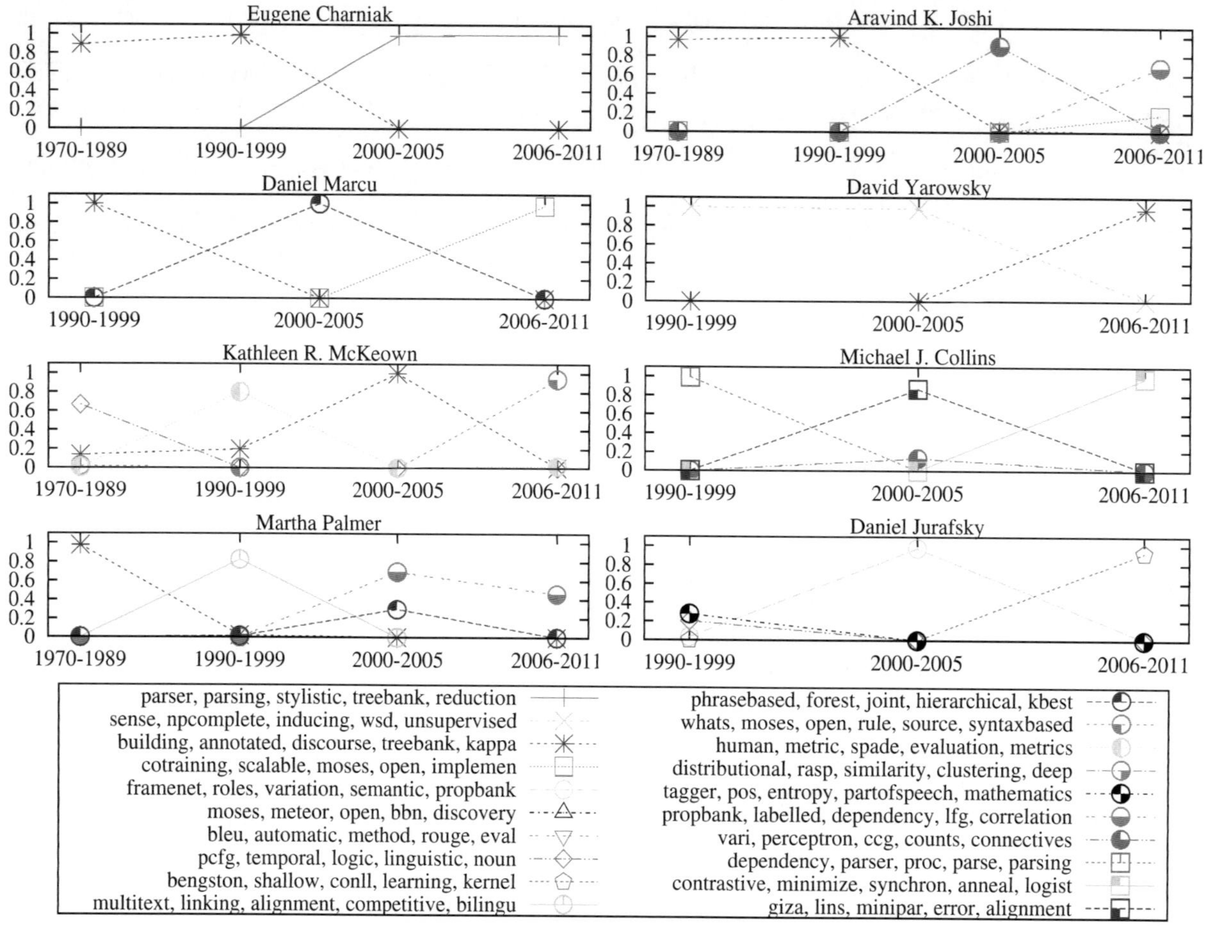

Figure 4: Posterior probability of faction alignment over time periods for eight researchers with significant publication records in at least three periods. The key for each entry contains the five highest weighted words in the deviation vectors for the faction's incoming citations. For each author, we show factions with which he or she is associated with probability > 0.1 in at least one time period.

2002; Ibáñez et al., 2009; Nallapati et al., 2008) and analyze authorship (Rosen-Zvi et al., 2004; Johri et al., 2011).

Assigning author factions can be seen as network classification problem, where the goal is to label nodes in a network such that there is (i) a correlation between a node's label and its observed attributes and (ii) a correlation between labels of interconnected nodes (Sen et al., 2008). Such collective network-based approaches have been used on scientific literature to classify papers/web pages into its subject categories (Kubica et al., 2002; Getoor, 2005; Angelova and Weikum, 2006). If we knew the word distributions between factions beforehand, learning the author factions in our model would be equivalent to the network classification task, where our edge weights are proportional to the probability of coauthorship multiplied by the probability of observing the citation words given the author's faction labels.

6 Conclusion

In this work, we have defined factions in terms of how authors talk about each other's work, going beyond co-authorship and citation graph representations of a research community. We take a first step toward computationally modeling faction formation by using a latent author faction model and applied it to the ACL community, revealing both factions and how they cite each other. We also extended the model to capture authors' faction changes over time.

Acknowledgments

The authors thank members of the ARK group and the anonymous reviewers for helpful feedback. We gratefully acknowledge technical assistance from Matthew Fiorillo. This research was supported in part by an A*STAR fellowship to Y. Sim, NSF grant IIS-0915187 to N. Smith, and the Center for Intelligent Information Retrieval and NSF grant IIS-0910884 for D. Smith.

References

G. Andrew and J. Gao. 2007. Scalable training of L_1-regularized log-linear models. In *Proc. of ICML*.

R. Angelova and G. Weikum. 2006. Graph-based text classification: learn from your neighbors. In *Proc. of SIGIR*.

S. Bergsma, D. Yarowsky, and K. Church. 2011. Using large monolingual and bilingual corpora to improve coordination disambiguation. In *Proc. of ACL*.

D. M. Blei, A. Y. Ng, and M. I. Jordan. 2003. Latent Dirichlet allocation. *The Journal of Machine Learning Research*, 3:993–1022.

E. Charniak. 2000. A maximum-entropy-inspired parser. In *Proc. of NAACL*.

I. S. Dhillon, Y. Guan, and B. Kulis. 2004. Kernel k-means: spectral clustering and normalized cuts. In *Proc. of KDD*.

L. Dietz, S. Bickel, and T. Scheffer. 2007. Unsupervised prediction of citation influences. In *Proc. of ICML*.

J. Eisenstein, A. Ahmed, and E. P. Xing. 2011. Sparse additive generative models of text. In *Proc. of ICML*.

M. A. T. Figueiredo. 2003. Adaptive sparseness for supervised learning. *IEEE Transactions on Pattern Analysis and Machine Intelligence*, 25(9):1150–1159.

N. Garera, C. Callison-Burch, and D. Yarowsky. 2009. Improving translation lexicon induction from monolingual corpora via dependency contexts and part-of-speech equivalences. In *Proc. of CoNLL*.

S. Gerrish and D. M. Blei. 2010. A language-based approach to measuring scholarly impact. In *Proc. of ICML*.

L. Getoor. 2005. Link-based classification. In *Advanced Methods for Knowledge Discovery from Complex Data*, pages 189–207. Springer.

D. Hall, D. Jurafsky, and C. D. Manning. 2008. Studying the history of ideas using topic models. In *Proc. of EMNLP*.

A. Ibáñez, P. Larrañaga, and C. Bielza. 2009. Predicting citation count of bioinformatics papers within four years of publication. *Bioinformatics*, 25(24):3303–3309.

N. Johri, D. Ramage, D. A. McFarland, and D. Jurafsky. 2011. A study of academic collaborations in computational linguistics using a latent mixture of authors model. In *Proc. of the ACL Workshop on Language Technology for Cultural Heritage, Social Sciences, and Humanities*.

M. M. Kessler. 1963. Bibliographic coupling between scientific papers. *American documentation*, 14(1):10–25.

J. Kubica, A. Moore, J. Schneider, and Y. Yang. 2002. Stochastic link and group detection. In *Proc. of AAAI*.

K. Lange and J. S. Sinsheimer. 1993. Normal/independent distributions and their applications in robust regression. *Journal of Computational and Graphical Statistics*, 2(2):175–198.

D. Marcu and W. Wong. 2002. A phrase-based, joint probability model for statistical machine translation. In *Proc. of EMNLP*.

A. McCallum, G. S. Mann, and D. Mimno. 2006. Bibliometric impact measures leveraging topic analysis. In *Proc. of JCDL*.

S. M. McNee, I. Albert, D. Cosley, P. Gopalkrishnan, S. K. Lam, A. M. Rashid, J. A. Konstan, and J. Riedl. 2002. On the recommending of citations for research papers. In *Proc. of CSCW*.

T. P. Minka. 2009. Estimating a Dirichlet distribution. Available online at `http://research.microsoft.com/en-us/um/people/minka/papers/dirichlet/minka-dirichlet.pdf`.

R. M. Nallapati, A. Ahmed, E. P. Xing, and W. W. Cohen. 2008. Joint latent topic models for text and citations. In *Proc. of KDD*.

F. Osareh. 1996. Bibliometrics, citation analysis and co-citation analysis: A review of literature I. *Libri*, 46(3):149–158.

R. Prasad, N. Dinesh, A. Lee, E. Miltsakaki, L. Robaldo, A. Joshi, and B. Webber. 2008. The Penn discourse treebank 2.0. In *Proc. of LREC*.

D. R. Radev, M. T. Joseph, B. Gibson, and P. Muthukrishnan. 2009a. A bibliometric and network analysis of the field of computational linguistics. *Journal of the American Society for Information Science and Technology*.

D. R. Radev, P. Muthukrishnan, and V. Qazvinian. 2009b. The ACL Anthology Network corpus. In *Proceedings of the Workshop on Text and Citation Analysis for Scholarly Digital Libraries*.

F. Radicchi, C. Castellano, F. Cecconi, V. Loreto, D. Parisi, and G. Parisi. 2004. Defining and identifying communities in networks. *Proceedings of the National Academy of Sciences of the United States of America*, 101(9):2658–2663.

M. Rosen-Zvi, T. Griffiths, M. Steyvers, and P. Smyth. 2004. The author-topic model for authors and documents. In *Proc. of UAI*.

V. Satuluri and S. Parthasarathy. 2011. Symmetrizations for clustering directed graphs. In *Proc. of International Conference on Extending Database Technology*.

P. Sen, G. Namata, M. Bilgic, L. Getoor, B. Galligher, and T. Eliassi-Rad. 2008. Collective classification in network data. *AI magazine*, 29(3):93.

H. Small. 1973. Co-citation in the scientific literature: A new measure of the relationship between two documents. *Journal of the American Society for information Science*, 24(4):265–269.

R. Tibshirani. 1996. Regression shrinkage and selection via the lasso. *Journal of the Royal Statistical Society. Series B (Methodological)*, 58(1):267–288.

G. C. G. Wei and M. A. Tanner. 1990. A Monte Carlo implementation of the EM algorithm and the poor man's data augmentation algorithms. *Journal of the American Statistical Association*, 85(411):699–704.

H. D. White and B. C. Griffith. 1981. Author cocitation: A literature measure of intellectual structure. *Journal of the American Society for Information Science*, 32(3):163–171.

D. Yogatama, M. Heilman, B. O'Connor, C.Dyer, B. R. Routledge, and N. A. Smith. 2011. Predicting a scientific community's response to an article. In *Proc. of EMNLP*.

He Said, She Said: Gender in the ACL Anthology

Adam Vogel
Stanford University
av@cs.stanford.edu

Dan Jurafsky
Stanford University
jurafsky@stanford.edu

Abstract

Studies of gender balance in academic computer science are typically based on statistics on enrollment and graduation. Going beyond these coarse measures of gender participation, we conduct a fine-grained study of gender in the field of Natural Language Processing. We use topic models (Latent Dirichlet Allocation) to explore the research topics of men and women in the ACL Anthology Network. We find that women publish more on dialog, discourse, and sentiment, while men publish more than women in parsing, formal semantics, and finite state models. To conduct our study we labeled the gender of authors in the ACL Anthology mostly manually, creating a useful resource for other gender studies. Finally, our study of historical patterns in female participation shows that the proportion of women authors in computational linguistics has been continuously increasing, with approximately a 50% increase in the three decades since 1980.

1 Introduction

The gender imbalance in science and engineering is particularly striking in computer science, where the percentage of graduate students in computer science that are women seems to have been declining rather than increasing recently (Palma, 2001; Beaubouef and Zhang, 2011; Spertus, 1991; Hill et al., 2010; Singh et al., 2007).

While many studies have examined enrollment and career advancement, less attention has been paid to gender differences in scientific publications. This paper studies author gender in the Association for Computational Linguistics Anthology Network (AAN) corpus (Radev et al., 2009), (based on the ACL Anthology Reference Corpus (Bird et al., 2008)) from which we used 13,000 papers by approximately 12,000 distinct authors from 1965 to 2008.

The AAN corpus disambiguates author names, but does not annotate these names for gender. We first performed a mostly-manual annotation of the gender of each author (details in Section 2). We make these annotation available as a useful resource for other researchers.[1]

We then study a number of properties of the ACL authors. We first address surface level questions regarding the balance of genders in publications. In 2008, women were granted 20.5% of computer science PhDs (CRA, 2008). Does this ratio hold also for the percentages of papers written by women in computational linguistics as well? We explore differences in publication count between genders, looking at total publications and normalized values like publications per year and trends over time.

Going beyond surface level analysis, we then turn to document content. We utilize Latent Dirichlet Allocation (LDA) topic models (Blei et al., 2003) to study the difference in topics that men and women write about.

2 Determining Gender

The gender of an author is in general difficult to determine automatically with extremely high precision. In many languages, there are gender-differentiated names for men and women that can make gender-assignment possible based on gen-

[1] http://nlp.stanford.edu/projects/gender.shtml

dered name dictionaries. But the fact that ACL authors come from many different language background makes this method prone to error. For example, while U.S. Census lists of frequently occurring names by gender (Census, 2012) can resolve a large proportion of commonly occurring names from authors in the United States and Canada, they incorrectly list the name "Jan" as female. It turns out that authors in the ACL Anthology who are named "Jan" are in fact male, since the name is a very common male name in many parts of Europe, and since US female researchers named "Jan" often use the full form of their name rather than the shortening "Jan" when publishing. Furthermore, a significant percentage of ACL authors have Chinese language names, which are much less clearly linked with personal names (e.g., Weiwei Sun is female whereas Weiwei Ding is male).

We found that Chinese names as well as ambiguous names like "Jan" were poorly predicted by online name gender website algorithms we looked at, leading to a high error rate. To insure high precision, we therefore instead chose to annotate the authors in the corpus with a high-precision method; mainly hand labeling the names but also using some automatic help.

We used unambiguous name lists for various languages to label a large proportion of the name; for example we used the subset of given names (out of the 4221 first names reported in the 1990 U.S. Census) that were unambiguous (occurring consistently with only one gender in all of our name lists) used morphological gender for languages like Czech or Bulgarian which mark morphological gender on names, and relied on lists of Indian and Basque names (from which we had removed any ambiguous names). For all ambiguous names, we next used our personal cognizance of many of the ACL authors, also asking for help from ACL researchers in China, Taiwan, and Singapore (to help label Chinese names of researchers they were familiar with) and other researchers for help on the Japanese and Korean names. Around 1100 names were hand-labeled from personal cognizance or photos of the ACL researchers on their web pages. The combination of name lists and personal cognizance left only 2048 names (15% of the original 12,692) still unlabeled. We then used a baby name website, `www.gpeters.com/names/`, originally designed for reporting the popularity and gender balance of first names, to find the gender of 1287 of these 2048 names.[2] The remaining 761 names remained unlabeled.

Gender	Total Papers	%	First Author Papers	%
Female	6772	33%	4034	27%
Male	13454	64%	10813	71%
Unknown	702	3%	313	2%

Table 1: Number of publications by gender. The total publications column shows the number of papers for which at least one author was a given gender, in any authorship position. The first authored publications column shows the number of papers for which a given gender is the first author.

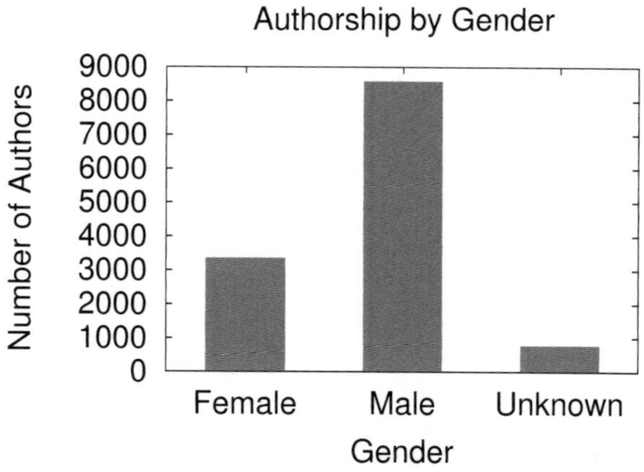

Figure 1: The total number of authors of a given gender.

3 Overall Statistics

We first discuss some overall gender statistics for the ACL Anthology. Figure 1 shows the number of authors of each gender. Men comprised 8573 of the 12692 authors (67.5%) and there were 3359 female authors (26.5%). We could not confidently determine the gender of 761 out of 12692 (6.0%) of the authors. Some of these are due to single letter first names or problems with ill-formatted data.

Table 1 lists the number of papers for each gender. About twice as many papers had at least one

[2] The gender balance of these 1287 automatically-determined names was 34% female, 66% male, slightly higher than the average for the whole corpus.

male author (64%) as had at least one female author (33%). The statistics for first authorship were slightly more skewed; women were the first author of 27% of papers, whereas men first authored 71%. In papers with at least one female author, the first author was a woman 60% of the time, whereas papers with at least one male author had a male first author 80% of the time. Thus men not only write more papers, but are also more frequently first authors.

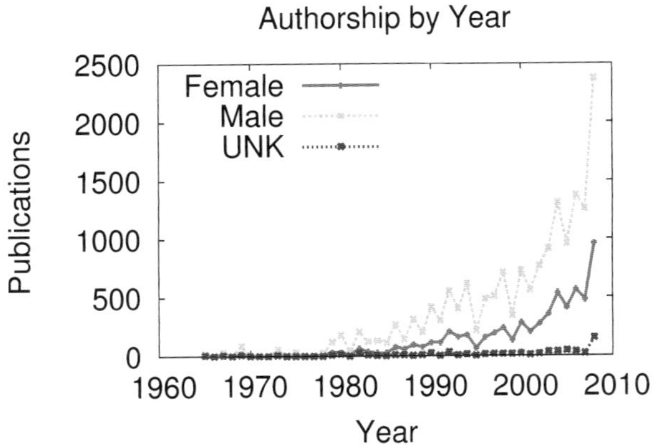

Figure 2: The number of authors of a given gender for a given year.

Figure 2 shows gender statistics over time, giving the number of authors of a given gender for a given year. An author is considered active for a year if he or she was an author of at least one paper. The number of both men and women authors increases over the years, reflecting the growth of computational linguistics.

Figure 3 shows the percentage of authors of a given gender over time. We overlay a linear regression of authorship percentage for each gender showing that the proportion of women is growing over time. The male best fit line has equation $y = -0.3025x + 675.49 (R^2 = 0.41, p = 1.95 \cdot 10^{-5})$ and the female best fit line is $y = 0.3429x - 659.48 (R^2 = 0.51, p = 1.48 \cdot 10^{-5})$. Female authorship percentage grew from 13% in 1980 to 27% in 2007, while male authorship percentage decreased from 79% in 1980 to 71% in 2007. Using the best fit lines as a more robust estimate, female authorship grew from 19.4% to 29.1%, a 50% relative increase.

This increase of the percentage of women authorship is substantial. Comparable numbers do not seem to exist for computer science in general, but according to the CRA Taulbee Surveys of computer science (CRA, 2008), women were awarded 18% of the PhDs in 2002 and 20.5% in 2007. In computational linguistics in the AAN, women first-authored 26% of papers in 2002 and 27% of papers in 2007. Although of course these numbers are not directly comparable, they at least suggest that women participate in computational linguistics research at least as much as in the general computer science population and quite possibly significantly more.

We next turn attention to how the most prolific authors of each gender compare. Figure 4 shows the number of papers published by the top 400 authors of each gender, sorted in decreasing order. We see that the most prolific authors are men.

There is an important confound in interpreting the number of total papers by men and the statistics on prolific authors. Since, as Figure 3 shows, there was a smaller proportion of women in the field in the early days of computational linguistics, and since authors publish more papers the longer they are in the field, it's important to control for length of service.

Figure 5 shows the average number of active years for each gender. An author is considered active in the years between his or her first and last publication in the anthology. Comparing the number of years of service for each gender, we find that on average men indeed have been in the field longer (t-test, $p = 10^{-6}$).

Accounting for this fact, Figure 6 shows the average number of publications per active year. Women published an average of 1.07 papers per year active, while men published 1.03 papers per active year. This difference is significant (t-test, $p = 10^{-3}$), suggesting that women are in fact slightly more prolific than men per active year.

In the field of Ecology, Sih and Nishikawa (1988) found that men and women published roughly the same number of papers per year of service. They used a random sample of 100 researchers in the field. In contrast, Symonds et al. (2006) found that men published more papers per year than women in ecology and evolutionary biology. This study also used random sampling, so it is unclear if the differing results are caused by a sampling error or by some other source.

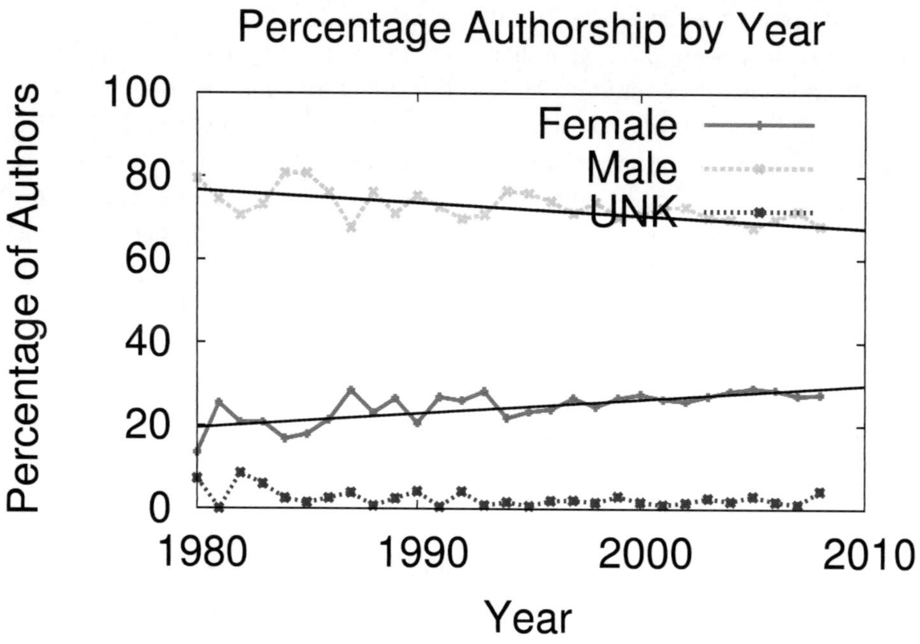

Figure 3: The percentage of authors of a given gender per year. Author statistics before 1980 are sparse and noisy, so we only display percentages from 1980 to 2008.

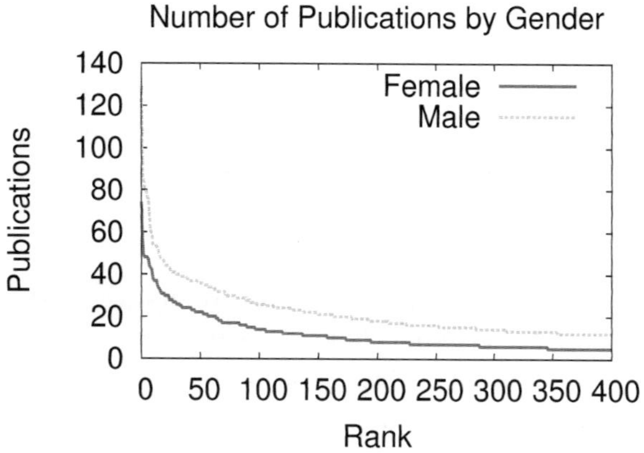

Figure 4: The number of publications per author sorted in decreasing order.

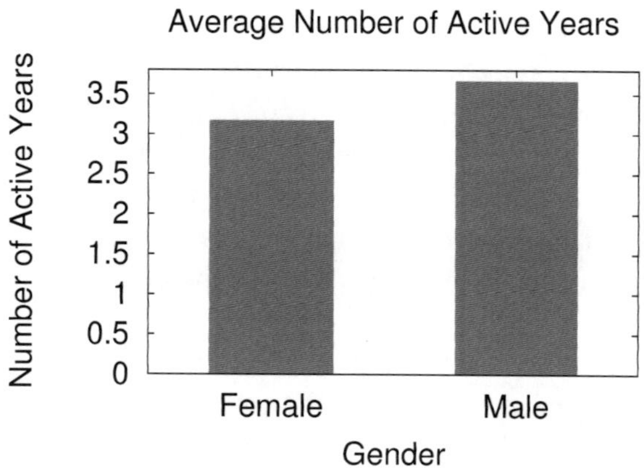

Figure 5: The average number of active years by gender

4 Topic Models

In this section we discuss the relationship between gender and document content. Our main tool is Latent Dirichlet Allocation (LDA), a model of the topics in a document. We briefly describe LDA; see (Blei et al., 2003) for more details. LDA is a generative model of documents, which models documents as a multinomial mixture of *topics*, which in turn are multinomial distributions over words. The generative story proceeds as follows: a document first picks the number of words N it will contain and samples a multinomial topic distribution $p(z|d)$ from a Dirichlet prior. Then for each word to be generated, it picks a topic z for that word, and then a word from the multinomial distribution $p(w|z)$.

Following earlier work like Hall et al. (2008), we ran LDA (Blei et al., 2003) on the ACL Anthology,

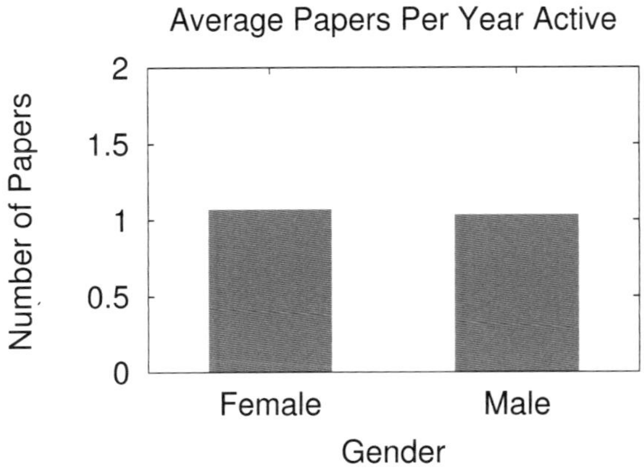

Figure 6: The average number of papers per active year, where an author is considered active in years between his or her first and last publication.

producing 100 generative topics. The second author and another senior expert in the field (Christopher D. Manning) collaboratively assigned labels to each of the 100 topics including marking those topics which were non-substantive (lists of function words or affixes) to be eliminated. Their consensus labeling eliminated 27 topics, leaving 73 substantive topics.

In this study we are interested in how documents written by men and women differ. We are mainly interested in $\Pr(Z|G)$, the probability of a topic being written about by a given gender, and $\Pr(Z|Y,G)$, the probability of a topic being written about by a particular gender in a given year. Random variable Z ranges over topics, Y over years, and G over gender. Our topic model gives us $\Pr(z|d)$, where d is a particular document. For a document $d \in D$, let d_G be the gender of the first author, and d_Y the year it was written.

To compute $\Pr(z|g)$, we sum over documents whose first author is gender g:

$$\begin{aligned}\Pr(z|g) &= \sum_{\{d \in D|d_G = g\}} \Pr(z|d)\Pr(d|g) \\ &= \sum_{\{d \in D|d_G = g\}} \frac{\Pr(z|d)}{|\{d \in D|d_G = g\}|}\end{aligned}$$

To compute $\Pr(z|y,g)$, we additionally condition on the year a document was written:

$$\begin{aligned}\Pr(z|y,g) &= \sum_{\{d \in D|d_Y = y\}} \Pr(z|d)\Pr(d|y,g) \\ &= \sum_{\{d \in D|d_Y = y, d_G = g\}} \frac{\Pr(z|d)}{|\{d \in D|d_Y = y, d_G = g\}|}\end{aligned}$$

To determine fields in which one gender publishes more than another, we compute the odds-ratio

$$\frac{\Pr(z|g = \text{female})(1 - \Pr(z|g = \text{female}))}{\Pr(z|g = \text{male})(1 - \Pr(z|g = \text{male}))}$$

for each of the 73 topics in our corpus.

5 Topic Modeling Results

Using the odds-ratio defined above, we computed the top eight male and female topics. The top female-published topics are speech acts + BDI, prosody, sentiment, dialog, verb subcategorization, summarization, anaphora resolution, and tutoring systems. Figure 9 shows the top words for each of those topics. Figure 7 shows how they have evolved over time.

The top male-published topics are categorial grammar + logic, dependency parsing, algorithmic efficiency, parsing, discriminative sequence models, unification based grammars, probability theory, and formal semantics. Figure 8 and 10 display these topics over time and their associated words.

There are interesting possible generalizations in these topic differences. At least in the ACL corpus, women tend to publish more in speech, in social and conversational topics, and in lexical semantics. Men tend to publish more in formal mathematical approaches and in formal syntax and semantics.

Of course the fact that a certain topic is more linked with one gender doesn't mean the other gender does not publish in this topic. In particular, due to the larger number of men in the field, there can be numerically more male-authored papers in a female-published topic. Instead, what our analysis yields are topics that each gender writes more about, when adjusted by the number of papers published by that gender in total.

Nonetheless, these differences do suggest that women and men in the ACL corpus may, at least to some extent, exhibit some gender-specific tendencies to favor different areas of research.

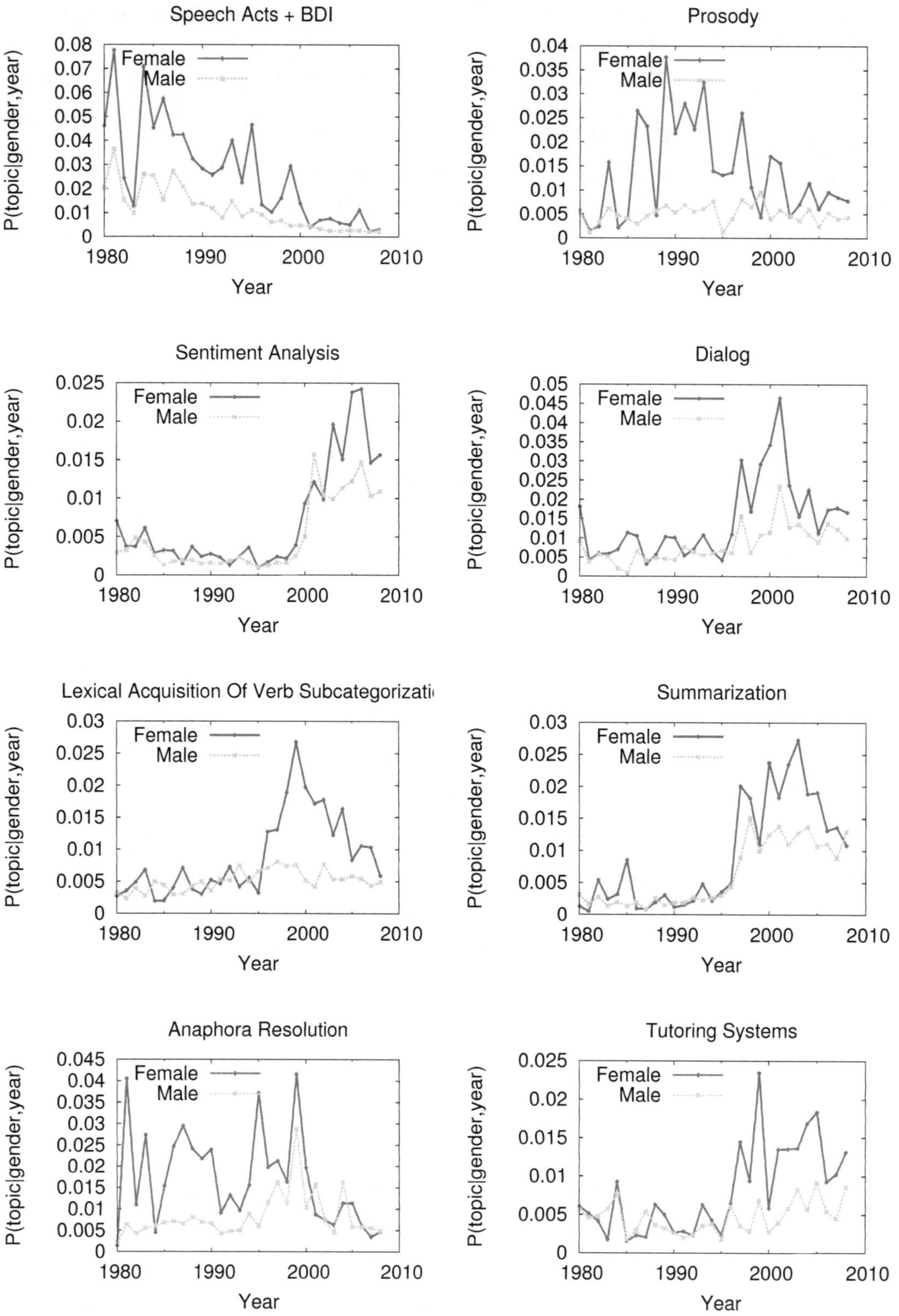

Figure 7: Plots of some topics for which $P(\text{topic}|\text{female}) > P(\text{topic}|\text{male})$. Note that the scale of the y-axis differs between plots.

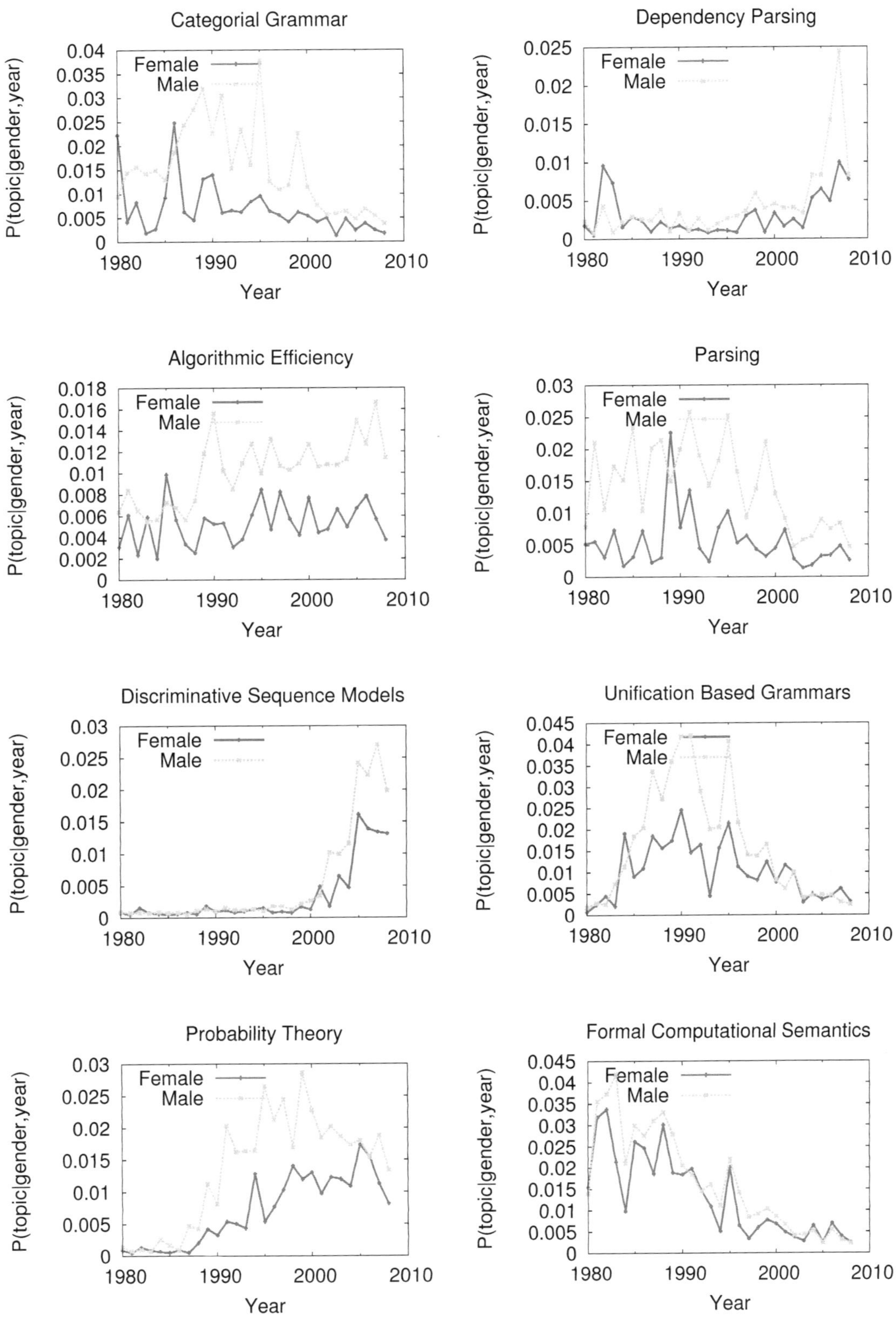

Figure 8: Plots of some topics for which $P(\text{topic}|\text{male}) > P(\text{topic}|\text{female})$. Note that the scale of the y-axis differs between plots.

Speech Acts + BDI	speaker utterance act hearer belief proposition acts beliefs focus evidence
Prosody	prosodic pitch boundary accent prosody boundaries cues repairs speaker phrases
Sentiment	question answer questions answers answering opinion sentiment negative trec positive
Dialog	dialogue utterance utterances spoken dialog dialogues act turn interaction conversation
Verb Subcategorization	class classes verbs paraphrases classification subcategorization paraphrase frames
Summarization	topic summarization summary document news summaries documents topics articles
Anaphora Resolution	resolution pronoun anaphora antecedent pronouns coreference anaphoric definite
Tutoring Systems	students student reading course computer tutoring teaching writing essay native

Figure 9: Top words for each topic that women publish in more than men

Categorial Grammar + Logic	proof logic definition let formula theorem every defined categorial axioms
Dependency Parsing	dependency dependencies head czech depen dependent treebank structures
Algorithmic Efficiency	search length size space cost algorithms large complexity pruning efficient
Parsing	grammars parse chart context-free edge edges production symbols symbol cfg
Discriminative Sequence Models	label conditional sequence random labels discriminative inference crf fields
Unification Based Grammars	unification constraints structures value hpsg default head grammars values
Probability Theory	probability probabilities distribution probabilistic estimation estimate entropy
Formal Semantics	semantics logical scope interpretation logic meaning representation predicate

Figure 10: Top words for each topic that men publish in more than women

6 Conclusion

Our study of gender in the ACL Anthology shows important gains in the percentage of women in the field over the history of the ACL (or at least the last 30 years of it). More concretely, we find approximately a 50% increase in the proportion of female authors since 1980. While women's smaller numbers means that they have produced less total papers in the anthology, they have equal (or even very slightly higher) productivity of papers per year.

In topics, we do notice some differing tendencies toward particular research topics. In current work, we are examining whether these differences are shrinking over time, as a visual overview of Figure 7 seems to suggest, which might indicate that gender balance in topics is a possible outcome, or possibly that topics first addressed by women are likely to to be taken up by male researchers. Additionally, other applications of topic models to the ACL Anthology allow us to study the topics a single author publishes in over time (Anderson et al., 2012). These techniques would allow us to study how gender relates to an author's topics throughout his or her career.

Our gender labels for ACL authors (available at `http://nlp.stanford.edu/projects/gender.shtml`) provide an important resource for other researchers to expand on the social study of computational linguistics research.

7 Acknowledgments

This research was generously supported by the Office of the President at Stanford University and the National Science Foundation under award 0835614.

Thanks to Steven Bethard and David Hall for creating the topic models, Christopher D. Manning for helping label the topics, and Chu-Ren Huang, Olivia Kwong, Heeyoung Lee, Hwee Tou Ng, and Nigel Ward for helping with labeling names for gender. Additional thanks to Martin Kay for the initial paper idea.

References

Ashton Anderson, Dan McFarland, and Dan Jurafsky. 2012. Towards a computational history of the acl: 1980 - 2008. In *ACL 2012 Workshop: Rediscovering 50 Years of Discoveries*.

Theresa Beaubouef and Wendy Zhang. 2011. Where are the women computer science students? *J. Comput. Sci. Coll.*, 26(4):14–20, April.

S. Bird, R. Dale, B.J. Dorr, B. Gibson, M. Joseph, M.Y. Kan, D. Lee, B. Powley, D.R. Radev, and Y.F. Tan.

2008. The ACL Anthology Reference Corpus: A reference dataset for bibliographic research in computational linguistics. In *LREC-08*, pages 1755–1759.

David M. Blei, Andrew Y. Ng, and Michael I. Jordan. 2003. Latent dirichlet allocation. *Journal of Machine Learning Research*, 3:993–1022, March.

US Census. 2012. First name frequency by gender. http://www.census.gov/genealogy/names/names_files.html.

CRA. 2008. CRA Taulbee Survey (web site). http://www.cra.org/resources/taulbee/.

David L.W. Hall, Daniel Jurafsky, and Christopher D. Manning. 2008. Studying the history of ideas using topic models. In *Proceedings of Conference on Empirical Methods on Natural Language Processing*.

Catherine Hill, Christianne Corbett, and Andresse St Rose. 2010. *Why So Few? Women in Science, Technology, Engineering, and Mathematics*. American Association of University Women.

Paul De Palma. 2001. Viewpoint: Why women avoid computer science. *Commun. ACM*, 44:27–30, June.

Dragomir R. Radev, Pradeep Muthukrishnan, and Vahed Qazvinian. 2009. The ACL Anthology Network corpus. In *Proceedings of the 2009 Workshop on Text and Citation Analysis for Scholarly Digital Libraries*, NLPIR4DL '09, pages 54–61, Stroudsburg, PA, USA. Association for Computational Linguistics.

Andrew Sih and Kiisa Nishikawa. 1988. Do men and women really differ in publication rates and contentiousness? an empirical survey. *Bulletin of the Ecological Society of America*, 69(1):pp. 15–18.

Kusum Singh, Katherine R Allen, Rebecca Scheckler, and Lisa Darlington. 2007. Women in computer-related majors: A critical synthesis of research and theory from 1994 to 2005. *Review of Educational Research*, 77(4):500–533.

Ellen Spertus. 1991. Why are there so few female computer scientists? Technical report, Massachusetts Institute of Technology, Cambridge, MA, USA.

Matthew R.E. Symonds, Neil J. Gemmell, Tamsin L. Braisher, Kylie L. Gorringe, and Mark A. Elgar. 2006. Gender differences in publication output: Towards an unbiased metric of research performance. *PLoS ONE*, 1(1):e127, 12.

Discourse Structure and Computation: Past, Present and Future

Bonnie Webber
School of Informatics
University of Edinburgh
Edinburgh UK EH8 9AB
bonnie.webber@ed.ac.uk

Aravind Joshi
Dept of Computer & Information Science
University of Pennsylvania
Philadelphia PA 19104-6228
joshi@seas.upenn.edu

Abstract

The discourse properties of text have long been recognized as critical to language technology, and over the past 40 years, our understanding of and ability to exploit the discourse properties of text has grown in many ways. This essay briefly recounts these developments, the technology they employ, the applications they support, and the new challenges that each subsequent development has raised. We conclude with the challenges faced by our current understanding of discourse, and the applications that meeting these challenges will promote.

1 Why bother with discourse?

Research in Natural Language Processing (NLP) has long benefitted from the fact that text can often be treated as simply a bag of words or a bag of sentences. But not always: *Position* often matters — e.g., It is well-known that the first one or two sentences in a news report usually comprise its best extractive summary. *Order* often matters – e.g., very different events are conveyed depending on how clauses and sentences are ordered.

(1) a. I said the magic words, and a genie appeared.

b. A genie appeared, and I said the magic words.

Adjacency often matters — e.g., attributed material may span a sequence of adjacent sentences, and contrasts are visible through sentence juxtaposition. *Context* always matters — e.g., All languages achieve economy through minimal expressions that can only convey intended meaning when understood in context.

Position, order, adjacency and context are intrinsic features of *discourse*, and research on discourse processing attempts to solve the challenges posed by context-bound expressions and the discourse structures that give rise, when linearized, to position, order and adjacency.

But challenges are not why Language Technology (LT) researchers should care about discourse: Rather, discourse can enable LT to overcome known obstacles to better performance. Consider automated summarization and machine translation: Humans regularly judge output quality in terms that include *referential clarity* and *coherence*. Systems can only improve here by paying attention to discourse — i.e., to linguistic features above the level of n-grams and single sentences. (In fact, we predict that as soon as cheap — i.e., non-manual – methods are found for reliably assessing these features — for example, using proxies like those suggested in (Pitler et al., 2010) — they will supplant, or at least complement today's common metrics, *Bleu* and *Rouge* that say little about what matters to human text understanding (Callison-Burch et al., 2006).)

Consider also work on *automated text simplification*: One way that human editors simplify text is by re-expressing a long complex sentence as a discourse sequence of simple sentences. Researchers should be able to automate this through understanding the various ways that information is conveyed in discourse. Other examples of LT applications already benefitting from recognizing and applying discourse-level information include automated assessment of student essays (Burstein and Chodorow, 2010); summarization (Thione et al., 2004), information extraction (Patwardhan and Riloff, 2007; Eales et al., 2008; Maslennikov and Chua, 2007), and more recently, statistical machine translation (Foster et al., 2010). These are described in more detail in (Webber et al., 2012).

Our aim here then, on this occasion of ACL's 50th Annual Meeting, is to briefly describe the evolution of computational approaches to discourse structure, reflect on where the field currently stands, and what new challenges it faces in trying to deliver on its promised benefit to Language Technology.

2 Background

2.1 Early Methods

The challenges mentioned above are not new. Question-Answering systems like LUNAR (Woods, 1968; Woods, 1978) couldn't answer successive questions without resolving context-bound expressions such as pronouns:

(2) What is the concentration of silicon in breccias?
⟨*breccia1, parts per million*⟩
⟨*breccia2, parts per million*⟩
⟨...⟩
What is *it* in volcanics? (Woods, 1978)

Early systems for human interaction with animated agents, including SHRDLU (Winograd, 1973) and HOMER (Vere and Bickmore, 1990), faced the same challenge. And early message understanding systems couldn't extract relevant information (like when a sighted submarine submerged – "went sinker") without recognizing relations implicit in the structure of a message, as in

(3) VISUAL SIGHTING OF PERISCOPE FOLLOWED BY ATTACK WITH ASROC AND TORPEDO. WENT SINKER. LOOSEFOOT 722/723 CONTINUE SEARCH. (Palmer et al., 1993)

The same was true of early systems for processing narrative text (under the rubric *story understanding*). They took on the problem of recognizing events that had probably happened but hadn't been mentioned in the text, given the sequence of events that had been (Lehnert, 1977; Rumelhart, 1975; Schank and Abelson, 1977; Mandler, 1984).

Since these early systems never saw more than a handful of examples, they could successfully employ straight-forward, but *ad hoc* methods to handle the discourse problems the examples posed. For example, LUNAR used a single 10-position ring buffer to store discourse entities associated with both the user's and the system's referring expressions, resolving pronouns by looking back through the buffer for an appropriate entity and over-writing previous buffer entries when the buffer was full.

The next wave of work in computational discourse processing sought greater generality through stronger theoretical grounding, appealing to then-current theories of discourse such as *Centering Theory* (Grosz et al., 1986; Grosz et al., 1995), used as a basis for anaphor resolution (Brennan et al., 1987; Walker et al., 1997; Tetreault, 2001) and text generation (Kibble and Power, 2000), *Rhetorical Structure Theory* (Mann and Thompson, 1988), used as a basis for text generation (Moore, 1995) and document summarization (Marcu, 2000b), and Grosz and Sidner's theory of discourse based on intentions (Grosz and Sidner, 1986a) and shared plans (Grosz and Sidner, 1990), used in developing animated agents (Johnson and Rickel, 2000). Issues related to fully characterizing centering are explored in great detail in (Kehler, 1997) and (Poesio et al., 2004).

The approaches considered during this period never saw more than a few handfuls of examples. But, as has been clear from developments in PoS-tagging, Named Entity Recognition and parsing, Language Technology demands approaches that can deal with whatever data are given them. So subsequent work in computational discourse processing has similarly pursued robustness through the use of data-driven approaches that are usually able to capture the most common forms of any phenomenon (ie, the 80% at the high end of the Zipfian distribution), while giving up on the long tail. This is described in Section 3.

2.2 Early Assumptions

While early work focussed on the correct assumption that much was implicit in text and had to be inferred from the explicit sequence of sentences that constituted a text, work during the next period focussed on the underlying structure of discourse and its consequences. More specificaly, it assumed that the sequence of sentences constituting the text were covered by a single tree structure, similar to the single tree structure of phrases and clauses covering the

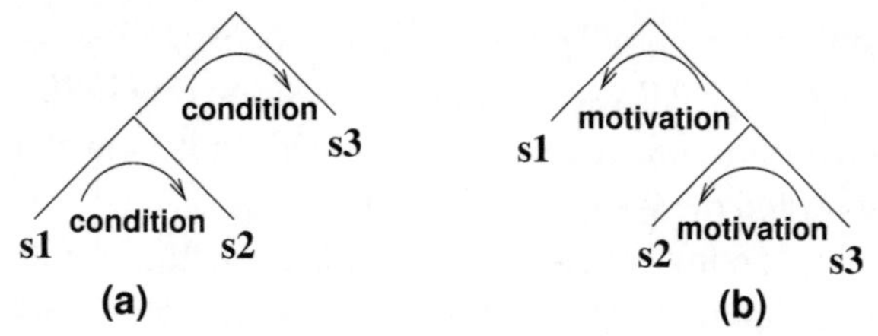

Figure 1: Proposed discourse structures for Ex. 4: (a) In terms of informational relations; (b) in terms of intentional relations

words in a sentence. At issue though was the nature of the structure.

One issue concerned the nature of the relation between parent and child nodes in a discourse tree, and/or the relation between siblings. While *Rhetorical Structure Theory* (Mann and Thompson, 1988) posited a single discourse relation holding between any two *discourse units* (i.e., units projecting to adjacent text spans), Moore and Pollack (1992) gave an example of a simple discourse (Ex. 4) in which different choices about the discourse relation holding between pairs of units, implied different and non-isomorphic structures.

(4) Come home by 5:00. $_{s1}$ Then we can go to the hardware store before it closes. $_{s2}$ That way we can finish the bookshelves tonight. $_{s3}$

Example 4 could be analysed purely in terms of information-based discourse relations, in which $s1$ specified the CONDITION under which $s2$ held, which in turn specified the CONDITION under which $s3$ held. This would make $s1$ subordinate to $s2$, which in turn would be subordinate to $s3$, as in Figure 1a. Alternatively, Example 4 could be analysed purely in terms of intention-based (pragmatic) relations, in which $s2$ would be MOTIVATION for $s1$, while $s3$ would be MOTIVATION for $s2$. This would make $s3$ subordinate to $s2$, which in turn would be subordinate to $s1$, as in Figure 1b. In short, the choice of relation was not merely a matter of labels, but had structural implications as well.

Another issue during this period concerned the nature of discourse structure: Was it really a tree? Sibun (1992), looking at people's descriptions of the layout of their house or apartment, argued that they resembled different ways of linearizing a graph of the rooms and their connectivity through doors and halls. None of these linearizations were trees. Similarly, Knott *et al.* (2001), looking at transcriptions of museum tours, argued that each resembled a linear sequence of trees, with one or more topic-based connections between their root nodes — again, not a single covering tree structure. Wiebe (1993), looking at simple examples such as

(5) The car was finally coming toward him. $_{s1}$
He finished his diagnostic tests, $_{s2}$
feeling relief. $_{s3}$
But then the car started to turn right. $_{s4}$

pointed multiple lexical items explicitly relating a clause to multiple other clauses. Here, but would relate $s4$ to $s3$ via a CONTRAST relation, while then would relate $s4$ to $s2$ via a temporal SUCCESSION relation.

The most well-known of work from this period is that of Mann and Thompson (1988), Grosz and Sidner (1986b), Moore and Moser (1996), Polanyi and van den Berg (1996), and Asher and Lascarides (2003).[1]

The way out of these problems was also a way to achieve the robustness required of any Language Technology, and that lay in the growing consensus towards the view that discourse does not have a single monolithic hierarchical structure. Rather, different aspects of a discourse give rise to different structures, possibly with different formal properties (Stede, 2008; Stede, 2012; Webber et al., 2012). These different structures we describe in the next section, while the fact that this can't be the end of the story, we take up in Section 4.

3 The Situation Today

Recent years have seen progress to differing degrees on at least four different types of discourse structures: topic structure, functional structure, event structure, and a structure of coherence relations. First we say a bit about the structures, and then about the resources employed in recognizing and labelling them.

3.1 Types of discourse structures

Topic structure and *automated topic segmentation* aims to break a discourse into a linear sequence of

[1]For a historical account and assessent of work in automated anaphora resolution in this period and afterwards, we direct the reader to Strube (2007), Ng (2010) and Stede (2012).

topics such the geography of a country, followed by its history, its demographics, its economy, its legal structures, etc. Segmentation is usually done on a sentence-by-sentence basis, with segments not assumed to overlap. Methods for topic segmenation emply semantic, lexical and referential similarity or, more recently, language models (Bestgen, 2006; Chen et al., 2009; Choi et al., 2001; Eisenstein and Barzilay, 2008; Galley et al., 2003; Hearst, 1997; Malioutov and Barzilay, 2006; Purver et al., 2006; Purver, 2011).

Functional structure and *automated functional segmentation* aims to identify sections within a discourse that serve different functions. These functions are genre-specific. In the case of scientific journals, high-level sections generally include the *Background* (work that motivates the objectives of the work and/or the hypothesis or claim being tested), followed by its *Methods*, and *Results*, ending with a *Discussion* of the results or outcomes, along with conclusions to be drawn. Finer-grained segments might include the advantage of a new method (*method-new-advantage*) or of an old method (*method-old-advantage*) or the disadvantage of one or the other (Liakata et al., 2010). Again, segmentation is usually done on a sentence-by-sentence basis, with sentences not assumed to fill more than one function. Methods for functional segmentation have employed specific cue words and phrases, as well as more general language models (Burstein et al., 2003; Chung, 2009; Guo et al., 2010; Kim et al., 2010; Lin et al., 2006; McKnight and Srinivasan, 2003; Ruch et al., 2007; Mizuta et al., 2006; Palau and Moens, 2009; Teufel and Moens, 2002; Teufel et al., 2009; Agarwal and Yu, 2009). The BIO approach to sequential classication (Beginning/Inside/Outside) used in Named Entity Recognition has also proved useful (Hirohata et al., 2008), recognizing that the way the start of a functional segement is signalled may differ from how it is continued.

Note that topic segmentation and functional segmentation are still not always distinguished. For example, in (Jurafsky and Martin, 2009), the term *discourse segmentation* is used to refer to any segmentation of a discourse into a "high-level" linear structure. Nevertheless, segmentation by function exploits different features (and in some cases, different methods) than segmentation by topic, so they are worth keeping distinct.

Attention to event structure and the identification of events within a text is a more recent phenomena, after a hiatus of over twenty years. Here we just point to work by (Bex and Verheij, 2010; Chambers and Jurafsky, 2008; Do et al., 2011; Finlayson, 2009).

The *automated identification of discourse relations* aims to identify discourse relations such as CONDITION and MOTIVATION, as in Example 4, and CONTRAST and SUCCESSION, as in Example 5. These have also been called *coherence relations* or *rhetorical relations*. Methods used depend on whether or not a text is taken to be divisible into a covering sequence of a non-overlapping *discourse units* related to adjacent units by *discourse relations* as in Rhetorical Structure Theory (Mann and Thompson, 1988) or to both adjacent and non-adjacent units as in the Discourse GraphBank (Wolf and Gibson, 2005). If such a cover is assumed, methods involve parsing a text into units using lexical and punctuational cues, followed by labelling the relation holding between them (Marcu, 2000a; Marcu, 2000b; Wolf and Gibson, 2005). If text is not assumed to be divisible into discourse units, then methods involve finding evidence for discourse relations (including both explicit words and phrases, and clausal and sentential adjacency) and their arguments, and then labelling the sense of the identified relation (Elwell and Baldridge, 2008; Ghosh et al., 2011; Lin et al., 2010; Lin, 2012; Prasad et al., 2010a; Wellner, 2008; Wellner and Pustejovsky, 2007).

3.2 Resources for discourse structure

All automated systems for segmenting and labelling text are grounded in data — whether the data has informed the manual creation of rules or has been a source of features for an approach based on machine learning. In the case of topic structure and high-level functional structure, there is now a substantial amount of data that is freely available. For other types of discourse structure, manual annotation has been required and, depending on the type of structure, different amounts are currently available.

More specifically, work on topic structure and segmentation has been able to take advantage of the large, free, still-growing *wikipedia*, where articles on similar topics tend to show similar explicit segmentation into sub-topics. This is certainly the case with the English wikipedia. If similar wikipedia evolving in other languages lack explicit segmentation, it may be that cross-lingual techniques may be able to project explicit segmentation from English-language articles.

With respect to high-level functional structure, some work on automated segmentation has been able to exploit explicit author-provided indicators of structure, such as the author-structured abstracts now required by bio-medical journals indexed by MedLine. Researchers have used these explicitly structured abstracts to segment abstracts that lack explicit structure (Chung, 2009; Guo et al., 2010; Hirohata et al., 2008; Lin et al., 2006).

For all other kinds of discourse structures, dedicated manual annotation has been required, both for segmentation and labelling, and many of these resources have been made available for other researchers. For *fine-grained functional structure*, there is the ART corpus (Liakata et al., 2010)[2].

For *discourse relations* annotated in the RST framework, there is the RST Discourse TreeBank of English text (Carlson et al., 2003), available through the Linguistic Data Consortium (LDC), as well as similarly annotated corpora in Spanish (da Cunha et al., 2011), Portugese (Pardo et al., 2008) and German (Stede, 2004).

For *discourse relations* annotated in the *lexically-grounded* approach first described in (Webber and Joshi, 1998), there is the Penn Discourse TreeBank (Prasad et al., 2008) in English, as well as corpora in Modern Standard Arabic (Al-Saif and Markert, 2010; Al-Saif and Markert, 2011), Chinese (Xue, 2005; Zhou and Xue, 2012), Czech (Mladová et al., 2008), Danish (Buch-Kromann et al., 2009; Buch-Kromann and Korzen, 2010), Dutch (van der Vliet et al., 2011), Hindi (Oza et al., 2009), and Turkish (Zeyrek and Webber, 2008; Zeyrek et al., 2009; Zeyrek et al., 2010). Also available are discourse-annotated journal articles in biomedicine (Prasad et al., 2011) and discourse-annotated dialogue (Tonelli et al., 2010).

[2]http://www.aber.ac.uk/en/cs/research/cb/projects/art/art-corpus/

4 New challenges

Although the largely empirically-grounded, multi-structure view of discourse addresses some of the problems that previous computational approaches encountered, it also reveals new ones, while leaving some earlier problems still unaddressed.

4.1 Evidence for discourse structures

The first issue has to do with what should be taken as evidence for a particular discourse structure. While one could simply consider all features that can be computed reliably and just identify the most accurate predictors, this is both expensive and, in the end, unsatisfying.

With *topic structure*, content words do seem to provide compelling evidence for segmentation, either using language models or semantic relatedness. On the other hand, this might be improved through further evidence in the form of *entity chains*, as explored earlier in (Kan et al., 1998), but using today's more accurate approaches to automated coreference recognition (Strube, 2007; Charniak and Elsner, 2009; Ng, 2010).

Whatever the genre, evidence for *function structure* seems to come from the frequency and distribution of closed-class words, particular phrases (or phrase patterns), and in the case of speech, intonation. So, for example, Niekrasz (2012) shows that what he calls *participant-relational features* that indicate the participants relationships to the text provide convincing evidence for segmenting oral narrative by the type of narrative activity taking place. These features include the distribution and frequency of first and second person pronouns, tense, and intonation. But much work remains to be done in this area, in establishing what provides reliable evidence within a genre and what evidence might be stable across genres.

Evidence for discourse relations is what we have given significant thought to, as the Penn Discourse TreeBank (Prasad et al., 2008) and related corpora mentioned in Section 3.2 aim to ground each instance of a discourse relation in the evidence that supports it. The issue of evidence is especially important because none of these corpora has yet been completely annotated with discourse relations. Completing the annotation and developing robust automated segmentation techniques requires identifying what elements of the language provide evidence for coherence relations, and under what conditions.

The two main types of evidence for discourse relations in English are the presence of a discourse connective and sentence adjacency. Discourse connectives annotated in the PDTB 2.0 come from a list of subordinating and coordinating conjunctions, and discourse adverbials — a subset of those identified by Forbes-Riley *et al* (2006). Subsequently, Prasad *et al.* (2010b) used Callison-Burch's technique for identifying syntax-constrained paraphrases (Callison-Burch, 2008) to identify additional discourse connectives, some of which don't appear in the PDTB corpus and some of which appear in the corpus but were not identified and annotated as discourse connectives. English isn't alone in lacking a complete list of discourse connectives: While German has the massive *Handbuch de deutschen Konnektoren* (Pasch et al., 2003), even this resource has been found to be incomplete through clever application of automated tagging and word-alignment of parallel corpora (Versley, 2010).

Evidence for discourse relations in the PDTB also comes from lexical or phrasal elements that are outside the initial set of conjunctions and discourse adverbials. This evidence has been called *alternative lexicalization* or *AltLex* (Prasad et al., 2010b), and includes (in English) clause-initial *what's more* (Example 6) and *that means* (Example 7).

(6) A search party soon found the unscathed aircraft in a forest clearing much too small to have allowed a conventional landing. *What's more*, the seven mail personnel aboard were missing. [wsj_0550]

(7) The two companies each produce market pulp, containerboard and white paper. *That means* goods could be manufactured closer to customers, saving shipping costs, he said. [wsj_0317]

The discovery of these other forms of evidence[3] raises the question of **when** it is that a word or phrase signals a discourse relation. For example, only 15 of the 33 tokens of *that means* in the PDTB were annotated as evidence of a discourse relation. While the three paragraph-initial instances were left unannotated due to resource limitations (ie, no paragraph initial sentences were annotated unless they contained an explicit discourse connective), the majority were ignored because they followed an explicit connective.

As Wiebe's example (5) showed, there can be multiple explicit discourse connectives in a clause, each of which is evidence for a separate discourse relation (albeit possibly between the same arguments). All of these are annotated in the PDTB – eg, both *but* and *then* in

(8) Congress would have 20 days to reject the package with a 50% majority, but then a President could veto that rejection. [wsj_1698]

The question is whether an *AltLex* in the context of an explicit connective also provides evidence of a distinct discourse relation — for example, with the conjunction with *But* in

(9) At a yearling sale, a buyer can go solo and get a horse for a few thousand dollars. But *that means* paying the horse's maintenance; on average, it costs $25,000 a year to raise a horse. [wsj_1174]

As noted above, the PDTB 2.0 also admits sentence adjacency as evidence for one, or even two, implicit discourse relations, as in

(10) *And some investors fault Mr. Spiegel's life style*; [Implicit = because, for instance] **he earns millions of dollars a year and flies around in Columbia's jet planes**. [wsj_0179]

Here, the implicit token of *because* is associated with a discourse relation labelled CONTINGENCY.CAUSE.REASON, while the implicit token of *for instance* is associated with one labelled EXPANSION.RESTATEMENT.SPECIFICATION.

The question is whether sentence adjacency could also serve as evidence for a distinct discourse relation, even when there is also an explicit discourse adverbial, as in the following three instances of *instead*. Here, Ex. 11 can be paraphrased as *And instead*, Ex. 12 as *But instead*, and Ex.13 as *So instead*.

(11) But many banks are turning away from strict price competition. Instead, they are trying to

[3] which English is not alone in having, cf. (Rysova, 2012)

build customer loyalty by bundling their services into packages and targeting them to small segments of the population. [wsj_0085]

(12) The tension was evident on Wednesday evening during Mr. Nixon's final banquet toast, normally an opportunity for reciting platitudes about eternal friendship. Instead, Mr. Nixon reminded his host, Chinese President Yang Shangkun, that Americans haven't forgiven China's leaders for the military assault of June 3-4 that killed hundreds, and perhaps thousands, of demonstrators. [wsj_0093]

(13) Since stars are considerably more massive than planets, such wobbles are small and hard to see directly. Instead, Dr Marcy and others like him look for changes that the wobbles cause in the wavelength of the light from the star. [*The Economist*, 10 November 2007]

These examples suggest that the presence of an explicit connective should not, in all cases, be considered evidence for the absense of an implicit connective. Once the set of explicit connectives have been identified that can co-occur with each other (including *for example* and *for instance*, as well as *instead*), automated parsers for coherence relations can be made to consider the presence of an implicit connective whenever one of these is seen.

4.2 Variability in discourse annotation

Another issue relates to variability in annotating discourse structure: Inter-annotator agreement can be very low in annotating pragmatic and discourse-related phenomena. While we will illustrate the point here in terms of annotating coherence relations, for other examples, the general point is illustrated in papers from the DGfS Workshop on *Beyond Semantics*[4] and in an upcoming special issue of the journal *Discourse and Dialogue* devoted to the same topic.

The Penn *Wall Street Journal* corpus contains twenty-four (24) reports of *errata* in previously-appearing articles. Twenty-three (23) consist of a single pair of sentences, with no explicit discourse connective signalling the relation between them.[5] One sentence reports the error, and the other, the correct statement – e.g.

(14) VIACOM Inc.'s loss narrowed to $21.7 million in the third quarter from $56.9 million a year ago. Thursday's edition misstated the narrowing. [wsj_1747]

In twenty of the errata (class **C1**), the correct statement is given in the first sentence and the error, in the second; In the other three (class **C2**), it is the other way around. One might think that the two sentences in the twenty **C1** reports would be annotated as having the same discourse relation holding between them, and the same with the two sentences in the three **C2** reports. But that is not the case: The twenty **C1** reports presented to annotators at different times ended up being labelled with **six** different discourse relations. There was even variability in labelling the three members of the **C2** class: They were labelled with one discourse relation, and one with a completely different one.

What should one conclude from this variability? One possibility is that there is one right answer, and annotators just vary in their ability to identify it. This would mean it would be beneficial to have a large troop of annotators (so that the majority view could prevail). Another possibility is that there is more than one right answer, which would imply multi-label classification so that multiple labels could hold to different degrees. A third possibility reflects the view from *Beyond Semantics* that it is often very hard to transfer results from theoretical linguistics based on toy examples to naturally-occurring texts. In this case, variability is a consequence of the still *exploratory nature* of much discourse annotation. In the case of errata, while clearly **some** relation holds between the pair of sentences, it may actually not be any of those used in annotating the PDTB. That is, as Grosz and Sidner (1986b) argued several years ago, the sentences may only be related by their *communicative intentions* – one sentence intended to draw the reader's attention to the specific error that was made (so that the reader knows what was mis-stated), the other intended to correct it. One might then take the sense annotation of discourse relations as still exploratory in the wide range of corpora being annotated with this information (cf. Section 3.2).

[4] http://www.linguistics.ruhr-uni-bochum.de/beyondsem/

[5] The other report contains three sentences, again with no explicit connectives.

4.3 Systematic relations between discourse structures

Fortunately for approaches to automated discourse structure recognition, the lack of isomorphism between different discourse structures does not necessarily mean that they are completely independent. This belief that different aspects of discourse would be related, is what led Grosz and Sidner (1986b) to propose a theory that linked what they called the *intentional structure* of discourse, with its linguistic structure and with the reader or listener's cognitive attentional structure.

With respect to the different types of discourse structure considered here, (Lin, 2012) has considered the possibility of systematic relations between Teufel's *Argumentative Zone* labelling of scientific texts in a corpus developed for her PhD thesis (Teufel, 1999) and PDTB-style discourse relations, both within and across sentences. This is certainly worth additional study, for the value it can bring to automated methods of discourse structure recognition.

4.4 Intentional structure

When computational discourse processing turned to machine learning methods based on reliably-identifiable features, it abandoned (at least temporarily) the centrality of pragmatics and speaker intentions to discourse. That is, there were few or no features that directly indicated or could serve as reliable proxies for what role speaker intended his/her utterance to play in the larger discourse. But both Niekrasz' work on meeting segmentation (Section 4.1) and the discussion in Section 4.2 of errata and variability in their labelling draws new attention to this old question, and not just to Moore and Pollack's observation (Section 3) that *intentional* and *informational* characterizations may confer different, non-isomorphic structures over a text. It may also be the case that neither structure may provide a complete cover: A new visit is warranted.

4.5 Discourse and inference

Not only were intentions abandoned in the move to data-intensive methods, so was inference and issues of how readers and listeners recover information that isn't explicit. What's missing can be an unmentioned event, with classic examples coming from the *restaurant script* (Lehnert, 1977), where someone enters a restaurant, sits down at a table and gives their order to a waiter, where unmentioned *inter alia* is an event in which the person becomes informed of what items the restaurant has to offer, say through being given a menu. Or it can be an unmentioned fact, such as that *program trading* involves the computer-executed trading of a basket of fifteen or more stocks. The latter explains the annotation of an implicit EXPANSION.RESTATEMENT.GENERALIZATION relation between the two sentences in

(15) "You're not going to stop the idea of trading a basket of stocks," says Vanderbilt's Prof. Stoll. "Program trading is here to stay, and computers are here to stay, and we just need to understand it." [wsj_0118]

The problem here with inference is when labelling an implicit coherence relation requires inferred information about its arguments, those arguments may have quite different features than when all the information needed to label the relation is explicit.

5 Conclusion

There are still large challenges ahead for computational discourse modelling. But we are hopeful that greater openness to how information is conveyed through discourse, as well as richer modelling techniques developed for other problems, will allow needed progress to be made. If we can improve system performance in recognizing the roles that utterances are meant to play in discourse in one genre, perhaps it will help us generalize and transport this intention recognition between genres. We also hope for progress in finding more ways to take advantage of unannotated data in discourse research; in understanding more about inter-dependencies between features of different types of discourse structure; in continuing to carry out related computational discourse research and development in multiple languages and genres, so as to widen the access to the knowledge gained; and in exploiting discourse in Language Technology applications, including information extraction and SMT.

References

Shashank Agarwal and Hong Yu. 2009. Automatically classifying sentences in full-text biomedical articles into introduction, methods, results and discussion. *Bioinformatics*, 25(23):3174–3180.

Amal Al-Saif and Katja Markert. 2010. The Leeds Arabic Discourse Treebank: Annotating discourse connectives for Arabic. In *Proceedings, 7th International Conference on Language Resources and Evaluation (LREC 2010)*.

Amal Al-Saif and Katja Markert. 2011. Modelling discourse relations for Arabic. In *Proceedings, Empirical Methods in Natural Language Processing*, pages 736–747.

Nicholas Asher and Alex Lascarides. 2003. *Logics of Conversation*. Cambridge University Press, Cambridge UK.

Yves Bestgen. 2006. Improving text segmentation using Latent Semantic Analysis: A reanalysis of Choi, Wiemer-Hastings, and Moore (2001). *Computational Linguistics*, 32(1):5–12.

Floris Bex and Bart Verheij. 2010. Story schemes for argumentation about the facts of a crime. In *Proceedings, AAAI Fall Symposium on Computational Narratives*, Menlo Park CA. AAAI Press.

Susan E. Brennan, Marilyn Walker Friedman, and Carl J. Pollard. 1987. A centering approach to pronouns. In *Proceedings of the 25th Annual Meeting, Association for Computational Linguistics*, pages 155–162, Stanford University, Stanford CA.

Matthias Buch-Kromann and Iørn Korzen. 2010. The unified annotation of syntax and discourse in the Copenhagen Dependency Treebanks. In *Proceedings of the Fourth Linguistic Annotation Workshop*, pages 127–131, July.

Matthias Buch-Kromann, Iørn Korzen, and Henrik Høeg Müller. 2009. Uncovering the 'lost' structure of translations with parallel treebanks. In Fabio Alves, Susanne Göpferich, and Inger Mees, editors, *Copenhagen Studies of Language: Methodology, Technology and Innovation in Translation Process Research*, Copenhagen Studies of Language, vol. 38, pages 199–224. Copenhagen Business School.

Jill Burstein and Martin Chodorow. 2010. Progress and new directions in technology for automated essay evaluation. In R Kaplan, editor, *The Oxford Handbook of Applied Linguistics*, pages 487–497. Oxford University Press, 2 edition.

Jill Burstein, Daniel Marcu, and Kevin Knight. 2003. Finding the WRITE stuff: Automatic identification of discourse structure in student essays. *IEEE Intelligent Systems: Special Issue on Advances in Natural Language Processing*, 18:32–39.

Chris Callison-Burch, Miles Osborne, and Philipp Koehn. 2006. Re-evaluating the role of bleu in machine translation research. In *11th Conference of the European Chapter of the Association for Computational Linguistics*, pages 249–256, Trento, Italy.

Chris Callison-Burch. 2008. Syntactic constraints on paraphrases extracted from parallel corpora. In *EMNLP '08: Proceedings of the Conference on Empirical Methods in Natural Language Processing*.

Lynn Carlson, Daniel Marcu, and Mary Ellen Okurowski. 2003. Building a discourse-tagged corpus in the framework of rhetorical structure theory. In J. van Kuppevelt & R. Smith, editor, *Current Directions in Discourse and Dialogue*. Kluwer, New York.

Nathanael Chambers and Dan Jurafsky. 2008. Unsupervised learning of narrative event chains. In *Proceedings, Annual Meeting of the Association for Computational Linguistics: Human Language Technologies*, pages 789–797.

Eugene Charniak and Micha Elsner. 2009. Em works for pronoun anaphora resolution. In *Proc. European Chapter of the Association for Computational Linguistics*.

Harr Chen, S. R. K. Branavan, Regina Barzilay, and David Karger. 2009. Global models of document structure using latent permutations. In *Proceedings, Annual Conference of the North American Chapter of the Association for Computational Linguistics (NAACL)*, pages 371–379.

Freddy Y. Y. Choi, Peter Wiemer-Hastings, and Johanna Moore. 2001. Latent Semantic Analysis for text segmentation. In *EMNLP '01: Proceedings of the Conference on Empirical Methods in Natural Language Processing*, pages 109–117.

Grace Chung. 2009. Sentence retrieval for abstracts of randomized controlled trials. *BMC Medical Informatics and Decision Making*, 10(9), February.

Iria da Cunha, Juan-Manuel Torres-Moreno, and Gerardo Sierra. 2011. On the development of the rst spanish treebank. In *Proc. 5th Linguistic Annotation Workshop*, pages 1–10, Portland OR.

Quang Xuan Do, Yee Seng Chan, and Dan Roth. 2011. Minimally supervised event causality identification. In *Proceedings, Conference on Empirical Methods in Natural Language Processing*, pages 294–303.

James Eales, Robert Stevens, and David Robertson. 2008. Full-text mining: Linking practice, protocols and articles in biological research. In *Proceedings of the BioLink SIG, ISMB 2008*.

Jacob Eisenstein and Regina Barzilay. 2008. Bayesian unsupervised topic segmentation. In *EMNLP '08: Proceedings of the Conference on Empirical Methods in Natural Language Processing*, pages 334–343.

Robert Elwell and Jason Baldridge. 2008. Discourse connective argument identication with connective specic rankers. In *Proceedings of the IEEE Conference on Semantic Computing (ICSC-08)*.

Mark Finlayson. 2009. Deriving narrative morphologies via analogical story merging. In *Proceedings, 2nd International Conference on Analogy*, pages 127–136.

Katherine Forbes-Riley, Bonnie Webber, and Aravind Joshi. 2006. Computing discourse semantics: The predicate-argument semantics of discourse connectives in D-LTAG. *Journal of Semantics*, 23:55–106.

George Foster, Pierre Isabelle, and Roland Kuhn. 2010. Translating structured documents. In *Proceedings of AMTA*.

Michel Galley, Kathleen McKeown, Eric Fosler-Lussier, and Hongyan Jing. 2003. Discourse segmentation of multi-party conversation. In *Proceedings of the 41st Annual Conference of the Association for Computational Linguistics*.

Sucheta Ghosh, Sara Tonelli, Giuseppe Riccardi, and Richard Johansson. 2011. End-to-end discourse parser evaluation. In *Proceedings, IEEE Conference on Semantic Computing (ICSC-11)*.

Barbara Grosz and Candace Sidner. 1986a. Attention, intention and the structure of discourse. *Computational Linguistics*, 12(3):175–204.

Barbara Grosz and Candace Sidner. 1986b. Attention, intention and the structure of discourse. *Computational Linguistics*, 12(3):175–204.

Barbara Grosz and Candace Sidner. 1990. Plans for discourse. In Philip Cohen, Jerry Morgan, and Martha Pollack, editors, *Intentions in Communication*, pages 417–444. MIT Press.

Barbara Grosz, Aravind Joshi, and Scott Weinstein. 1986. Towards a computational theory of discourse interpretation. Widely circulated unpublished manuscript.

Barbara Grosz, Aravind Joshi, and Scott Weinstein. 1995. Centering: A framework for modelling the local coherence of discourse. *Computational Linguistics*, 21(2):203–225.

Yufan Guo, Anna Korhonen, Maria Liakata, Ilona Silins, Lin Sun, and Ulla Stenius. 2010. Identifying the information structure of scientific abstracts. In *Proceedings of the 2010 BioNLP Workshop*, July.

Marti Hearst. 1997. TextTiling: Segmenting text into multi-paragraph subtopic passages. *Computational Linguistics*, 23(1):33–64.

Kenji Hirohata, Naoki Okazaki, Sophia Ananiadou, and Mitsuru Ishizuka. 2008. Identifying sections in scientic abstracts using conditional random fields. In *Proceedings of the 3rd International Joint Conference on Natural Language Processing*, pages 381–388.

W. Lewis Johnson and Jeff Rickel. 2000. Animated pedagogical agents: Face-to-face interaction in interactive learning environments. *Int'l J. Artificial Intelligence in Education*, 11:47–78.

Dan Jurafsky and James Martin. 2009. *Speech and Language Processing*. Prentice-Hall, Englewood Cliffs NJ, 2 edition.

Min-Yen Kan, Judith Klavans, and Kathleen McKeown. 1998. Linear segmentation and segment significance. In *Proceedings of the Sixth Workshop on Very Large Corpora*.

Andrew Kehler. 1997. Current theories of centering for pronoun intepretation: A critical evaluation. *Computational Linguistics*, 23(3):467–475.

Rodger Kibble and Richard Power. 2000. An integrated framework for text planning and pronominalisation. In *Proc. of the First International Conference on Natural Language Generation*, pages 77–84, Mitzpe Ramon, Israel, June.

Su Nam Kim, David Martinez, and Lawrence Cavedon. 2010. Automatic classification of sentences for evidence based medicine. In *Proc. ACM 4th Int'l Workshop on Data and Text Mining in Biomedical informatics*, pages 13–22.

Alistair Knott, Jon Oberlander, Mick O'Donnell, and Chris Mellish. 2001. Beyond elaboration: The interaction of relations and focus in coherent text. In T Sanders, J Schilperoord, and W Spooren, editors, *Text Representation:Linguistic and psycholinguistic aspects*, pages 181–196. John Benjamins Publishing.

Wendy Lehnert. 1977. A conceptual theory of question answering. In *Proc 5th International Joint Conference on Artificial Intelligence*, pages 158–164.

Maria Liakata, Simone Teufel, Advaith Siddharthan, and Colin Batchelor. 2010. Corpora for the conceptualisation and zoning of scientific papers. In *Proceedings of the 7th International Conference on Language Resources and Evaluation (LREC 2010)*.

Jimmy Lin, Damianos Karakos, Dina Demner-Fushman, and Sanjeev Khudanpur. 2006. Generative content models for structural analysis of medical abstracts. In *Proceedings of the HLT-NAACL Workshop on BioNLP*, pages 65–72.

Ziheng Lin, Hwee Tou Ng, and Min-Yen Kan. 2010. A PDTB-styled end-to-end discourse parser. Technical report, Department of Computing, National University of Singapore, November. http://arxiv.org/abs/1011.0835.

Ziheng Lin. 2012. *Discourse Parsing: Inferring Discourse Structure, Modelling Coherence, and its Applications*. Ph.D. thesis, National University of Singapore.

Igor Malioutov and Regina Barzilay. 2006. Minimum cut model for spoken lecture segmentation. In *Proceedings of the 21st International Conference on Computational Linguistics and the 44th annual meeting of the Association for Computational Linguistics*.

Jean Mandler. 1984. *Stories, scripts, and scenes: Aspects of schema theory*. Lawrence Erlbaum Associates, Hillsdale NJ.

William Mann and Sandra Thompson. 1988. Rhetorical Structure Theory: Toward a functional theory of text organization. *Text*, 8(3):243–281.

Daniel Marcu. 2000a. The rhetorical parsing of unrestricted texts: A surface-based approach. *Computational Linguistics*, 26(3):395–448.

Daniel Marcu. 2000b. *The theory and practice of discourse parsing and summarization*. MIT Press.

Mstislav Maslennikov and Tat-Seng Chua. 2007. A multi-resolution framework for information extraction from free text. In *Proceedings of the 45th Annual Meeting of the Association of Computational Linguistics*, pages 592–599. Association for Computational Linguistics.

Larry McKnight and Padmini Srinivasan. 2003. Categorization of sentence types in medical abstracts. In *Proceedings of the AMIA Annual Symposium*, pages 440–444.

Yoko Mizuta, Anna Korhonen, Tony Mullen, and Nigel Collier. 2006. Zone analysis in biology articles as a basis for information extraction. *International Journal of Medical Informatics*, 75:468487.

Lucie Mladová, Šárka Zikánová, and Eva Hajičová. 2008. From sentence to discourse: Building an annotation scheme for discourse based on the Prague Dependency Treebank. In *Proceedings of the 6th International Conference on Language Resources and Evaluation (LREC 2008)*.

Johanna Moore and Martha Pollack. 1992. A problem for RST: The need for multi-level discouse analysis. *Computational Linguistics*, 18(4):537–544.

Johanna Moore. 1995. *Participating in Explanatory Dialogues*. MIT Press, Cambridge MA.

Megan Moser and Johanna Moore. 1996. Toward a synthesis of two accounts of discourse structure. *Computational Linguistics*, 22(3):409–419.

Vincent Ng. 2010. Supervised noun phrase coreference research: The first 15 years. In *Proc. 48th Annual Meeting of the Association for Computational Linguistics*, pages 1396–1411, Uppsala, Sweden.

John Niekrasz. 2012. *Toward Summarization of Communicative Activities in Spoken Conversation*. Ph.D. thesis, University of Edinburgh.

Umangi Oza, Rashmi Prasad, Sudheer Kolachina, Dipti Misra Sharma, and Aravind Joshi. 2009. The hindi discourse relation bank. In *Proc. 3rd ACL Language Annotation Workshop (LAW III)*, Singapore, August.

Raquel Mochales Palau and Marie-Francine Moens. 2009. Argumentation mining: the detection, classification and structure of arguments in text. In *Proc. 12th International Conference on Artificial Intelligence and Law*, ICAIL '09, pages 98–107. ACM.

Martha Palmer, Carl Weir, Rebecca Passonneau, and Tim Finin. 1993. The kernal text understanding system. *Artificial Intelligence*, 63:17–68.

Thiago Alexandre Salgueiro Pardo, Maria das Gracas Volpe Nunes, and Lucia Helena Machado Rino. 2008. Dizer: An automatic discourse analyzer for brazilian portuguese. *Lecture Notes in Artificial Intelligence*, 3171:224–234.

Renate Pasch, Ursula Brausse, Eva Breindl, and Ulrich Wassner. 2003. *Handbuch der deutschen Konnektoren*. Walter de Gruyter, Berlin.

Siddharth Patwardhan and Ellen Riloff. 2007. Effective information extraction with semantic affinity patterns and relevant regions. In *Proceedings of the 2007 Conference on Empirical Methods in Natural Language Processing (EMNLP-07)*.

Emily Pitler, Annie Louis, and Ani Nenkova. 2010. Automatic evaluation of linguistic quality in multi-document summarization. In *Proc., 48th Annual Meeting of the Association for Computational Linguistics*, pages 544–554, Uppsala, Sweden.

Massimo Poesio, Rosemary Stevenson, Barbara Di Eugenio, and Janet Hitzeman. 2004. Centering: A parametric theory and its instantiations. *Computational Linguistics*, 30(3):300–363.

Livia Polanyi and Martin H. van den Berg. 1996. Discourse structure and discourse interpretation. In P. Dekker and M. Stokhof, editors, *Proceedings of the Tenth Amsterdam Colloquium*, pages 113–131, University of Amsterdam.

Rashmi Prasad, Nikhil Dinesh, Alan Lee, Eleni Miltsakaki, and et al. 2008. The Penn Discourse Treebank 2.0. In *Proceedings of the 6th International Conference on Language Resources and Evaluation*.

Rashmi Prasad, Aravind Joshi, and Bonnie Webber. 2010a. Exploiting scope for shallow discourse parsing. In *Proceedings of the 7th International Conference on Language Resources and Evaluation (LREC 2010)*.

Rashmi Prasad, Aravind Joshi, and Bonnie Webber. 2010b. Realization of discourse relations by other means: Alternative lexicalizations. In *Proceedings, International Conf. on Computational Linguistics (COLING)*.

Rashmi Prasad, Susan McRoy, Nadya Frid, Aravind Joshi, and Hong Yu. 2011. The Biomedical Discourse

Relation Bank. *BMC Bioinformatics*, 12(188):18 pages. http://www.biomedcentral.com/1471-2015/12/188.

Matthew Purver, Tom Griffiths, K.P. Körding, and Joshua Tenenbaum. 2006. Unsupervised topic modelling for multi-party spoken discourse. In *Proceedings, International Conf. on Computational Linguistics (COLING) and the Annual Meeting of the Association for Computational Linguistics*, pages 17–24.

Matthew Purver. 2011. Topic segmentation. In Gokhan Tur and Renato de Mori, editors, *Spoken Language Understanding: Systems for Extracting Semantic Information from Speech*. Wiley, Hoboken NJ.

Patrick Ruch, Celia Boyer, Christine Chichester, Imad Tbahriti, Antoine Geissbühler, Paul Fabry, and et al. 2007. Using argumentation to extract key sentences from biomedical abstracts. *International Journal of Medical Informatics*, 76(2–3):195–200.

David Rumelhart. 1975. Notes on a schema for stories. In Dan Bobrow and Alan Collins, editors, *Representation and Understanding: Studies in Cognitive Science*. Academic Press, New York.

Magdalena Rysova. 2012. Alternative lexicalizations of discourse connectives in czech. In *Proc. 8th Int'l Conf. Language Resources and Evaluation (LREC 2012)*.

Roger Schank and Robert Abelson. 1977. *Scripts, Plans, Goals and Understanding: an Inquiry into Human Knowledge Structures*. Lawrence Erlbaum, Hillsdale NJ.

Penni Sibun. 1992. Generating text without trees. *Computational Intelligence*, 8(1):102–122.

Manfred Stede. 2004. The Potsdam Commentary Corpus. In *ACL Workshop on Discourse Annotation*, Barcelona, Spain, July.

Manfred Stede. 2008. RST revisted: Disentangling nuclearity. In Cathrine Fabricius-Hansen and Wiebke Ramm, editors, *'Subordination' versus 'Coordination' in Sentence and Text*, pages 33–59. John Benjamins, Amsterdam.

Manfred Stede. 2012. *Discourse Processing*. Morgan & Claypool Publishers.

Michael Strube. 2007. Corpus-based and machine learning approaches to anaphora resolution. In Monika Schwarz-Friesel, Manfred Consten, and Mareile Knees, editors, *Anaphors in Text: Cognitive, formal and applied approaches to anaphoric reference*, pages 207–222. John Benjamins Publishing.

Joel Tetreault. 2001. A corpus-based evaluation of centering and pronoun resolution. *Computational Linguistics*, 27(4):507–520.

Simone Teufel and Marc Moens. 2002. Summarizing scientific articles - experiments with relevance and rhetorical status. *Computational Linguistics*, 28:409–445.

Simone Teufel, Advaith Siddharthan, and Colin Batchelor. 2009. Towards discipline-independent argumentative zoning: evidence from chemistry and computational linguistics. In *Proceedings, Conference on Empirical Methods in Natural Language Processing*, pages 1493–1502.

Simone Teufel. 1999. *Argumentative Zoning: Information Extraction from Scientific Text*. Ph.D. thesis, University of Edinburgh.

Gian Lorenzo Thione, Martin van den Berg, Livia Polanyi, and Chris Culy. 2004. Hybrid text summarization: combining external relevance measures with structural analysis. In *Proceedings of the ACL 2004 Workshop Text Summarization Branches Out*.

Sara Tonelli, Guiseppe Riccardi, Rashmi Prasad, and Aravind Joshi. 2010. Annotation of discourse relations for conversational spoken dialogs. In *Proc. 7th Int'l Conf. Language Resources and Evaluation (LREC 2010)*.

Nynke van der Vliet, Ildikó Berzlánovich, Gosse Bouma, Markus Egg, and Gisela Redeker. 2011. Building a discourse-annotated Dutch text corpus. In *Bochumer Linguistische Arbeitsberichte*, pages 157–171.

Steven Vere and Timothy Bickmore. 1990. A basic agent. *Computational Intelligence*, 6(1):41–60.

Yannick Versley. 2010. Discovery of ambiguous and unambiguous discourse connectives via annotation projection. In *Workshop on the Annotation and Exploitation of Parallel Corpora (AEPC)*. NODALIDA.

Marilyn Walker, Aravind Joshi, and Ellen Prince. 1997. *Centering in Discourse*. Oxford University Press, Oxford, England.

Bonnie Webber and Aravind Joshi. 1998. Anchoring a lexicalized tree-adjoining grammar for discourse. In *Coling/ACL Workshop on Discourse Relations and Discourse Markers*, pages 86–92, Montreal, Canada.

Bonnie Webber, Markus Egg, and Valia Kordoni. 2012. Discourse structure and language technology. *Natural Language Engineering*.

Ben Wellner and James Pustejovsky. 2007. Automatically identifying the arguments of discourse connectives. In *Proceedings of the 2007 Conference on Empirical Methods in Natural Language Processing (EMNLP-07)*.

Ben Wellner. 2008. *Sequence Models and Ranking Methods for Discourse Parsing*. Ph.D. thesis, Brandeis University.

Janyce Wiebe. 1993. Issues in linguistic segmentation. In *Workshop on Intentionality and Structure in Discourse Relations, Association for Computational Linguistics*, pages 148–151, Ohio StateUniversity.

Terry Winograd. 1973. A procedural model of language understanding. In Roger Schank and Ken Colby, editors, *Computer Models of Thought and Language*, pages 152–186. W.H. Freeman. Reprinted in Grosz et al. (eds), Readings in Natural Language Processing. Los Altos CA: Morgan Kaufmann Publishers, 1986, pp.249-266.

Florian Wolf and Edward Gibson. 2005. Representing discourse coherence: A corpus-based study. *Computational Linguistics*, 31:249–287.

William Woods. 1968. Procedural semantics for a question-answering machine. In *Proceedings of the AFIPS National Computer Conference*, pages 457–471, Montvale NJ. AFIPS Press.

William Woods. 1978. Semantics and quantification in natural language question answering. In *Advances in Computers*, volume 17, pages 1–87. Academic Press, New York.

Nianwen Xue. 2005. Annotating discourse connectives in the chinese treebank. In *ACL Workshop on Frontiers in Corpus Annotation II*, Ann Arbor MI.

Deniz Zeyrek and Bonnie Webber. 2008. A discourse resource for Turkish: Annotating discourse connectives in the METU corpus. In *Proceedings of the 6th Workshop on Asian Language Resources (ALR6).*

Deniz Zeyrek, Ümut Deniz Turan, Cem Bozsahin, Ruket Çakıcı, and et al. 2009. Annotating Subordinators in the Turkish Discourse Bank. In *Proceedings of the 3rd Linguistic Annotation Workshop (LAW III).*

Deniz Zeyrek, Işın Demirşahin, Ayışığı Sevdik-Çallı, Hale Ögel Balaban, İhsan Yalçınkaya, and Ümut Deniz Turan. 2010. The annotation scheme of the Turkish Discourse Bank and an evaluation of inconsistent annotations. In *Proceedings of the 4th Linguistic Annotation Workshop (LAW III).*

Yuping Zhou and Nianwen Xue. 2012. Pdtb-style discourse annotation of chinese text. In *Proc. 50th Annual Meeting of the ACL*, Jeju Island, Korea.

Extracting glossary sentences from scholarly articles: A comparative evaluation of pattern bootstrapping and deep analysis

Melanie Reiplinger[1] **Ulrich Schäfer**[2] **Magdalena Wolska**[1*]

[1]Computational Linguistics, Saarland University, D-66041 Saarbrücken, Germany
[2]DFKI Language Technology Lab, Campus D 3 1, D-66123 Saarbrücken, Germany
{mreiplin,magda}@coli.uni-saarland.de, ulrich.schaefer@dfki.de

Abstract

The paper reports on a comparative study of two approaches to extracting definitional sentences from a corpus of scholarly discourse: one based on bootstrapping lexico-syntactic patterns and another based on deep analysis. Computational Linguistics was used as the target domain and the ACL Anthology as the corpus. Definitional sentences extracted for a set of well-defined concepts were rated by domain experts. Results show that both methods extract high-quality definition sentences intended for automated glossary construction.

1 Introduction

Specialized glossaries serve two functions: Firstly, they are *linguistic resources* summarizing the terminological basis of a specialized domain. Secondly, they are *knowledge resources*, in that they provide definitions of concepts which the terms denote. Glossaries find obvious use as sources of reference. A survey on the use of lexicographical aids in specialized translation showed that glossaries are among the top five resources used (Durán-Muñoz, 2010). Glossaries have also been shown to facilitate reception of texts and acquisition of knowledge during study (Weiten et al., 1999), while self-explanation of reasoning by referring to definitions has been shown to promote understanding (Aleven et al., 1999). From a machine-processing point of view, glossaries may be used as input for domain ontology induction; see, e.g. (Bozzato et al., 2008).

*Corresponding author

The process of glossary creation is inherently dependent on expert knowledge of the given domain, its concepts and language. In case of scientific domains, which constantly evolve, glossaries need to be regularly maintained: updated and continually extended. Manual creation of specialized glossaries is therefore costly. As an alternative, fully- and semi-automatic methods of glossary creation have been proposed (see Section 2).

This paper compares two approaches to corpus-based extraction of definitional sentences intended to serve as input for a specialized glossary of a scientific domain. The bootstrapping approach acquires lexico-syntactic patterns characteristic of definitions from a corpus of scholarly discourse. The deep approach uses syntactic and semantic processing to build structured representations of sentences based on which 'is-a'-type definitions are extracted. In the present study we used Computational Linguistics (CL) as the target domain of interest and the ACL Anthology as the corpus.

Computational Linguistics, as a specialized domain, is rich in technical terminology. As a cross-disciplinary domain at the intersection of linguistics, computer science, artificial intelligence, and mathematics, it is interesting as far as glossary creation is concerned in that its scholarly discourse ranges from descriptive informal to formal, including mathematical notation. Consider the following two descriptions of *Probabilistic Context-Free Grammar (PCFG)*:

(1) A **PCFG** is a CFG in which each production $A \rightarrow \alpha$ in the grammar's set of productions R is associated with an emission probabil-

ity $P(A \to \alpha)$ that satisfies a normalization constraint

$$\sum_{\alpha:A\to\alpha\in R} P(A \to \alpha) = 1$$

and a consistency or tightness constraint [...]

(2) A **PCFG** defines the probability of a string of words as the sum of the probabilities of all admissible phrase structure parses (trees) for that string.

While (1) is an example of a genus-differentia definition, (2) is a valid description of PCFG which neither has the typical copula structure of an "is-a"-type definition, nor does it contain the level of detail of the former. (2) is, however, well-usable for a glossary. The bootstrapping approach extracts definitions of both types. Thus, at the subsequent glossary creation stage, alternative entries can be used to generate glossaries of different granularity and formal detail; e.g., targeting different user groups.

Outline. Section 2 gives an overview of related work. Section 3 presents the corpora and the preprocessing steps. The bootstrapping procedure is summarized in Section 4 and deep analysis in Section 5. Section 6 presents the evaluation methodology and the results. Section 7 presents an outlook.

2 Related Work

Most of the existing definition extraction methods – be it targeting definitional question answering or glossary creation – are based on mining part-of-speech (POS) and/or lexical patterns typical of definitional contexts. Patterns are then filtered heuristically or using machine learning based on features which refer to the contexts' syntax, lexical content, punctuation, layout, position in discourse, etc.

DEFINDER (Muresan and Klavans, 2002), a rule-based system, mines definitions from online medical articles in lay language by extracting sentences using cue-phrases, such as "x is the term for y", "x is defined as y", and punctuation, e.g., hyphens and brackets. The results are analyzed with a statistical parser. Fahmi and Bouma (2006) train supervised learners to classify concept definitions from medical pages of the Dutch Wikipedia using the "is a" pattern and apply a lexical filter (stopwords) to the classifier's output. Besides other features, the position of a sentence within a document is used, which, due to the encyclopaedic text character of the corpus, allows to set the baseline precision at above 75% by classifying the first sentences as definitions. Westerhout and Monachesi (2008) use a complex set of grammar rules over POS, syntactic chunks, and entire definitory contexts to extract definition sentences from an eLearning corpus. Machine learning is used to filter out incorrect candidates. Gaudio and Branco (2009) use only POS information in a supervised-learning approach, pointing out that lexical and syntactic features are domain and language dependent. Borg et al. (2009) use genetic programming to learn rules for typical linguistic forms of definition sentences in an eLearning corpus and genetic algorithms to assign weights to the rules. Velardi et al. (2008) present a fully-automatic end-to-end methodology of glossary creation. First, TermExtractor acquires domain terminology and GlossExtractor searches for definitions on the web using google queries constructed from a set of manually lexical definitional patterns. Then, the search results are filtered using POS and chunk information as well as term distribution properties of the domain of interest. Filtered results are presented to humans for manual validation upon which the system updates the glossary. The entire process is automated.

Bootstrapping as a method of linguistic pattern induction was used for learning hyponymy/is-a relations already in the early 90s by Hearst (1992). Various variants of the procedure – for instance, exploiting POS information, double pattern-anchors, semantic information – have been recently proposed (Etzioni et al., 2005; Pantel and Pennacchiotti, 2006; Girju et al., 2006; Walter, 2008; Kozareva et al., 2008; Wolska et al., 2011). The method presented here is most similar to Hearst's, however, we acquire a large set of general patterns over POS tags alone which we subsequently optimize on a small manually annotated corpus subset by lexicalizing the verb classes.

3 The Corpora and Preprocesssing

The corpora. Three corpora were used in this study. At the initial stage two development corpora were used: a digitalized early draft of the Jurafsky-

Martin textbook (Jurafsky and Martin, 2000) and the WeScience Corpus, a set of Wikipedia articles in the domain of Natural Language Processing (Ytrestøl et al., 2009).[1] The former served as a source of seed domain terms with definitions, while the latter was used for seed pattern creation.

For acquisition of definitional patterns and pattern refinement we used the *ACL Anthology*, a digital archive of scientific papers from conferences, workshops, and journals on Computational Linguistics and Language Technology (Bird et al., 2008).[2] The corpus consisted of 18,653 papers published between 1965 and 2011, with a total of 66,789,624 tokens and 3,288,073 sentences. This corpus was also used to extract sentences for the evaluation using both extraction methods.

Preprocessing. The corpora have been sentence and word-tokenized using regular expression-based sentence boundary detection and tokenization tools. Sentences have been part-of-speech tagged using the TnT tagger (Brants, 2000) trained on the Penn Treebank (Marcus et al., 1993).[3]

Next, domain terms were identified using the C-Value approach (Frantzi et al., 1998). *C-Value* is a domain-independent method of automatic multi-word term recognition that rewards high frequency and high-order n-gram candidates, but penalizes those which frequently occur as sub-strings of another candidate. 10,000 top-ranking multi-word token sequences, according to C-Value, were used.

Domain terms. The set of domain terms was compiled from the following sub-sets: 1) the 10,000 automatically identified multi-word terms, 2) the set of terms appearing on the margins of the Jurafsky-Martin textbook; the intuition being that these are domain-specific terms which are likely to be defined or explained in the text along which they appear, 3) a set of 5,000 terms obtained by expanding frequent abbreviations and acronyms retrieved from the ACL Anthology corpus using simple pattern matching. The token spans of domain terms have been marked in the corpora as these are used in the course of definition pattern acquisition (Section 4.2).

[1]`http://moin.delph-in.net/WeScience`

[2]`http://aclweb.org/anthology/`

[3]The accuracy of tokenization and tagging was not verified.

Seed terms	machine translation		language model
	neural network		reference resolution
	finite(-|)state automaton		hidden markov model
	speech synthesis		semantic role label(l)?ing
	context(-|)free grammar		ontology
	generative grammar		dynamic programming
	mutual information		
Seed patterns		T	.* (is|are|can be) used
		T	.* called
		T	.* (is|are) composed
		T	.* involv(es|ed|e|ing)
		T	.* perform(s|ed|ing)?
		T	\\(or .*? \\)
	task of .*	T	.*? is
	term	T	.*? refer(s|red|ring)?

Table 1: Seed domain terms (top) and seed patterns (bottom) used for bootstrapping; `T` stands for a domain term.

4 Bootstrapping Definition Patterns

Bootstrapping-based extraction of definitional sentences proceeds in two stages: First, aiming at recall, a large set of *lexico-syntactic patterns* is acquired: Starting with a small set of seed terms and patterns, term and pattern "pools" are iteratively augmented by searching for matching sentences from the ACL Anthology while acquiring candidates for definition terms and patterns. Second, aiming at precision, general patterns acquired at the first stage are systematically optimized on set of annotated extracted definitions.

4.1 Seed Terms and Seed Patterns

As seed terms to initialize pattern acquisition, we chose terms which are likely to have definitions. Specifically, from the top-ranked multi-word terms, ordered by C-value, we selected those which were also in either the Jurafsky-Martin term list or the list of expanded frequent abbreviations. The resulting 13 seed terms are shown in the top part of Table 1.

Seed definition patterns were created by inspecting definitional contexts in the Jurafsky-Martin and WeScience corpora. First, 12 terms from Jurafsky-Martin and WeScience were selected to find domain terms with which they co-occurred in simple "is-a" patterns. Next, the corpora were searched again to find sentences in which the term pairs in "is-a" relation occur. Non-definition sentences were discarded.

Finally, based on the resulting definition sentences, 22 seed patterns were constructed by transforming the definition phrasings into regular expressions. A subset of the seed phrases extracted in this way is shown in the bottom part of Table 1.[4]

4.2 Acquiring Patterns

Pattern acquisition proceeds in two stages: First, based on seed sets, candidate defining terms are found and ranked. Then, new patterns are acquired by instantiating existing patterns with pairs of likely co-occurring domain terms, searching for sentences in which the term pairs co-occur, and creating POS-based patterns. These steps are summarized below.

Finding definiens candidates. Starting with a set of seed terms and a set of definition phrases, the first stage finds sentences with the seed terms in the `T`-placeholder position of the seed phrases. For each term, the set of extracted sentences is searched for candidate defining terms (other domain terms in the sentence) to form term-term pairs which, at the second stage, will be used to acquire new patterns.

Two situations can occur: a sentence may contain more than one domain term (other than one of the seed terms) or the same domain terms may be found to co-occur with multiple seed terms. Therefore, term-term pairs are ranked.

Ranking. Term-term pairs are ranked using four standard measures of association strength: 1) *co-occurrence* count, 2) *pointwise mutual information (PMI)*, 3) *refined PMI*; compensates bias toward low-frequency events by multiplying PMI with co-occurrence count (Manning and Schütze, 1999), and 4) *mutual dependency (MD)*; compensates bias toward rare events by subtracting co-occurrence's self-information (entropy) from its PMI (Thanopoulos et al., 2002). The measures are calculated based on the corpus for co-occurrences within a 15-word window.

Based on experimentation, mutual dependency was found to produce the best results and therefore it was used in ranking definiens candidates in the final evaluation of patterns. The top-k candidates make up the set of defining terms to be used in the pattern acquisition stage. Table 2 shows the top-20 candidate defining terms for the term "Lexical Functional Grammar", according to mutual dependency.

Domain term	Candidate defining terms
lexical functional grammar (LFG)	phrase structure grammar
	formal system
	functional unification grammar
	grammatical representation
	phrase structure
	generalized phrase
	functional unification
	binding theory
	syntactic theories
	functional structure
	grammar formalism(s)
	grammars
	linguistic theor(y|ies)

Table 2: Candidate defining phrases of the term "Lexical Functional Grammar (LFG)".

Pattern and domain term acquisition. At the pattern acquisition stage, definition patterns are retrieved by 1) coupling terms with their definiens candidates, 2) extracting sentences that contain the pair within the specified window of words, and finally 3) creating POS-based patterns corresponding to the extracted sentences. All co-occurrences of each term together with each of its defining terms within the fixed window size are extracted from the POS-tagged corpus. At each iteration also new definiendum and definiens terms are found by applying the new abstracted patterns to the corpus and retrieving the matching domain terms.

The newly extracted sentences and terms are filtered (see "Filtering" below). The remaining data constitute new instances for further iterations. The linguistic material between the two terms in the extracted sentences is taken to be an instantiation of a potential definition pattern for which its POS pattern is created as follows:

- The defined and defining terms are replaced by placeholders, `T` and `DEF`,
- All the material outside the `T` and `DEF` anchors is removed; i.e. the resulting patterns have the form `'T ... DEF'` or `'DEF ... T'`
- Assuming that the fundamental elements of a definition pattern, are verbs and noun phrases,

[4]Here and further in the paper, regular expressions are presented in Perl notation.

all tags except verb, noun, modal and the infinitive marker "to" are replaced with by placeholders denoting any string; punctuation is preserved, as it has been observed to be informative in detecting definitions (Westerhout and Monachesi, 2008; Fahmi and Bouma, 2006),

- Sequences of singular and plural nouns and proper nouns are replaced with noun phrase placeholder, `NP`; it is expanded to match complex noun phrases when applying the patterns to extract definition sentences.

The new patterns and terms are then fed as input to the acquisition process to extract more sentences and again abstract new patterns.

Filtering. In the course of pattern acquisition information on term-pattern co-occurrence frequencies is stored and relative frequencies are calculated: 1) for each term, the percentage of seed patterns it occurs with, and 2) for each pattern, the percentage of seed terms it occurs with. These are used in the bootstrapping cycles to filter out terms which do not occur as part of a sufficient number of patterns (possibly false positive definiendum candidates) and patterns which do not occur with sufficient number of terms (insufficient generalizing behavior).

Moreover, the following filtering rules are applied: Abstracted POS-pattern sequences of the form `'T .+ DEF'`[5] and `'DEF T'` are discarded; the former because it is not informative, the latter because it is rather an indicator of compound nouns than of definitions. From the extracted sentences, those containing negation are filtered out; negation is contra-indicative of definition (Pearson, 1996). For the same reason, auxiliary constructions with "do" and "have" are excluded unless, in case of the latter, "have" is followed by a two past participle tags as in, e.g., "has been/VBN defined/VBN (as)."

4.3 Manual Refinement

While the goal of the bootstrapping stage was to find as many candidate patterns for good definition terms as possible, the purpose of the refinement stage is to aim at precision. Since the automatically extracted patterns consist only of verb and noun phrase tags between the definiendum and its defining term anchors, they are too general.

[5] '.+' stands for at least one arbitrary character.

#	Definitions	#	Non-definitions
25	is/VBZ	24	is/VBZ
8	represents/VBZ	14	contains/VBZ
6	provides/VBZ	9	employed/VBD
6	contains/VBZ	6	includes/VBZ
6	consists/VBZ	4	reflects/VBZ
3	serves/VBZ	3	uses/VBZ
3	describes/VBZ	3	typed/VBN
3	constitutes/VBZ	3	provides/VBZ
3	are/VBP	3	learning/VBG

Table 3: Subset of verbs occurring in sentences matched by the most frequently extracted patterns.

In order to create more precise patterns, we tuned the pattern sequences based on a small development sub-corpus of the extracted sentences which we annotated. The development corpus was created by extracting sentences using the most frequent patterns instantiated with the term which occurred with the highest percentage of seed patterns. The term "ontology" appeared with more than 80% of the patterns and was used for this purpose. The sentences were then manually annotated as to whether they are true-positive or false examples of definitions (101 and 163 sentences, respectively).

Pattern tuning was done by investigating which verbs are and which are not indicative of definitions based on the positive and negative example sentences. Table 3 shows the frequency distribution of verbs (or verb sequences) in the annotated corpus which occurred more than twice. Abstracting over POS sequences of the sentences containing definition-indicative verbs, we created 13 patterns, extending the automatically found patterns, that yielded 65% precision on the development set, matching 51% of the definition sentences, and reducing noise to 17% non-definitions. Patterns resulting from verb tuning were used in the evaluation. Examples of the tuned patterns are shown below:

```
T VBZ DT JJ? NP .* DEF
T , NP VBZ IN NP .* DEF
T , .+ VBZ DT .+ NP .* DEF
T VBZ DT JJ? NP .* DEF
```

The first pattern matches our both introductory

example definitions of the term "PCFG" (cf. Section 1) with `'T'` as a placeholder for the term itself, `'NP'` denoting a noun phrase, and `'DEF'` one of the term's defining phrases, in the first case, (1), "grammar", in the second case, (2), "probabilities". The examples annotated with matched pattern elements are shown below:[6]

> [PCFG]$_{\mathrm{T}}$ [is]$_{\mathrm{VBZ}}$ [a]$_{\mathrm{DT}}$ [CFG]$_{\mathrm{NP}}$ [in which each production $A \rightarrow \alpha$ in the]$_{.*}$ [grammar]$_{\mathrm{DEF}}$'s set of productions R is associated with an emission probability ...
>
> A [PCFG]$_{\mathrm{T}}$ [defines]$_{\mathrm{VBZ}}$ [the]$_{\mathrm{DT}}$ [probability]$_{\mathrm{DEF}}$ of a string of words as the sum of the probabilities of all admissible phrase structure parses (trees) for that string.

5 Deep Analysis for Definition Extraction

An alternative, largely domain-independent approach to the extraction of definition sentences is based on the sentence-semantic index generation of the ACL Anthology Searchbench (Schäfer et al., 2011).

Deep syntactic parsing with semantic predicate-argument structure extraction of each of the approx. 3.3 million sentences in the 18,653 papers ACL Anthology corpus is used for our experiments. We briefly describe how in this approach we get from the sentence text to the semantic representation.

The preprocessing is shared with the bootstrapping-based approach for definition sentence extraction, namely PDF-to-text extraction, sentence boundary detection (SBR), and trigram-based POS tagging with TnT (Brants, 2000). The tagger output is combined with information from a named entity recognizer that in addition delivers hypothetical information on citation expressions. The combined result is delivered as input to the deep parser PET (Callmeier, 2000) running the open source HPSG grammar (Pollard and Sag, 1994) grammar for English (ERG; Flickinger (2002)).

The deep parser is made robust and fast through a careful combination of several techniques; e.g.: (1) *chart pruning*: directed search during parsing to increase performance and coverage for longer sentences (Cramer and Zhang, 2010); (2) *chart mapping*: a framework for integrating preprocessing information from PoS tagger and named entity recognizer in exactly the way the deep grammar expects it (Adolphs et al., 2008)[7]; (3) a statistical parse ranking model (WeScience; (Flickinger et al., 2010)).

The parser outputs sentence-semantic representation in the MRS format (Copestake et al., 2005) that is transformed into a dependency-like variant (Copestake, 2009). From these DMRS representations, predicate-argument structures are derived. These are indexed with structure (semantic subject, predicate, direct object, indirect object, adjuncts) using a customized Apache Solr[8] server. Matching of arguments is left to Solr's standard analyzer for English with stemming; exact matches are ranked higher than partial matches.

The basic semantics extraction algorithm consists of the following steps: 1) calculate the closure for each (D)MRS elementary predication based on the EQ (variable equivalence) relation and group the predicates and entities in each closure respectively; 2) extract the relations of the groups, which results in a graph as a whole; 3) recursively traverse the graph, form one semantic tuple for each predicate, and fill information under its scope, i.e. subject, object, etc.

The semantic structure extraction algorithm generates multiple predicate-argument structures for coordinated sentence (sub-)structures in the index. Moreover, explicit negation is recognized and negated sentences are excluded for the task for the same reasons as in the bootstrapping approach above (see Section 4.2, "Filtering").

Further details of the deep parsing approach are described in (Schäfer and Kiefer, 2011). In the Searchbench online system[9], the definition extraction can by tested with any domain term `T` by using statement queries of the form '**s:T p:is**'.

6 Evaluation

For evaluation, we selected 20 terms, shown in Table 4, which can be considered *domain terms* in the

[6] Matching pattern elements in square brackets; tags from the pattern subscripted.

[7] PoS tagging, e.g., helps the deep parser to cope with words unknown to the deep lexicon, for which default entries based on the PoS information are generated on the fly.

[8] `http://lucene.apache.org/solr`

[9] `http://aclasb.dfki.de`

integer linear programming (ILP)
conditional random field (CRF)
support vector machine (SVM)
latent semantic analysis (LSA)
combinatory categorial grammar (CCG)
lexical-functional grammar (LFG)
probabilistic context-free grammar (PCFG)
discourse representation theory (DRT)
discourse representation structure (DRS)
phrase-based machine translation (PSMT;PBSMT)
statistical machine translation (SMT)
multi-document summarization (MDS)
word sense disambiguation (WSD)
semantic role labeling (SRL)
coreference resolution
conditional entropy
cosine similarity
mutual information (MI)
default unification (DU)
computational linguistics (CL)

Table 4: Domain-terms used in the rating experiment

domain of computational linguistics. Five general terms, such as 'English text' or 'web page', were also included in the evaluation as a control sample; since general terms of this kind are not likely to be defined in scientific papers in CL, their definition sentences were of low quality (false positives). We do not include them in the summary of the evaluation results for space reasons. "Computational linguistics", while certainly a domain term in the domain, is not likely to be defined in the articles in the ACL Anthology, however, the term as such should rather be included in a glossary of computational linguistics, therefore, we included it in the evaluation.

Due to the lack of a gold-standard glossary definitions in the domain, we performed a rating experiment in which we asked domain experts to judge top-ranked definitional sentences extracted using the two approaches. Below we briefly outline the evaluation setup and the procedure.

6.1 Evaluation Data

A set of definitional sentences for the 20 domain terms was extracted as follows:

Lexico-syntactic patterns (LSP). For the lexico-syntactic patterns approach, sentences extracted by the set of refined patterns (see Section 4.3) were considered for evaluation only if they contained at least one of the term's potential defining phrases as identified by the first stage of the glossary extraction (Section 4.2). Acronyms were allowed as fillers of the domain term placeholders.

The candidate evaluation sentences were ranked using single linkage clustering in order to find subsets of similar sentences. `tf.idf`-based cosine between vectors of lemmatized words was used as a similarity function. As in (Shen et al., 2006), the longest sentence was chosen from each of the clusters. Results were ranked by considering the size of the clusters as a measure of how likely it represents a definition. The larger the cluster, the higher it was ranked. Five top-ranked sentences for each of the 20 terms were used for the evaluation.

Deep analysis (DA). The only pattern used for deep analysis extraction was 'subject:`T` predicate:**is**', with '**is**' restricted by the HPSG grammar to be the copula relation and not an auxiliary such as in passive constructions, etc. Five top-ranked sentences – as per the Solr's matching algorithm – extracted with this pattern were used for the evaluation.

In total, 200 candidate definition sentences for 20 domain terms were evaluated, 100 per extraction methods. Examples of candidate glossary sentences extracted using both methods, along with their ratings, are shown in the appendix.

6.2 Evaluation Method

Candidate definition sentences were presented to 6 human domain experts by a web interface displaying one sentence at a time in random order. Judges were asked to rate sentences on a 5-point ordinal scale with the following descriptors:[10]

5: The passage provides a precise and concise description of the concept

4: The passage provides a good description of the concept

3: The passage provides useful information about the concept, which could enhance a definition

[10]Example definitions at each scale point selected by the authors were shown for the concept "hidden markov model".

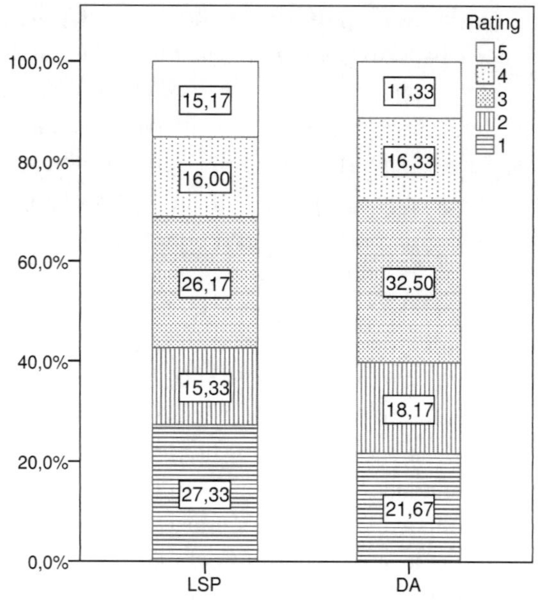

Figure 1: Distribution of ratings across the 5 scale points; LSP: lexico-syntactic patterns, DA: deep analysis

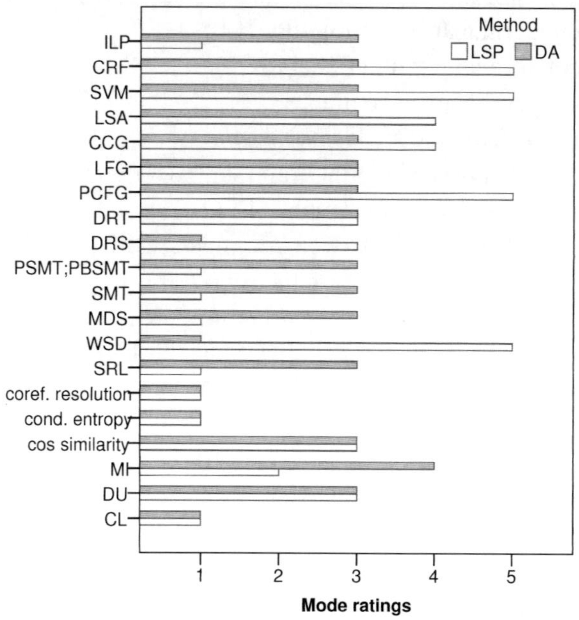

Figure 2: Mode values of ratings per method for the individual domain terms; see Table 4

2: The passage is not a good enough description of the concept to serve as a definition; for instance, it's too general, unfocused, or a subconcept/superconcept of the target concept is defined instead

1: The passage does not describe the concept at all

The judges participating in the rating experiment were PhD students, postdoctoral researchers, or researchers of comparable expertise, active in the areas of computational linguistics/natural language processing/language technology. One of the raters was one of the authors of this paper. The raters were explicitly instructed to think along the lines of "what they would like to see in a glossary of computational linguistics terms".

6.3 Results

Figure 1 shows the distribution of ratings across the five scale points for the two systems. Around 57% of the LSP ratings and 60% of DA ratings fall within the top three scale-points (positive ratings) and 43% and 40%, respectively, within the bottom two scale-points (low ratings). Krippendorff's ordinal α (Hayes and Krippendorff, 2007) was 0.66 (1,000 bootstrapped samples) indicating a modest degree of agreement, at which, however, tentative conclusions can be drawn.

Figure 2 shows the distribution of mode ratings of the individual domain terms used in the evaluation. Definitions of 6 terms extracted using the LSP method were rated most frequently at 4 or 5 as opposed to the majority of ratings at 3 for most terms in case of the DA method.

A Wilcoxon signed-rank test was conducted to evaluate whether domain experts favored definitional sentences extracted by one the two methods.[11] The results indicated no significant difference between ratings of definitions extracted using LSP and DA ($Z = 0.43$, $p = 0.68$).

Now, considering that the ultimate purpose of the sentence extraction is glossary creation, we were also interested in how the top-ranked sentences were rated; that is, assuming we were to create a glossary using only the highest ranked sentences (according to the methods' ranking schemes; see Section 6.1) we wanted to know whether one of the methods proposes rank-1 candidates with higher ratings, independently of the magnitude of the difference. A sign test indicated no statistical difference in ratings of the rank-1 candidates between the two methods.

[11] Definition sentences for each domain term were paired by their rank assigned by the extraction methods: rank-1 DA sentence with rank-1 LSP, etc.; see Section 6.1.

7 Conclusions and Future Work

The results show that both methods have the potential of extracting good quality glossary sentences: the majority of the extracted sentences provide at least useful information about the domain concepts. However, both methods need improvement.

The rating experiment suggests that the concept of definition quality in a specialized domain is largely subjective (borderline acceptable agreement overall and $\alpha = 0.65$ for rank-1 sentences). This calls for a modification of the evaluation methodology and for additional tests of consistency of ratings. The low agreement might be remedied by introducing a blocked design in which groups of judges would evaluate definitions of a small set of concepts with which they are most familiar, rather than a large set of concepts from various CL sub-areas.

An analysis of the extracted sentences and their ratings[12] revealed that deep analysis reduces noise in sentence extraction. Bootstrapping, however, yields more candidate sentences with good or very good ratings. While in the present work pattern refinement was based only on verbs, we observed that also the presence and position of (wh-)determiners and prepositions might be informative. Further experiments are needed 1) to find out how much specificity can be allowed without blocking the patterns' productivity and 2) to exploit the complementary strengths of the methods by combining them.

Since both approaches use generic linguistic resources and preprocessing (POS-tagging, named-entity extraction, etc.) they can be considered domain-independent. To our knowledge, this is, however, the first work that attempts to identify definitions of Computational Linguistics concepts. Thus, it contributes to evaluating pattern bootstrapping and deep analysis in the context of the definition extraction task in our own domain.

Acknowledgments

The C-Value algorithm was implemented by Mihai Grigore. We are indebted to our colleagues from the Computational Linguistics department and DFKI in Saarbrücken who kindly agreed to participate in the rating experiment as domain experts. We are also grateful to the reviewers for their feedback. The work described in this paper has been partially funded by the German Federal Ministry of Education and Research, projects TAKE (FKZ 01IW08003) and Deependance (FKZ 01IW11003).

[12]Not included in this paper for space reasons

References

P. Adolphs, S. Oepen, U. Callmeier, B. Crysmann, D. Flickinger, and B. Kiefer. 2008. Some Fine Points of Hybrid Natural Language Parsing. In *Proceedings of the 6th LREC*, pages 1380–1387.

V. Aleven, K. R. Koedinger, and K. Cross. 1999. Tutoring Answer Explanation Fosters Learning with Understanding. In *Artificial Intelligence in Education*, pages 199–206. IOS Press.

S. Bird, R. Dale, B. Dorr, B. Gibson, M. Joseph, M.-Y. Kan, D. Lee, B. Powley, D. Radev, and Y. F. Tan. 2008. The ACL Anthology Reference Corpus: A Reference Dataset for Bibliographic Research in Computational Linguistics. In *Proceedings of the 6th LREC*, pages 1755–1759.

C. Borg, M. Rosner, and G. Pace. 2009. Evolutionary Algorithms for Definition Extraction. In *Proceedings of the 1st Workshop on Definition Extraction*, pages 26–32.

L. Bozzato, M. Ferrari, and A. Trombetta. 2008. Building a Domain Ontology from Glossaries: A General Methodology. In *Proceedings of the 5th Workshop on Semantic Web Applications and Perspectives*, pages 1–10.

T. Brants. 2000. TnT – a statistical part-of-speech tagger. In *Proceedings of ANLP*, pages 224–231.

U. Callmeier. 2000. PET – A Platform for Experimentation with Efficient HPSG Processing Techniques. *Natural Language Engineering*, 6(1):99–108.

A. Copestake, D. Flickinger, I. A. Sag, and C. Pollard. 2005. Minimal Recursion Semantics: an Introduction. *Research on Language and Computation*, 3(2–3):281–332.

A. Copestake. 2009. Slacker semantics: why superficiality, dependency and avoidance of commitment can be the right way to go. In *Proceedings of the 12th EACL Conference*, pages 1–9.

B. Cramer and Y. Zhang. 2010. Constraining robust constructions for broad-coverage parsing with precision grammars. In *Proceedings of the 23rd COLING Conference*, pages 223–231.

I. Durán-Muñoz, 2010. *eLexicography in the 21st century: New challenges, new applications*, volume 7, chapter Specialised lexicographical resources: a survey of translators' needs, pages 55–66. Presses Universitaires de Louvain.

O. Etzioni, M. Cafarella, D. Downey, A-M. Popescu, T. Shaked, S. Soderland, D.S. Weld, and A. Yates. 2005. Unsupervised named-entity extraction from the Web: an experimental study. *Artificial Intelligence*, 165:91–134.

I. Fahmi and G. Bouma. 2006. Learning to identify definitions using syntactic features. In *Proceedings of the EACL Workshop on Learning Structured Information in Natural Language Applications*, pages 64–71.

D. Flickinger, S. Oepen, and G. Ytrestøl. 2010. WikiWoods: Syntacto-semantic annotation for English Wikipedia. In *Proceedings of the 7th LREC*, pages 1665–1671.

D. Flickinger. 2002. On building a more efficient grammar by exploiting types. In *Collaborative Language Engineering. A Case Study in Efficient Grammar-based Processing*, pages 1–17. CSLI Publications, Stanford, CA.

K. Frantzi, S. Ananiadou, and H. Mima. 1998. Automatic recognition of multi-word terms: the C-value/NC-value method. In *Proceedings of the 2nd European Conference on Research and Advanced Technology for Digital Libraries*, pages 585–604.

R. Del Gaudio and A. Branco. 2009. Language independent system for definition extraction: First results using learning algorithms. In *Proceedings of the 1st Workshop on Definition Extraction*, pages 33–39.

R. Girju, A. Badulescu, and D. Moldovan. 2006. Automatic discovery of part-whole relations. *Computational Linguistics*, 32(1):83–135.

A. F. Hayes and K. Krippendorff. 2007. Answering the call for a standard reliability measure for coding data. *Communication Methods and Measures*, 1(1):77–89.

M. A. Hearst. 1992. Automatic acquisition of hyponyms from large text corpora. In *Proceedings of the 14th COLING Conference*, pages 539–545.

D. Jurafsky and J. H. Martin. 2000. *Speech and Language Processing: An Introduction to Natural Language Processing, Computational Linguistics and Speech Recognition.* Prentice Hall Series in Artificial Intelligence. 2nd Ed. Online draft (June 25, 2007).

Z. Kozareva, E. Riloff, and E. Hovy. 2008. Semantic Class Learning from the Web with Hyponym Pattern Linkage Graphs. In *Proceedings of the 46th ACL Meeting*, pages 1048–1056.

C. D. Manning and H. Schütze. 1999. *Foundations of statistical natural language processing.* MIT Press, Cambridge, MA, USA.

M. P. Marcus, B. Santorini, and M. A. Marcinkiewicz. 1993. Building a large annotated corpus of English. The Penn Treebank. *Computational Linguistics*, 19:313–330.

S. Muresan and J. Klavans. 2002. A method for automatically building and evaluating dictionary resources. In *Proceedings of the 3rd LREC*, pages 231–234.

P. Pantel and M. Pennacchiotti. 2006. Espresso: Leveraging Generic Patterns for Automatically Harvesting Semantic Relations. In *Proceedings of the 21st COLING and the 44th ACL Meeting*, pages 113–120.

J. Pearson. 1996. The expression of definitions in specialised texts: A corpus-based analysis. In *Proceedings of Euralex-96*, pages 817–824.

C. Pollard and I. A. Sag. 1994. *Head-Driven Phrase Structure Grammar.* Studies in Contemporary Linguistics. University of Chicago Press, Chicago.

U. Schäfer and B. Kiefer. 2011. Advances in deep parsing of scholarly paper content. In R. Bernardi, S. Chambers, B. Gottfried, F. Segond, and I. Zaihrayeu, editors, *Advanced Language Technologies for Digital Libraries*, number 6699 in LNCS, pages 135–153. Springer.

U. Schäfer, B. Kiefer, C. Spurk, J. Steffen, and R. Wang. 2011. The ACL Anthology Searchbench. In *Proceedings of ACL-HLT 2011, System Demonstrations*, pages 7–13, Portland, Oregon, June.

Y. Shen, G. Zaccak, B. Katz, Y. Luo, and O. Uzuner. 2006. Duplicate Removal for Candidate Answer Sentences. In *Proceedings of the 1st CSAIL Student Workshop*.

A. Thanopoulos, N. Fakotakis, and G. Kokkinakis. 2002. Comparative evaluation of collocation extraction metrics. In *Proceedings of the 3rd Language Resources Evaluation Conference*, pages 620–625.

P. Velardi, R. Navigli, and P. D'Amadio. 2008. Mining the Web to Create Specialized Glossaries. *IEEE Intelligent Systems*, pages 18–25.

S. Walter. 2008. Linguistic description and automatic extraction of definitions from german court decisions. In *Proceedings of the 6th LREC*, pages 2926–2932.

W. Weiten, D. Deguara, E. Rehmke, and L. Sewell. 1999. University, Community College, and High School Students' Evaluations of Textbook Pedagogical Aids. *Teaching of Psychology*, 26(1):19–21.

E. Westerhout and P. Monachesi. 2008. Creating glossaries using pattern-based and machine learning techniques. In *Proceedings of the 6th LREC*, pages 3074–3081.

M. Wolska, U. Schäfer, and The Nghia Pham. 2011. Bootstrapping a domain-specific terminological taxonomy from scientific text. In *Proceedings of the 9th International Conference on Terminology and Artificial Intelligence (TIA-11)*, pages 17–23. INALCO, Paris.

G. Ytrestøl, D. Flickinger, and S. Oepen. 2009. Extracting and annotating wikipedia sub-domains. In *Proceedings of the 7th Workshop on Treebanks and Linguistic Theories*, pages 185–197.

Appendix

Rated glossary sentences for 'word sense disambiguation (WSD)' and 'mutual information (MI)'. As shown in Figure 2, for WSD, mode ratings of LSP sentences were higher, while for MI it was the other way round.

word sense disambiguation (WSD)

mode ratings of LSP sentences:

WSD is the task of determining the sense of a polysemous word within a specific context (Wang et al., 2006).	5
Word sense disambiguation or WSD, the task of identifying the correct sense of a word in context, is a central problem for all natural language processing applications, and in particular machine translation: different senses of a word translate differently in other languages, and resolving sense ambiguity is needed to identify the right translation of a word.	4
Unlike previous applications of co-training and self-training to natural languagelearning, where one general classifier is build to cover the entire problem space, supervised word sense disambiguation implies a different classifier for each individual word, resulting eventually in thousands of different classifiers, each with its own characteristics (learning rate, sensitivity to new examples, etc.).	3
NER identifies different kinds of names such as "person", "location" or "date", while WSD distinguishes the senses of ambiguous words.	3
This paper presents a corpus-based approach to word sense disambiguation that builds an ensemble of Naive Bayesian classifiers, each of which is based on lexical features that represent co-occurring words in varying sized windows of context.	1

DA sentences:

Word Sense Disambiguation (WSD) is the task of formalizing the intended meaning of a word in context by selecting an appropriate sense from a computational lexicon in an automatic manner.	5
Word Sense Disambiguation(WSD) is the process of assigning a meaning to a word based on the context in which it occurs.	{4,5}
Word sense disambiguation (WSD) is a difficult problem in natural language processing.	2
word sense disambiguation, Hownet, sememe, co-occurrence Word sense disambiguation (WSD) is one of the most difficult problems in NLP.	{1,2}
There is a general concern within the field of word sense disambiguation about the inter-annotator agreement between human annotators.	1

mutual information (MI)

mode ratings of LSP sentences:

According to Fano (1961), if two points (words), x and y, have probabilities $P(x)$ and $P(y)$, then their mutual information, $I(x, y)$, is defined to be $I(x, y) = log_2 \frac{P(x,y)}{P(x)P(y)}$); informally, mutual information compares the probability of observing x and y together (the joint probability) with the probabilities of observing x and y independently (chance).	5
Mutual information, $I(v; c/s)$, measures the strength of the statistical association between the given verb v and the candidate class c in the given syntactic position s.	3
In this equation, $pmi(i, p)$ is the pointwise mutual information score (Church and Hanks, 1990) between a pattern, p (e.g. consist-of), and a tuple, i (e.g. engine-car), and max_{pmi} is the maximum PMI score between all patterns and tuples.	{1,3}
Note that while differential entropies can be negative and not invariant under change of variables, other properties of entropy are retained (Huber et al., 2008), such as the chain rule for conditional entropy which describes the uncertainty in Y given knowledge of X, and the chain rule for mutual information which describes the mutual dependence between X and Y.	2
The first term of the conditional probability measures the generality of the association, while the second term of the mutual information measures the co-occurrence of the association.	2

DA sentences:

Mutual information (Shannon and Weaver, 1949) is a measure of mutual dependence between two random variables.	4
3 Theory Mutual information is a measure of the amount of information that one random variable contains about another random variable.	4
Conditional mutual information is the mutual information of two random variables conditioned on a third one.	{1,3}
Thus, the mutual information is $log_2 5$ or 2.32 bits, meaning that the joint probability is 5 times more likely than chance.	1
Thus, the mutual information is $log_2 0$, meaning that the joint is infinitely less likely than chance.	1

Applying Collocation Segmentation to the ACL Anthology Reference Corpus

Vidas Daudaravičius
Vytautas Magnus University / Vileikos 8, Lithuania
v.daudaravicius@if.vdu.lt

Abstract

Collocation is a well-known linguistic phenomenon which has a long history of research and use. In this study I employ collocation segmentation to extract terms from the large and complex ACL Anthology Reference Corpus, and also briefly research and describe the history of the ACL. The results of the study show that until 1986, the most significant terms were related to formal/rule based methods. Starting in 1987, terms related to statistical methods became more important. For instance, *language model*, *similarity measure*, *text classification*. In 1990, the terms *Penn Treebank*, *Mutual Information* , *statistical parsing*, *bilingual corpus*, and *dependency tree* became the most important, showing that newly released language resources appeared together with many new research areas in computational linguistics. Although *Penn Treebank* was a significant term only temporarily in the early nineties, the corpus is still used by researchers today. The most recent significant terms are *Bleu score* and *semantic role labeling*. While *machine translation* as a term is significant throughout the ACL ARC corpus, it is not significant for any particular time period. This shows that some terms can be significant globally while remaining insignificant at a local level.

1 Introduction

Collocation is a well-known linguistic phenomenon which has a long history of research and use. The importance of the collocation paradigm shift is raised in the most recent study on collocations (Seretan, 2011). Collocations are a key issue for tasks like natural language parsing and generation, as well as real-life applications such as machine translation, information extraction and retrieval. Collocation phenomena are simple, but hard to employ in real tasks. In this study I introduce collocation segmentation as a language processing method, maintaining simplicity and clarity of use as per the n-gram approach. In the beginning, I study the usage of the terms *collocation* and *segmentation* in the ACL Anthology Reference Corpus (ARC), as well as other related terms such as *word*, *multi-word*, and *n-gram*. To evaluate the ability of collocation segmentation to handle different aspects of collocations, I extract the most significant collocation segments in the ACL ARC. In addition, based on a ranking like that of $TF\text{-}IDF$, I extract terms that are related to different phenomena of natural language analysis and processing. The distribution of these terms in ACL ARC helps to understand the main breakpoints of different research areas across the years. On the other hand, there was no goal to make a thorough study of the methods used by the ACL ARC, as such a task is complex and prohibitively extensive.

2 ACL Anthology Reference Corpus

This study uses the ACL ARC version 20090501. The first step was to clean and preprocess the corpus. First of all, files that were unsuitable for the analysis were removed. These were texts containing characters with no clear word boundaries, i.e., each character was separated from the next by whitespace. This problem is related to the extraction of text from .pdf format files and is hard to solve. Each file in the ACL ARC represents a single printed page. The file name encodes the document ID and page number, e.g., the file name *C04-1001_0007.txt* is made up of four parts: *C* is the publication type, *(20)04* is the year, *1001* is the document ID, and *0007* is the page number. The next step was to compile files of the same paper into a single document. Also, headers and footers that appear on each document page were removed, though they were not always easily recognized and, therefore, some of them remained. A few simple rules were then applied to remove line breaks, thus keeping each paragraph on a single line. Finally, documents that were smaller than 1 kB were also removed. The final corpus comprised 8,581 files with a total of 51,881,537 tokens.

3 Terms in the ACL ARC related to collocations

The list of terms related to the term *collocation* could be prohibitively lengthy and could include many aspects of *what it is* and *how it is used*. For simplicitys sake, a short list of related terms, including *word, collocation, multiword, token, unigram, bigram, trigram, collocation extraction* and *segmentation*, was compiled. Table 2 shows when these terms were introduced in the ACL ARC: some terms were introduced early on, others more recently. The term collocation was introduced nearly 50 years ago and has been in use ever since. This is not unexpected, as collocation phenomena were already being studied by the ancient Greeks (Seretan, 2011). Table 2 presents the first use of terms, showing that the terms *segmentation*, *collocation* and *multiword* are related to a similar concept of gathering consecutive words together into one unit.

Term	Count	Documents	Introduced in
word	218813	7725	1965
segmentation	11458	1413	1965
collocation	6046	786	1965
multiword	1944	650	1969
token	3841	760	1973
trigram	3841	760	1973/87
bigram	5812	995	1988
unigram	2223	507	1989
collocation extraction	214	57	1992

Table 1: Term usage in ACL ARC

While the term *collocation* has been used for many years, the first attempt to define what *a collocation is* could be related to the time period when statistics first began to be used in linguistics heavily. Until that time, *collocation* was used mostly in the sense of an expression produced by a particular syntactic rule. The first definition of collocation in ACL ARC is found in (Cumming, 1986).

(Cumming, 1986): *By "collocation" I mean lexical restrictions (restrictions which are not predictable from the syntactic or semantic properties of the items) on the modifiers of an item; for example, you can say* **answer the door** *but not* **answer the window**. *The phenomenon which I've called* **collocation is** *of particular interest in the context of a paper on the lexicon in text generation because this particular type of idiom is something which a generator needs to know about, while a parser may not.*

It is not the purpose of this paper to provide a definition of the term collocation, because at the moment there is no definition that everybody would agree upon. The introduction of *unigrams, bigrams* and *trigrams* in the eighties had a big influence on the use of collocations in practice. N-grams, as a substitute to collocations, started being used intensively and in many applications. On the other hand, n-grams are lacking in generalization capabilities and recent research tends to combine n-grams, syntax and semantics (Pecina, 2005) .

The following sections introduce collocation segmentation and apply it to extracting the most significant collocation segments to study the main breakpoints of different research areas in the ACL ARC.

4 Collocation Segmentation

The ACL ARC contains many different segmentation types: discourse segmentation (Levow, 2004), topic segmentation (Arguello and Rose, 2006), text segmentation (Li and Yamanishi, 2000), Chinese text segmentation (Feng et al., 2004), word segmentation (Andrew, 2006). Segmentation is performed by detecting boundaries, which may also be of several different types: syllable boundaries (Müller, 2006), sentence boundaries (Liu et al., 2004), clause boundaries (Sang and Dejean, 2001), phrase boundaries (Bachenko and Fitzpatrick, 1990), prosodic boundaries (Collier et al., 1993), morpheme bound-

Term	Source and Citation
word	(Culik, 1965) : 3. Translation "**word** by **word**". "Of the same simplicity and uniqueness is the decomposition of the sentence S in its single **words** w_1 , w_2 , ..., w_k separated by interspaces, so that it is possible to write s = (w_1 w_2 ... w_k) like at the text." A **word** is the result of a sentence decomposition.
segmentation	(Sakai, 1965): The statement "x is transformed to y" is a generalization of the original fact, and this generalization is not always true. The text should be checked before a transformational rule is applied to it. Some separate steps for this purpose will save the machine time. (1) A text to be parsed must consist of segments specified by the rule. The correct **segmentation** can be done by finding the tree structure of the text. Therefore, the concatenation rules must be prepared so as to account for the structure of any acceptable string.
Collocation	(Tosh, 1965): We shall include features such as lexical **collocation** (agent-action agreement) and transformations of semantic equivalence in a systematic description of a higher order which presupposes a morpho-syntactic description for each language [8, pp. 66-71]. The following analogy might be drawn: just as strings of alphabetic and other characters are taken as a body of data to be parsed and classified by a phrase structure grammar, we may regard the string of rule numbers generated from a phrase structure analysis as a string of symbols to be parsed and classified in a still higher order grammar [11; 13, pp. 67-83], for which there is as yet no universally accepted nomenclature.
multi-word	(Yang, 1969): When title indices and catalogs, subject indices and catalogs, business telephone directories, scientific and technical dictionaries, lexicons and idiom-and-phrase dictionaries, and other descriptive **multi-word** information are desired, the first character of each non-trivial word may be selected in the original word sequence to form a keyword. For example, the rather lengthy title of this paper may have a keyword as SADSIRS. Several known information systems are named exactly in this manner such as SIR (Raphael's Semantic Information Retrieval), SADSAM (Lindsay's Sentence Appraiser and Diagrammer and Semantic Analyzing Machine), BIRS (Vinsonhaler's Basic Indexing and Retrieval System), and CGC (Klein and Simmons' Computational Grammar Coder).
token	(Beebe, 1973): The type/**token** ratio is calculated by dividing the number of discrete entries by the total number of syntagms in the row.
trigram	(Knowles, 1973): sort of phoneme triples (**trigrams**), giving list of clusters and third-order information-theoretic values. (D'Orta et al., 1987): Such a model it called **trigram** language model. It is based on a very simple idea and, for this reason, its statistics can be built very easily only counting all the sequences of three consecutive words present in the corpus. On the other hand, its predictive power is very high.
bigram	(van Berkelt and Smedt, 1988): **Bigrams** are in general too short to contain any useful identifying information while tetragrams and larger n-gram are already close to average word length. (Church and Gale, 1989): Our goal is to develop a methodology for extending an n-gram model to an (n+l)-gram model. We regard the model for **unigrams** as completely fixed before beginning to study **bigrams**.
unigram	the same as bigram for (Church and Gale, 1989)
collocation extraction	(McKeown et al., 1992): Added syntactic parser to Xtract, a **collocation extraction** system, to further filter collocations produced, eliminating those that are not consistently used in the same syntactic relation.

Table 2: Terms introductions in ACL ARC.

aries (Monson et al., 2004), paragraph boundaries (Filippova and Strube, 2006), word boundaries (Rytting, 2004), constituent boundaries (Kinyon, 2001), topic boundaries (Tur et al., 2001).

Collocation segmentation is a new type of segmentation whose goal is to detect *fixed word sequences* and to segment a text into word sequences called collocation segments. I use the definition of a sequence in the notion of one or more. Thus, a collocation segment is a sequence of one or more consecutive words that collocates and have collocability relations. A collocation segment can be of any

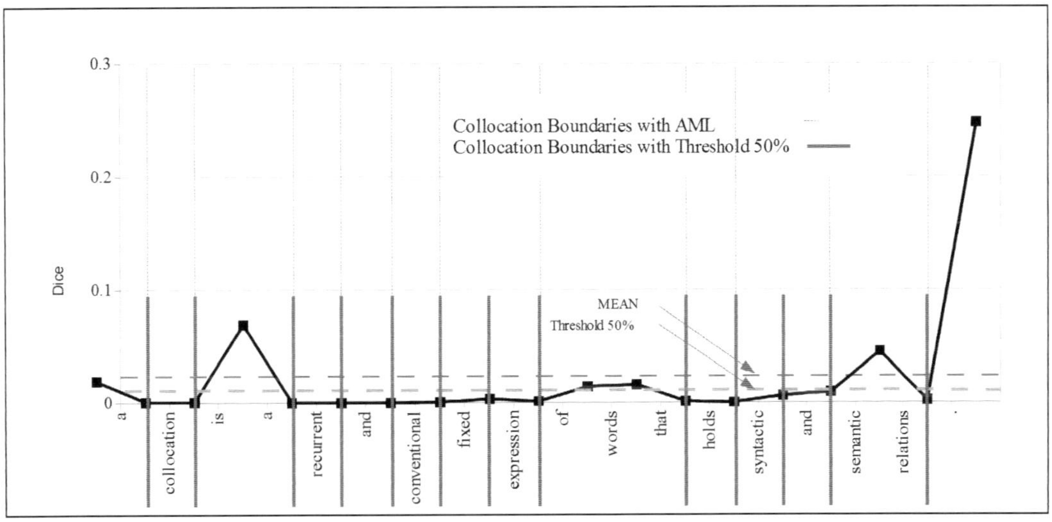

Figure 1: The collocation segmentation of the sentence *a collocation is a recurrent and conventional fixed expression of words that holds syntactic and semantic relations* . *(Xue et al., 2006).*

length (even a single word) and the length is not defined in advance. This definition differs from other collocation definitions that are usually based on n-gram lists (Tjong-Kim-Sang and S., 2000; Choueka, 1988; Smadja, 1993). Collocation segmentation is related to collocation extraction using syntactic rules (Lin, 1998). The syntax-based approach allows the extraction of collocations that are easier to describe, and the process of collocation extraction is well-controlled. On the other hand, the syntax-based approach is not easily applied to languages with fewer resources. Collocation segmentation is based on a discrete signal of associativity values between two consecutive words, and boundaries that are used to chunk a sequence of words.

The main differences of collocation segmentation from other methods are: (1) collocation segmentation does not analyze nested collocations it takes the longest one possible in a given context, while the n-gram list-based approach cannot detect if a collocation is nested in another one, e.g., *machine translation system*; (2) collocation segmentation is able to process long collocations quickly with the complexity of a bigram list size, while the n-gram list-based approach is usually limited to 3-word collocations and has high processing complexity.

There are many word associativity measures, such as Mutual Information (MI), T-score, Log-Likelihood, etc. A detailed overview of associativity measures can be found in (Pecina, 2010), and any of these measures can be applied to collocation segmentation. MI and Dice scores are almost similar in the sense of distribution of values (Daudaravicius and Marcinkeviciene, 2004), but the Dice score is always in the range between 0 and 1, while the range of the MI score depends on the corpus size. Thus, the Dice score is preferable. This score is used, for instance, in the collocation compiler XTract (Smadja, 1993) and in the lexicon extraction system Champollion (Smadja et al., 1996). Dice is defined as follows:

$$D(x_{i-1}; x_i) = \frac{2 \cdot f(x_{i-1}; x_i)}{f(x_{i-1}) + f(x_i)}$$

where $f(x_{i-1}; x_i)$ is the number of co-occurrence of x_{i-1} and x_i, and $f(x_{i-1})$ and $f(x_i)$ are the numbers of occurrence of x_{i-1} and x_i in the training corpus. If x_{i-1} and x_i tend to occur in conjunction, their Dice score will be high. The Dice score is sensitive to low-frequency word pairs. If two consecutive words are used only once and appear together, there is a good chance that these two words are highly related and form some new concept, e.g., a proper name. A text is seen as a changing curve of Dice values between two adjacent words (see Figure 1). This curve of associativity values is used to detect the boundaries of collocation segments, which can be done using a threshold or by following certain rules, as described in the following sections.

length	unique segments	segment count	word count	corpus coverage
1	289,277	31,427,570	31,427,570	60.58%
2	222,252	8,594,745	17,189,490	33.13%
3	72,699	994,393	2,983,179	5.75%
4	12,669	66,552	266,208	0.51%
5	1075	2,839	14,195	0.03%
6	57	141	846	0.00%
7	3	7	49	0.00%
Total	598,032	41,086,247	51,881,537	100%

Table 3: The distribution of collocation segments

2 word segments	CTFIDF
machine translation	10777
speech recognition	10524
training data	10401
language model	10188
named entity	9006
error rate	8280
test set	8083
maximum entropy	7570
sense disambiguation	7546
training set	7515
noun phrase	7509
our system	7352
question answering	7346
information retrieval	7338
the user	7198
word segmentation	7194
machine learning	7128
parse tree	6987
knowledge base	6792
information extraction	6675

3 word segments	CTFIDF
in terms of	4099
total number of	3926
th international conference	3649
is used to	3614
one or more	3449
a set of	3439
note that the	3346
it is not	3320
is that the	3287
associated with the	3211
large number of	3189
there is a	3189
support vector machines	3111
are used to	3109
extracted from the	3054
with the same	3030
so that the	3008
for a given	2915
it is a	2909
fact that the	2876

4 word segments	CTFIDF
if there is a	1690
human language technology conference	1174
is defined as the	1064
is used as the	836
human language technology workshop	681
could be used to	654
has not yet been	514
may be used to	508
so that it can	480
our results show that	476
would you like to	469
as well as an	420
these results show that	388
might be able to	379
it can also be	346
have not yet been	327
not be able to	323
are shown in table	320
is that it can	311
if there is an	305

5 word segments	CTFIDF
will not be able to	255
only if there is a	212
would not be able to	207
may not be able to	169
a list of all the	94
will also be able to	43
lexical information from a large	30
should not be able to	23
so that it can also	23
so that it would not	23
was used for this task	23
indicate that a sentence is	17
a list of words or	16
because it can also be	16
before or after the predicate	16
but it can also be	16
has not yet been performed	16
if the system has a	16
is defined as an object	16
is given by an expression	16

Table 4: Top 20 segments for the segment length of two to five words.

4.1 Setting segment boundaries with a Threshold

A boundary can be set between two adjacent words in a text when the Dice value is lower than a certain threshold. We use a dynamic threshold which defines the range between the minimum and the average associativity values of a sentence. Zero equals the minimum associativity value and 100 equals the average value of the sentence. Thus, the threshold value is expressed as a percentage between the minimum and the average associativity values. If the threshold is set to 0, then no threshold filtering is used and no collocation segment boundaries are set using the threshold. The main purpose of using a threshold is to keep only strongly connected tokens. On the other hand, it is possible to set the threshold to the maximum value of associativity values. This would make no words combine into more than single word segments, i.e., collocation segmentation would be equal to simple tokenization. In general, the threshold makes it possible to move from only single-word segments to whole-sentence segments by changing the threshold from the minimum to the maximum value of the sentence. There is no reason to use the maximum value threshold, but this helps to understand how the threshold can be used. (Daudaravicius and Marcinkeviciene, 2004) uses a global constant threshold which produces very long collocation segments that are like the clichs used in legal documents and hardly related to collocations. A dynamic threshold allows the problem of very long segments to be reduced. In this study I used a threshold level of 50 percent. An example of threshold is shown in Figure 1. In the example, if the threshold is 50 percent then segmentation is as follows: *a* | *collocation* | *is a* | *recurrent* | *and* | *conventional* | *fixed* | *expression* | *of words that* | *holds* | *syntactic* | *and* | *semantic relations* | . To reduce the problem of long segments even more, the Average Minimum Law can also be used, as described in the following section.

4.2 Setting segment boundaries with Average Minimum Law

(Daudaravicius, 2010) introduces the Average Minimum Law (AML) for setting collocation segmentation boundaries. AML is a simple rule which is applied to three adjacent associativity values and is expressed as follows:

$$boundary(x_{i-2}, x_{i-1}) = \\ = \begin{cases} True & \frac{D(x_{i-3}; x_{i-2}) + D(x_{i-1}; x_i)}{2} < D(x_{i-2}; x_{i-1}) \\ False & otherwise \end{cases}$$

The boundary between two adjacent words in the text is set where the Dice value is lower than the average of the preceding and following Dice values. In order to apply AML to the first two or last two words, I use sequence beginning and sequence ending as tokens and calculate the associativity between the beginning of the sequence and the first word, and the last word and the end of the sequence as shown in Figure 1. AML can be used together with Threshold or alone. The recent study of (Daudaravicius, 2012) shows that AML is able to produce segmentation that gives the best text categorization results, while the threshold degrades them. On the other hand, AML can produce collocation segments where the associativity values between two adjacent words are very low (see Figure 1). Thus, for lexicon extraction tasks, it is a good idea to use AML and a threshold together.

5 Collocation segments from the ACL ARC

Before the collocation segmentation, the ACL ARC was preprocessed with lowercasing and tokenization. No stop-word lists, taggers or parsers were used, and all punctuation was kept. Collocation segmentation is done on a separate line basis, i.e., for each text line, which is usually a paragraph, the average and the minimum combinability values are determined and the threshold is set at 50 percent, midway between the average and the minimum. The Average Minimum Law is applied in tandem. The tool *CoSegment* for collocation segmentation is available at (`http://textmining.lt/`).

Table 3 presents the distribution of segments by length, i.e., by the number of words. The length of collocation segments varies from 1 to 7 words. In the ACL ARC there are 345,455 distinct tokens. After segmentation, the size of the segment list was 598,032 segments, almost double the length of the single word list. The length of the bigram list is

4,484,358, which is more than 10 times the size of the word list and 7 times that of the collocation segment list. About 40 percent of the corpus comprises collocation segments of two or more words, showing the amount of *fixed language* present therein. The longest collocation segment is *described in section 2 . 2 ,* which contains seven words (when punctuation is included as words). This shows that collocation segmentation with a threshold of 50 percent and AML diverges to one-, two- or three-word segments. Despite that, the list size of collocation segments is much shorter than the list size of bigrams, and shorter still than that of trigrams.

After segmentation, it was of interest to find the most significant segments used in the ACL ARC. For this purpose I used a modified TF-IDF which is defined as follows:

$$CTFIDF(x) = TF(x)*ln\left(\frac{N - D(x) + 1}{D(x) + 1}\right)$$

where $TF(x)$ is the raw frequency of segment x in the corpus, N is the total number of documents in the corpus, and $D(x)$ is the number of documents in which the segment x occurs. Table 4 presents the top 20 collocation segments for two-, three-, four- and five-word segments of items that contain alphabetic characters only. The term *machine translation* is the most significant in CTFIDF terms. This short list contains many of the main methods and datasets used in daily computational linguistics research, such as: *error rate*, *test set*, *maximum entropy*, *training set*, *parse tree*, *unknown words*, *word alignment*, *Penn Treebank*, *language models*, *mutual information*, *translation model*, etc. These terms show that computational linguistics has its own terminology, methods and tools to research many topics.

Finally, 76 terms of two or more words in length with the highest CTFIDF values were selected. The goal was to try to find how significant terms were used yearly in the ACL ARC. The main part of the ACL ARC was compiled using papers published after 1995. Therefore, for each selected term, the average CTFIDF value of each document for each year was calculated. This approach allows term usage throughout the history of the ACL to be analysed, and reduces the influence of the unbalanced amount of published papers. Only those terms whose average CTFIDF in any year was higher than 20 were kept. For instance, the term *machine translation* had to be removed, as it was not significant throughout all the years. Each term was ranked by the year in which its average CTFIDF value peaked. The ranked terms are shown in Table 5. For instance, the peak of the CTFIDF average of the term *statistical parsing* occurred in 1990, of the term *language model* in 1987, and of the term *bleu score* in 2006. The results (see Table 5) show the main research trends and time periods of the ACL community. Most of the terms with CTFIDF peaks prior to 1986 are related to formal/rule-based methods. Beginning in 1987, terms related to statistical methods become more important. For instance, *language model*, *similarity measure*, and *text classification*. The year 1990 stands out as a kind of breakthrough. In this year, the terms *Penn Treebank*, *Mutual Information*, *statistical parsing*, *bilingual corpus*, and *dependency tree* became the most important terms, showing that newly released language resources were supporting many new research areas in computational linguistics. Despite the fact that *Penn Treebank* was only significant temporarily, the corpus is still used by researchers today. The most recent important terms are *Bleu score* and *semantic role labeling*.

This study shows that collocation segmentation can help in term extraction from large and complex corpora, which helps to speed up research and simplify the study of ACL history.

6 Conclusions

This study has shown that collocation segmentation can help in term extraction from large and complex corpora, which helps to speed up research and simplify the study of ACL history. The results show that the most significant terms prior to 1986 are related to formal/rule based research methods. Beginning in 1987, terms related to statistical methods (e.g., *language model*, *similarity measure*, *text classification*) become more important. In 1990, a major turning point appears, when the terms *Penn Treebank*, *Mutual Information*, *statistical parsing*, *bilingual corpus*, and *dependency tree* become the most important, showing that research into new areas of computational linguistics is supported by the publication of new language resources. The *Penn Treebank*, which was only significant temporarily, it still used today. The most recent terms are *Bleu score* and *semantic role labeling*. While *machine translation* as a term is significant throughout the ACL ARC, it is not significant in any particular time period. This shows that some terms can be significant globally, but insignificant at a local level.

References

Galen Andrew. 2006. A hybrid markov/semi-markov conditional random field for sequence segmentation. In *Proceedings of the 2006 Conference on Empirical Methods in Natural Language Processing*, pages 465–472, Sydney, Australia, July. Association for Computational Linguistics.

Jaime Arguello and Carolyn Rose. 2006. Topic-segmentation of dialogue. In *Proceedings of the Analyzing Conversations in Text and Speech*, pages 42–49, New York City, New York, June. Association for Computational Linguistics.

J. Bachenko and E. Fitzpatrick. 1990. A computational grammar of discourse-neutral prosodic phrasing in english. *Computational Linguistics*, 16:155–170.

Ralph D. Beebe. 1973. The frequency distribution of english syntagms. In *Proceedings of the International Conference on Computational Linguistics, COLING*.

Y. Choueka. 1988. Looking for needles in a haystack, or locating interesting collocational expressions in large textual databases. In *Proceedings of the RIAO Conference on User-Oriented Content-Based Text and Image Handling*, pages 21–24, Cambridge, MA.

Kenneth W. Church and William A. Gale. 1989. Enhanced good-turing and cat.cal: Two new methods for estimating probabilities of english bigrams (abbreviated version). In *Speech and Natural Language: Proceedings of a Workshop Held at Cape Cod*.

René Collier, Jan Roelof de Pijper, and Angelien Sanderman. 1993. Perceived prosodic boundaries and their phonetic correlates. In *Proceedings of the workshop on Human Language Technology*, HLT '93, pages 341–345, Stroudsburg, PA, USA. Association for Computational Linguistics.

Karel Culik. 1965. Machine translation and connectedness between phrases. In *International Conference on Computational Linguistics, COLING*.

Susanna Cumming. 1986. The lexicon in text generation. In *Strategic Computing - Natural Language Workshop: Proceedings of a Workshop Held at Marina del Rey*.

V. Daudaravicius and R Marcinkeviciene. 2004. Gravity counts for the boundaries of collocations. *International Journal of Corpus Linguistics*, 9(2):321–348.

Vidas Daudaravicius. 2010. The influence of collocation segmentation and top 10 items to keyword assignment performance. In Alexander F. Gelbukh, editor, *CICLing*, volume 6008 of *Lecture Notes in Computer Science*, pages 648–660. Springer.

Vidas Daudaravicius. 2012. Automatic multilingual annotation of eu legislation with eurovoc descriptors. In *In Proceedings of the 8th International Conference on Language Resources and Evaluation (LREC'2012)*.

Paolo D'Orta, Marco Ferretti, Alessandro Martelli, and Stefano Scarci. 1987. An automatic speech recognition system for the italian language. In *Third Conference of the European Chapter of the Association for Computational Linguistics*.

Haodi Feng, Kang Chen, Xiaotie Deng, and Weimin Zheng. 2004. Accessor variety criteria for chinese word extraction. *Computational Linguistics*, 30:75–93.

Katja Filippova and Michael Strube. 2006. Using linguistically motivated features for paragraph boundary identification. In *Proceedings of the 2006 Conference on Empirical Methods in Natural Language Processing*, pages 267–274, Sydney, Australia, July. Association for Computational Linguistics.

Alexandra Kinyon. 2001. A language independent shallow-parser compiler. In *Proceedings of 39th Annual Meeting of the Association for Computational Linguistics*, pages 330–337, Toulouse, France, July. Association for Computational Linguistics.

F. Knowles. 1973. The quantitative syntagmatic analysis of the russian and polish phonological systems. In *Computational And Mathematical Linguistics: Proceedings of the International Conference on Computational Linguistics, COLING*.

Gina-Anne Levow. 2004. Prosodic cues to discourse segment boundaries in human-computer dialogue. In Michael Strube and Candy Sidner, editors, *Proceedings of the 5th SIGdial Workshop on Discourse and Dialogue*, pages 93–96, Cambridge, Massachusetts, USA, April 30 - May 1. Association for Computational Linguistics.

Hang Li and Kenji Yamanishi. 2000. Topic analysis using a finite mixture model. In *2000 Joint SIGDAT Conference on Empirical Methods in Natural Language Processing and Very Large Corpora*, pages 35–44, Hong Kong, China, October. Association for Computational Linguistics.

D. Lin. 1998. Extracting collocations from text corpora. In *First Workshop on Computational Terminology*, Montreal.

Yang Liu, Andreas Stolcke, Elizabeth Shriberg, and Mary Harper. 2004. Comparing and combining generative and posterior probability models: Some advances in sentence boundary detection in speech. In Dekang Lin and Dekai Wu, editors, *Proceedings of EMNLP 2004*, pages 64–71, Barcelona, Spain, July. Association for Computational Linguistics.

Kathleen McKeown, Diane Litman, and Rebecca Passonneau. 1992. Extracting constraints on word usage from large text corpora. In *Speech and Natural Language: Proceedings of a Workshop Held at Harriman*.

Christian Monson, Alon Lavie, Jaime Carbonell, and Lori Levin. 2004. Unsupervised induction of natural language morphology inflection classes. In *Proceedings of the Seventh Meeting of the ACL Special Interest Group in Computational Phonology*, pages 52–61, Barcelona, Spain, July. Association for Computational Linguistics.

Karin Müller. 2006. Improving syllabification models with phonotactic knowledge. In *Proceedings of the Eighth Meeting of the ACL Special Interest Group on Computational Phonology and Morphology at HLT-NAACL 2006*, pages 11–20, New York City, USA, June. Association for Computational Linguistics.

Pavel Pecina. 2005. An extensive empirical study of collocation extraction methods. In *Proceedings of the ACL Student Research Workshop*, pages 13–18, Ann Arbor, Michigan, June. Association for Computational Linguistics.

Pavel Pecina. 2010. Lexical association measures and collocation extraction. *Language Resources and Evaluation*, 44(1-2):137–158.

C. Anton Rytting. 2004. Segment predictability as a cue in word segmentation: Application to modern greek. In *Proceedings of the Seventh Meeting of the ACL Special Interest Group in Computational Phonology*, pages 78–85, Barcelona, Spain, July. Association for Computational Linguistics.

Itiroo Sakai. 1965. Some mathematical aspects on syntactic discription. In *International Conference on Computational Linguistics, COLING*.

Erik F. Tjong Kim Sang and Herve Dejean. 2001. Introduction to the conll-2001 shared task: clause identification. In *Proceedings of the ACL 2001 Workshop on Computational Natural Language Learning*, Toulouse, France, July. Association for Computational Linguistics.

Violeta Seretan. 2011. *Syntax-Based Collocation Extraction*, volume 44 of *Text, Speech and Language Technology*. Springer.

Frank Smadja, Vasileios Hatzivassiloglou, and Kathleen R. McKeown. 1996. Translating collocations for bilingual lexicons: A statistical approach. *Computational Linguistics*, 22:1–38.

Frank Smadja. 1993. Retrieving collocations from text: Xtract. *Computational Linguistics*, 19:143–177.

E. Tjong-Kim-Sang and Buchholz S. 2000. Introduction to the conll-2000 shared task: Chunking. In *Proc. of CoNLL-2000 and LLL-2000*, pages 127–132, Lisbon, Portugal.

L. W. Tosh. 1965. Data preparation for syntactic translation. In *International Conference on Computational Linguistics, COLING*.

Gokhan Tur, Andreas Stolcke, Dilek Hakkani-Tur, and Elizabeth Shriberg. 2001. Integrating prosodic and lexical cues for automatic topic segmentation. *Computational Linguistics*, 27:31–57.

Brigitte van Berkelt and Koenraad De Smedt. 1988. Triphone analysis: A combined method for the correction of orthographical and typographical errors. In *Proceedings of the Second Conference on Applied Natural Language Processing*, pages 77–83, Austin, Texas, USA, February. Association for Computational Linguistics.

Nianwen Xue, Jinying Chen, and Martha Palmer. 2006. Aligning features with sense distinction dimensions. In *Proceedings of the COLING/ACL 2006 Main Conference Poster Sessions*, pages 921–928, Sydney, Australia, July. Association for Computational Linguistics.

Shou-Chuan Yang. 1969. A search algorithm and data structure for an efficient information system. In *International Conference on Computational Linguistics, COLING*.

	65	67	69	73	75	78	79	80	81	82	83	84	85	86	87	88	89	90	91	92	93	94	95	96	97	98	99	00	01	02	03	04	05	06
parsing algorithm	25						2	9	5	13					13	7											10			10				
lexical entry			36		21		4						14												9						13			11
source language		11	21				4			15						9					12													
word senses		10		31					22	12			6	10	7	7	19	17		13						6			9				9	
target language		11	15		24		2			18			5			11				10	13				10		17							
brown corpus							4	36		16			6			30			21	18	21	20	6		14			9	29					
logical form							8	21	11	17	13	2	6	9	18	12	19	15	16	16	17	14	8		13	8			11	11		10	10	
semantic representation				9		4	3			21	9						11																	
multi - word											22																21	9						
reference resolution							4	7	8					41	9		30	17	13	16	18		9			9	23			14		12		
language model											9				34		11	19	14	13	12	18				7		13	11			12	10	9
text generation			24					17	9	25	25		13	9	29			19		12			7											
spoken language		6															37	23	20	19	21	13		14										
speech recognition													12			11	33	19	21	19	16	16												
similarity measure			13													13	33	17				15									10			
text classification																		55		23	17									11	16			
statistical parsing																		30																
tree adjoining grammars												3		14		22	19	29	19	15		13					12		11					
mutual information																12	17	27	12	15			9	11				15						
penn treebank																		26					6											
bilingual corpus																		22		11		19			9			11	9	16	17	12	11	
dependency tree	10	8	9							11	8			9	7	10		21		15			12		11			13	16		11	16	15	11
pos tagging																			23		14			10	11			10		10	10	11	13	9
spontaneous speech				16												8	34	22	20	42	16	17		18				9			13	10		
text categorization																			21	25								16	9	15	14	12		10
feature selection																			20	11	51				10	7	10	11	9	12	14	15	10	10
translation model																		28	27			49						17	11	15	18	15	14	10
spelling correction									10	14	9		7			17		17	16	19		42	9	27	26			15	10	17	10	13	19	16
edit distance																						37		21			13	16	10	14	11	12	15	12
target word																							42		13	9		12	9	16	14	20	13	11
speech synthesis							3	8			11			9		8	14	18	16		11		29		9				11	11		10		10
search engine																					27			31	16			12	20		11		9	10
maximum entropy																			22	12	22	25		27	12	10	10	9		12	10			
lexical rules				12		6	2	10					5	18	9		11		36			18	8	24	46		21	18	11		11			
annotation scheme																						15		14	31		21	14	15	11	18		10	
coreference resolution																							11	21	34	37		10	16	27	20	22	16	27
text summarization														15												36	17	14		13	13	13	12	
naive bayes																									32	23	43	14	12	13	23	20	12	17
trigram model																		20		20	16	13		13		14	38	10	13	11	13			10
named entity																						20	12	14	11	14	31	12	10	19	16		10	11
anaphora resolution									5						10	9						15	17	10			29	13	21	11		12	12	11
word segmentation																				20	19	26		16	16	13		10	11	20	31	26	24	30
word alignment																								10	13		19	20		11	24	24	22	17
semantic role labeling																																25	25	28
bleu score																														12	18	16	14	21
	65	67	69	73	75	78	79	80	81	82	83	84	85	86	87	88	89	90	91	92	93	94	95	96	97	98	99	00	01	02	03	04	05	06

Table 5: The list of selected terms and the yearly importance in terms of CTFIDF.

Text Reuse with ACL: (Upward) Trends

Parth Gupta and Paolo Rosso
Natural Language Engineering Lab - ELiRF
Department of Information Systems and Computation
Universidad Politécnica de Valencia, Spain
`http://www.dsic.upv.es/grupos/nle`
`{pgupta,prosso}@dsic.upv.es`

Abstract

With rapidly increasing community, a plethora of conferences related to Natural Language Processing and easy access to their proceedings make it essential to check the integrity and novelty of the new submissions. This study aims to investigate the trends of text reuse in the ACL submissions, if any. We carried a set of analyses on two spans of five years papers (the past and the present) of ACL using a publicly available text reuse detection application to notice the behaviour. In our study, we found some strong reuse cases which can be an indicator to establish a clear policy to handle text reuse for the upcoming editions of ACL. The results are anonymised.

1 Introduction

Text reuse refers to using the original text again in a different work. The text reuse in its most general form can be of two types: verbatim (quotations, definitions) and modified (paraphrasing, boilerplate text, translation). Although, the text reuse can be legal or illegal from a publishing authority perspective about the accreditation to the original author, more importantly it involves the ethical issues, especially in the scientific work.

There is a fuzzy line between the text reuse and the plagiarism and often this line is legislative. There are no straight-forward measures to declare a work as plagiarism and hence the publishing houses usually deploy their own rules and definitions to deal with plagiarism. For example, IEEE[1] and ACM[2] both consider the reuse as plagiarism in case of:

1. unaccredited reuse of text;
2. accredited large portion of text without proper delineation or quotes to the complete reused portion.

IEEE does not allow reusing large portion of own previous work, generally referred as self reuse or self plagiarism, without delineation, while ACM allows it provided the original source being explicitly cited.

With the advent of a large number of conferences and their publicly available proceedings, it is extremely easy to access the information on the desired topic to *refer* to and to *reuse*. Therefore, it becomes essential to check the authenticity and the novelty of the submitted text before the acceptance. It becomes nearly impossible for a human judge (reviewer) to discover the source of the submitted work, if any, unless the source is already known. Automatic plagiarism detection applications identify such potential sources for the submitted work and based on it a human judge can easily take the decision.

Unaccredited text reuse is often referred to as plagiarism and there has been abundant research about the same (Bouville, 2008; Loui, 2002; Maddox, 1995). Self plagiarism is another related issue, which is less known but not less unethical.

[1] `http://www.ieee.org/publications_standards/publications/rights/ID_Plagiarism.html`

[2] `http://www.acm.org/publications/policies/plagiarism_policy`

There has been limited research on the nature of self-plagiarism and its limit to the acceptability (Bretag and Mahmud, 2009; Collberg and Kobourov, 2005). In theory, the technologies to identify either of them do not differ at the core and there have been many approaches to it (Bendersky and Croft, 2009; Hoad and Zobel, 2003; Seo and Croft, 2008). The text reuse can also be present in the cross-language environment (Barrón-Cedeño et al., 2010; Potthast et al., 2011a). Since few years, PAN organises competitions at CLEF[3] (PAN@CLEF) on plagiarism detection (Potthast et al., 2010; Potthast et al., 2011b) and at FIRE[4] (PAN@FIRE) on cross-language text reuse (Barrón-Cedeño et al., 2011).

In the past, there has been an attempt to identify the plagiarism among the papers of ACL anthology in (HaCohen-Kerner et al., 2010), but it mainly aims to propose a new strategy to identify the plagiarism and uses the anthology as the corpus. In this study, we are concerned about the verbatim reuse and that too in large amount, only. We identify such strong text reuse cases in two spans of five years papers of ACL (conference and workshops) and analyse them to notice the trends in the past and the present based on their year of publication, paper type and the authorship. The detection method along with the subsection of the ACL anthology used are described in Section 2. Section 3 contains the details of the carried experiments and the analyses. Finally, in Section 4 we summarise the work with remarks.

2 Detection Method

The aim of this study is to investigate the trend of text reuse, and not proposing a new method. Looking at the importance of the replicability of the experiments, we use one of the publicly available tools to detect the text reuse. First we describe the best plagiarism detection system tested in (Potthast et al., 2010) and then explain how the tool we used works similarly. The partition of the ACL anthology used for the experiments is described in Section 2.1. The details of the system along with the detection method are presented in the Section 2.2.

[3]http://pan.webis.de/

[4]http://www.dsic.upv.es/grupos/nle/fire-workshop-clitr.html

Year	Long	Short	Workshop	Total
1993	47	0	68	115
1994	52	0	56	108
1995	56	0	15	71
1996	58	0	73	131
1997	73	0	232	305
2007	131	57	340	528
2008	119	68	363	550
2009	121	93	740	954
2010	160	70	772	1002
2011	164	128	783	1075

Table 1: The year-wise list of the number of accepted papers in ACL.

2.1 Data Partition

We crawled the long and short papers of the ACL conference and all the workshop papers from the ACL anthology of the years 1990-1997 and 2004-2011. We converted all the papers from the PDF format to plain text for processing using "pdftotext" utility available with "xpdf" package in linux[5]. The bibtex files available in the anthology are used for the author analysis. We investigate the trends over two span of five years (1993-97 and 2007-11) to depict the past and the present trends. The number of papers accepted for the mentioned categories in these years are listed in Table 1.

2.2 Reuse Identification

First, we describe how the best plagiarism detection system at PAN@CLEF 2010 works. Then we show that WCopyFind[6], the tool we used, works in a similar way.

2.2.1 State-of-the-art

The best system in PAN@CLEF 2010 edition was (Kasprzak and Brandejs, 2010). The overview of the system is as follows.

1. Preprocessing: The documents are processed to normalise the terms and word 5-gram chunks are made using MD5 hashing scheme.

[5]http://linux.die.net/man/1/pdftotext

[6]WCopyFind is freely available under GNU public license at http://plagiarism.bloomfieldmedia.com/z-wordpress/software/wcopyfind/. Version 4.1.1 is used.

2. Similarity: Inverted index of these chunks is created. Then for the given suspicious document, the source documents which contain at least 20 such chunks in common, are retrieved.

3. Annotation: The boundary of the exact fragments (cases) are annotated based on the position information of the common chunks. False positives are removed by neglecting the cases where the chunks are sparse (lay far from one another).

2.2.2 WCopyFind

For the identification of text reuse, we used an open source application WCopyFind. This system

Parameter	Value
Shortest Phrase to Match	6
Fewest Matches to Report	500
Ignore Punctuation	Yes
Ignore Outer Punctuation	Yes
Ignore Numbers	Yes
Ignore Letter Case	Yes
Skip Non-Words	Yes
Skip Long Words	No
Most Imperfections to Allow	0

Table 2: Parameters used of WCopyFind to identify the text reuse.

works very similarly to the approach explained in Sec. 2.2.1.[7] It handles the preprocessing by user defined variables as shown in Table 2 to tokenise the terms. Then it creates the word n-grams where n = *Shortest Phrase to Match* parameter and converts the chunks into 32-bit hash codes for similarity estimation. It outputs the reuse text portions among the documents in question explicitly as shown in Fig. 1. The system extends a wide variety of parameters with word and phrase-based similarity. We used the parameter values as depicted in Table 2. Most of the parameters are self-explanatory. We used word 6-grams for the identification because the value of n=6 is suggested by the developers of WCopyFind. Parameter "Fewest Matches to Report" interprets the number of words in the matching n-grams hence it is set to 500, which practically stands for ~85 word

[7]http://plagiarism.bloomfieldmedia.com/How_WCopyfind_and_Copyfind_Work.pdf

Figure 1: Screen-shot of the output of WCopyFind. The size is deliberately kept small to anonymise the case. Best viewed in color.

6-grams. There was a high overlap of the text among the papers in the "reference" section which can not be considered as reuse. To avoid this influence, we estimated the maximum words overlap of the reference section between two papers empirically, which turned out to be 200 words. Therefore, setting the threshold value to 500 words safely avoided high bibliographical similarity based false positives. In order to confirm the reliability of the threshold, we manually assessed 50 reported cases at random, in which 48 were actually cases of text reuse and only 2 were false positives.

3 Experiments

We carried out a number of experiments to understand the nature and the trends of text reuse among the papers of ACL. These experiments were carried for papers over two spans of five years to notice the trends.

3.1 At present

In this category, we carry out the experiments on papers within the most recent five years.

I. Text reuse in the papers among the same year submissions This experiment aimed to identify the text reuse among the papers accepted in the same year. Each year, ACL welcomes the work in many different formats like long, short, demo, student session and workshop papers. This analysis reveals the same or highly similar text submitted in multiple formats.

Fig. 2 shows the number of reuse cases identified among the papers accepted in the same year.

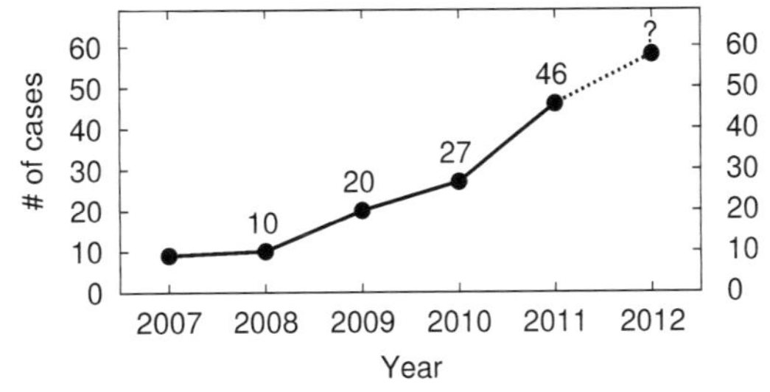

Figure 2: The text reuse cases identified among the papers of the same year submissions (span 2007-11).

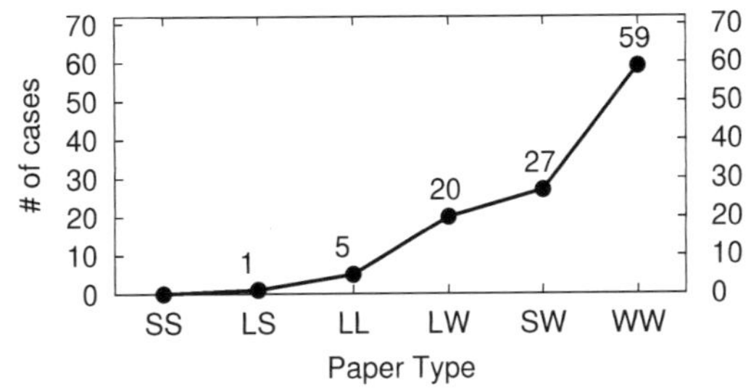

Figure 3: The text reuse cases based on the type of the papers involved. The 'L', 'S' and 'W' denote the long, short and workshop papers respectively. 'XY' refers to the cases of reuse involving one paper of type X and the other of type Y (span 2007-11).

We also analysed the types of the papers involved in these reuse cases. In the same year papers, it is difficult to decide the source and the target paper, because both are not published at the time of their review. Therefore, the number of cases based on the unordered pairs of the paper types involved in the reuse are shown in Fig. 3. It is noticeable from Fig. 2 and Table 1 that, although there is no big difference between the number of accepted papers in the last three years, the number of reuse cases are increasing rapidly. Moreover, Fig. 3 reveals that the chance of a workshop paper being involved in a reuse case with a long, short or another workshop paper is higher.

II. Text reuse in the papers from the previous year submissions This experiment aimed to depict the phenomenon of text reuse from an already published work, in this case, the ACL papers of the previous years. In this experimental setting, we considered the papers of a year 'X' as the target papers and the papers of the past three years from 'X' as the source papers. Fig. 4 depicts the reuse trend of

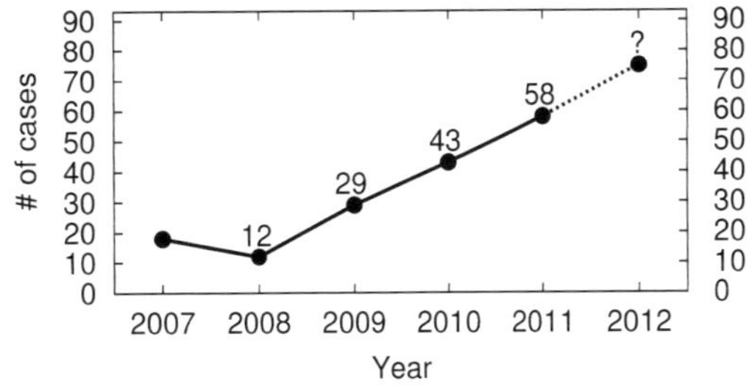

Figure 4: The text reuse cases in the papers of a year considering the papers of the past three years as the source (span 2007-11).

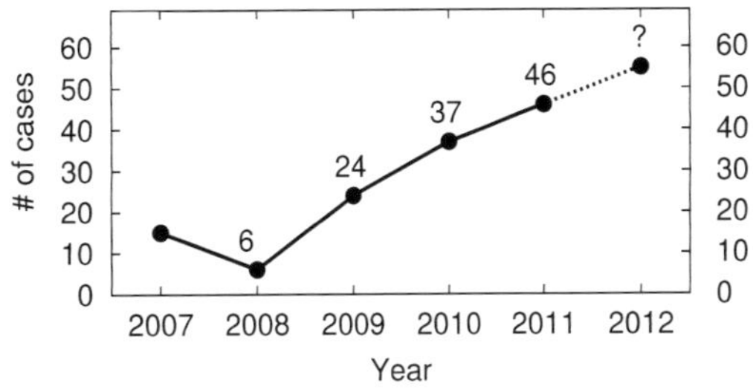

Figure 5: The text reuse cases in the papers of a year considering the papers of the immediate past year as the source (span 2007-11).

this nature over a span of five years.

We also carried a similar analysis considering only the immediate past year papers as the source. Fig. 5 presents the trend of such cases. It is noticeable from the Fig. 4 and 5 that the trend is upwards. Moreover, it is interesting to notice that the majority of the reuse cases involved the immediate past year papers as the source compared to the previous three year papers as the source.

We also analysed the trend of reuse based on the source and the target paper types and the findings are depicted in Fig. 6. Though the reuse cases involving the workshop papers are very high, there are noticeable amount of text reuse cases involving the papers where both of them (source and target) are of type long.

3.2 In retrospect

In this section we investigate the trends of text reuse in early 5 years papers i.e. papers from the span of years 1993-1997. Though the ACL Anthology contains papers from 1979, we chose this span because, for the consistency we wanted to include workshop

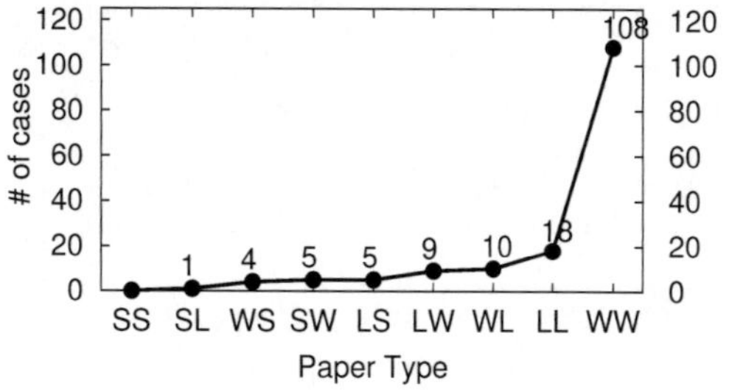

Figure 6: The text reuse trend based on the source and the target paper type. The 'L', 'S' and 'W' denote the long, short and workshop papers respectively. 'LS' refers to source is long paper and target is short paper, 'SL' refers to opposite and so on (span 2007-11).

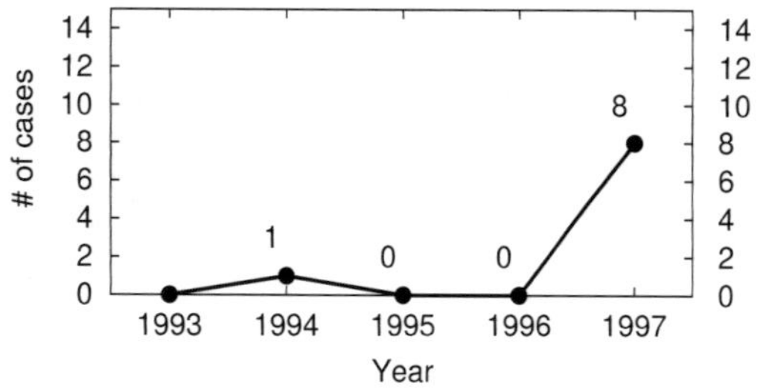

Figure 7: The text reuse cases identified among the papers of the same year submissions (span 1993-97).

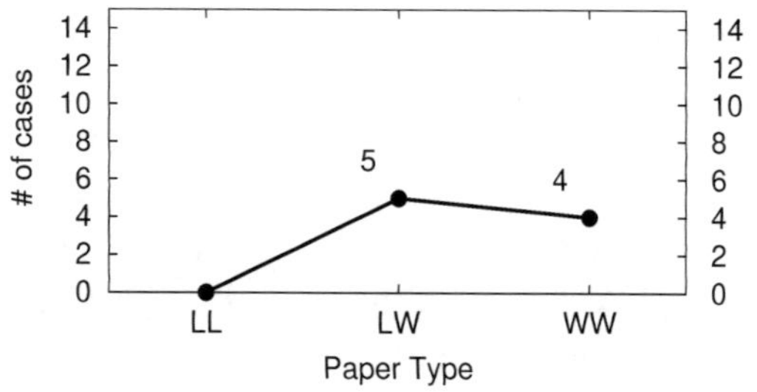

Figure 8: The text reuse cases based on the type of the papers involved. The 'L' and 'W' denote the long and workshop papers respectively. 'XY' refers to the cases of reuse involving one paper of type X and the other of type Y (span 1993-97).

papers in the experiments, which only started in 1990. So our first test year became 1993 considering previous three years papers to it serving as the source.

Figs. 7, 8, 9, 10 and 11 show the behaviour in the past years for the experiments described in Section 3.1. These results are relatively low compared to the behaviour in the present. To better understand this,

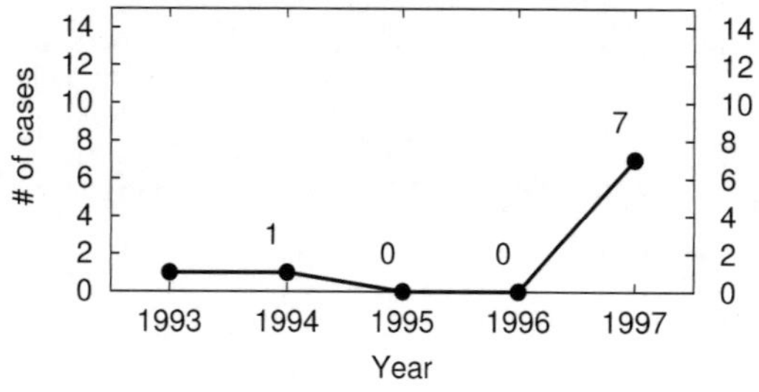

Figure 9: The text reuse cases in the papers of a year considering the papers of the past three years as the source (span 1993-97).

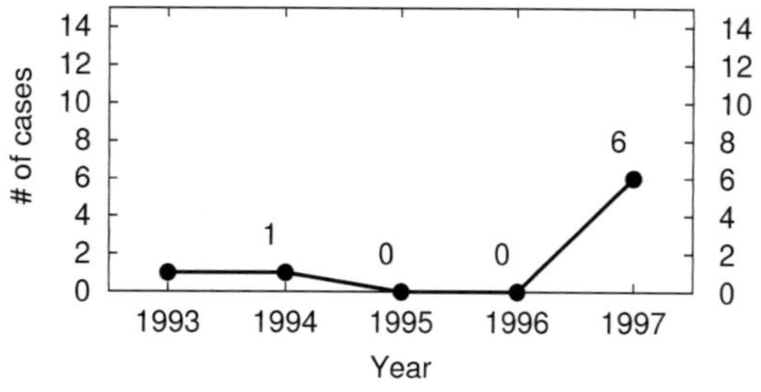

Figure 10: The text reuse cases in the papers of a year considering the papers of the immediate past year as the source (span 1993-97).

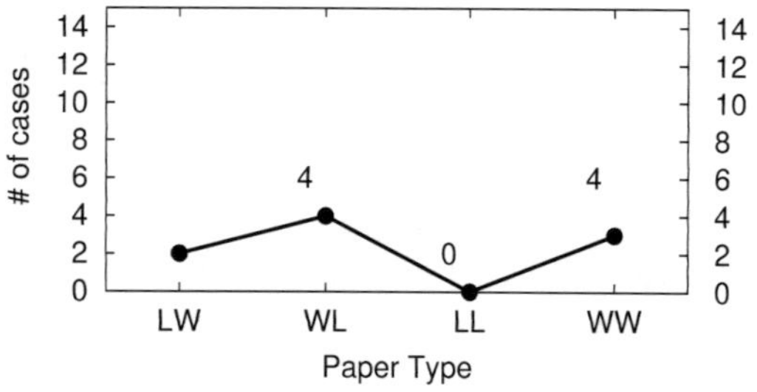

Figure 11: The text reuse trend based on the source and the target paper type. The 'L' and 'W' denote the long and workshop papers respectively. 'LW' refers to source is long paper and target is a workshop paper, 'WL' refers to opposite and so on (span 1993-97).

we present the number of text reuse cases in both the test spans as a relative frequency based on the total number of accepted papers in Table 3. It can be noticed from Table 3 that the reuse cases were quite a few in the past except the year 1997. Moreover, in the last five years the amount of text reuse cases have grown from 5.11% to 9.67%. In should also be noticed that in spite of these cases of text reuse, a large partition of the accepted papers (more than 90%) still remains free from text reuse.

Year	Tot. Cases	Tot. Accepted	% Cases
1993	1	115	0.87
1994	2	108	1.85
1995	0	71	0
1996	0	131	0
1997	15	305	4.92
2007	27	528	5.11
2008	22	550	4.00
2009	49	954	5.14
2010	70	1002	6.99
2011	104	1075	9.67

Table 3: The relative frequency of text reuse cases over the years.

3.3 Author analysis of the reuse cases

Finally we analysed the authorship of these text reuse cases and categorised them as self and cross reuse. If the two papers involved in text reuse share at least one common author then it is considered as a case of self reuse otherwise is reffered as cross reuse. The number of the self and cross reuse cases in the last five year papers are reported in Table 4. The self reuse cases are much higher than the cross reuse cases.

We also analysed the frequency of a particular author being involved in the text reuse cases. This analysis is presented in Fig. 12. This phenomenon follows the Zipf's power law i.e. a small set of authors (635 out of 8855 = less than 10%) refer to the reported cases of reuse in the last five years. More interestingly, only 80 authors (roughly 1% of the total authors) are involved in more than 5 cases of text reuse.

Reuse Type	**No. of Cases**
Self	232
Cross	17
Total	249

Table 4: Authorship of the text reuse cases. "Self" denotes that at least one author is common in the papers involved and "Cross" denotes otherwise.

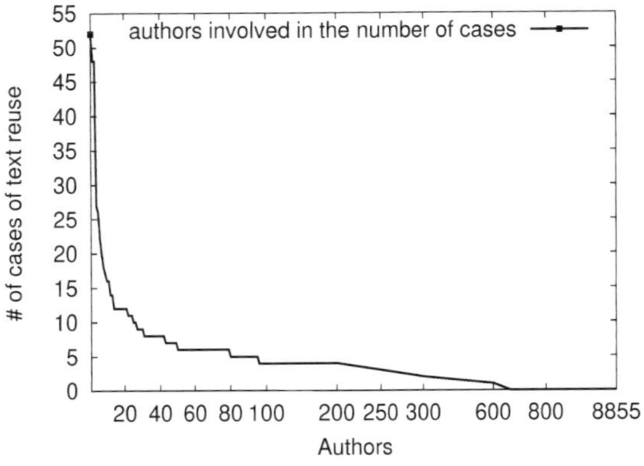

Figure 12: Involvement of an author in the number of text reuse cases.

4 Remarks

These cases are reported based on the verbatim copy of the text in the ACL proceedings only. We did not aim to detect any text reuse that is paraphrased, which in reality can not be neglected. The paraphrased cases of text reuse are even harder to detect, as remarked in (Stein et al., 2011): the state-of-the-art plagiarism detectors succeeded in detecting less than 30% of such plagiarised text fragments. Moreover, including the other major conferences and journals of the field, the number of reported cases may increase. The manual analysis revealed that, in some cases, the related work section is completely copied from another paper. There were many cases when two papers share a large portion of the text and differ mostly in the experiments and results section. This study revealed that self reuse is more prominent in the ACL papers compared to the cross reuse. The cross reuse could be a plagiarism case if the original authors are not acknowledged properly and explicitly. The ethicality and the acceptability of the self text reuse is arguable. Once more, the aim of this paper is not to judge the acceptability of the text reuse cases but to advocate the need of such systems to help in the review process. Text reuse in the same year submissions is also an eye opener because in such cases the text is novel but is used to publish in multiple formats and can stay unnoticed from the reviewers. In order to uphold the quality and the novelty of the work accepted in ACL, it is essential to implement a clear policy for text reuse and the technology to handle such reuse cases. We hope this work will help the ACL research community to consider handling the text reuse for the upcoming editions.

Acknowledgment

This work has been done in the framework of the VLC/CAMPUS Microcluster on Multimodal Interaction in Intelligent Systems and it has been partially funded by the European Commission as part of the WIQ-EI IRSES project (grant no. 269180) within the FP 7 Marie Curie People Framework, and by the Text-Enterprise 2.0 research project (TIN2009-13391-C04-03). We thank Rafael Banchs for his suggestions and ideas.

References

Alberto Barrón-Cedeño, Paolo Rosso, Eneko Agirre, and Gorka Labaka. 2010. Plagiarism detection across distant language pairs. In *Proceedings of the 23rd International Conference on Computational Linguistics*, COLING '10, Beijing, China, August 23-27.

Alberto Barrón-Cedeño, Paolo Rosso, Shobha Devi Lalitha, Paul Clough, and Mark Stevenson. 2011. Pan@fire: Overview of the cross-language !ndian text re-use detection competition. In *In Notebook Papers of FIRE 2011*, Mumbai, India, December 2-4.

Michael Bendersky and W. Bruce Croft. 2009. Finding text reuse on the web. In *Proceedings of the Second ACM International Conference on Web Search and Data Mining*, WSDM '09, pages 262–271, New York, NY, USA. ACM.

Mathieu Bouville. 2008. Plagiarism: Words and ideas. *Science and Engineering Ethics*, 14(3).

Tracey Bretag and Saadia Mahmud. 2009. Self-plagiarism or appropriate textual re-use? *Journal of Academic Ethics*, 7(3):193–205.

Christian Collberg and Stephen Kobourov. 2005. Self-plagiarism in computer science. *Commun. ACM*, 48(4):88–94, April.

Yaakov HaCohen-Kerner, Aharon Tayeb, and Natan Ben-Dror. 2010. Detection of simple plagiarism in computer science papers. In *Proceedings of the 23rd International Conference on Computational Linguistics*, COLING '10, pages 421–429, Beijing, China.

Timothy C. Hoad and Justin Zobel. 2003. Methods for identifying versioned and plagiarized documents. *J. Am. Soc. Inf. Sci. Technol.*, 54(3):203–215, February.

Jan Kasprzak and Michal Brandejs. 2010. Improving the reliability of the plagiarism detection system - lab report for pan at clef 2010. In Martin Braschler, Donna Harman, and Emanuele Pianta, editors, *CLEF (Notebook Papers/LABs/Workshops)*.

Michael C. Loui. 2002. Seven ways to plagiarize: handling real allegations of research misconduct. *Science and Engineering Ethics*, 8(4):529–539.

John Maddox. 1995. Plagiarism is worse than mere theft. *Nature*, 376(6543):721.

Martin Potthast, Alberto Barrón-Cedeño, Andreas Eiselt, Benno Stein, and Paolo Rosso. 2010. Overview of the 2nd international competition on plagiarism detection. In *Notebook Papers of CLEF 2010 LABs and Workshops*, CLEF '10, Padua, Italy, September 22-23.

Martin Potthast, Alberto Barrón-Cedeño, Benno Stein, and Paolo Rosso. 2011a. Cross-language plagiarism detection. *Language Resources and Evaluation*, 45(1):45–62.

Martin Potthast, Andreas Eiselt, Alberto Barrón-Cedeño, Benno Stein, and Paolo Rosso. 2011b. Overview of the 3rd international competition on plagiarism detection. In *Notebook Papers of CLEF 2011 LABs and Workshops*, CLEF '11, Amsterdam, The Netherlands, September 19-22.

Jangwon Seo and W. Bruce Croft. 2008. Local text reuse detection. In *Proceedings of the 31st annual international ACM SIGIR conference on Research and development in information retrieval*, SIGIR '08, pages 571–578, New York, NY, USA. ACM.

Benno Stein, Martin Potthast, Paolo Rosso, Alberto Barrón-Cedeño, Efstathios Stamatatos, and Moshe Koppel. 2011. Fourth international workshop on uncovering plagiarism, authorship, and social software misuse. *SIGIR Forum*, 45(1):45–48, May.

Integrating User-Generated Content in the ACL Anthology

Praveen Bysani
Web IR / NLP Group (WING)
National University of Singapore
13 Computing Link, Singapore 117590
bpraveen@comp.nus.edu.sg

Min-Yen Kan
Web IR / NLP Group (WING)
National University of Singapore
13 Computing Link, Singapore 117590
kanmy@comp.nus.edu.sg

Abstract

The ACL Anthology was revamped in 2012 to its second major version, encompassing faceted navigation, social media use, as well as author- and reader-generated content and comments on published work as part of the revised frontend user interface. At the backend, the Anthology was updated to incorporate its publication records into a database. We describe the ACL Anthology's previous legacy, redesign and revamp process and technologies, and its resulting functionality.

1 Introduction

To most of its users, the ACL Anthology[1] is a useful open-access repository of scholarly articles on the topics of computational linguistics and natural language processing. The liberal use and access policy granted by the Association of Computational Linguistics (ACL) to the authors of works published by the ACL makes discovery, access, and use of its research results easily available to both members and the general readership. The ACL Anthology initiative has contributed to the success of this mission, both as an archiving and dissemination vehicle for published works.

Started as a means to collect and preserve articles published by the ACL in 2001, the Anthology has since matured and now has well-defined workflows for its core missions. In 2009, the Anthology staff embarked to expand the Anthology's mission to meet two specific goals: on the backend, to enforce a proper data model onto the publication metadata; on the frontend, to expand the scope of the Anthology to encompass services that would best serve its constituents. Where possible, we adopted widely-deployed open source software, customizing it for the Anthology where needed.

With respect to the backend, the revamp adopted a database model to describe the publication metadata, implemented using MySQL. On top of this database layer, we chose Ruby on Rails as the application framework to interact with the data, and built suitable web interfaces to support both administrative and end-users. The backend also needed to support resource discovery by automated agents, and metadata export to sites that ingest ACL metadata.

With respect to the frontend, the Anthology website needed to meet the rising expectations in search and discovery of documents both by content and by fielded metadata. To satisfy both, we incorporated a faceted browsing interface that exposes metadata facets to the user. These metadata fields can be used to restrict subsequent browsing and searching actions to the values specified (e.g., *Year = 2001–2011*). Aside from resource discovery, the frontend also incorporated changes to support the workflow of readers and authors. We added both per-author and per-publication webpages. The publication pages invite the public to define content for the Anthology: anyone can report errors in the metadata, authors can supply revisions and errata, software and dataset links post-publication, readers can discuss the papers using the commenting framework

Praveen Bysani's work was supported from the National Research Foundations grant no. R-252-000-325-279.

[1] http://aclweb.org/anthology/; beta version 2 currently at http://aclantho3.herokuapp.com/.

in the system, and automated agents can use NLP and CL technology to extract, process and post information related to individual papers.

2 Revamp Design

Prior to our revamp, the Anthology's basic mission was to transcribe the metadata of ACL proceedings into a suitable form for the Web. To ensure widespread adoption, a simple XML format for the requisite metadata of *author* and *title* was created, with each ACL event's publication chair providing a single XML file describing the publications in each event and the details of the event (e.g., the volume's *booktitle* and *year*). Other fields were optional and could be included in the XML. The Anthology editor further added a unique identifier, an *Anthology ID*, for each publication record (e.g., "A00-1001"). Mandatory fields in the XML were extracted by a collection of programs to create the visible HTML pages in the Anthology website and the service export files, used to update the Association of Computing Machinery's (ACM) Portal[2] and the DBLP Computer Science Bibliography[3]. Prior to the revamp, this set of XML files – collected over various years – represented the canonical record of all publication data.

While easing adoption, storing canonical publication metadata as XML is not ideal. As it is stored across multiple files, even simple questions of inventory are hard to answer. As there was no set document type definition, the XML schema and enforcement of mandatory fields varied per document. In the revamp, we migrated the publication data into a database schema shown in Figure 1. The database form allows easy incorporation of additional fields that can be provided post-publication (including the Document Object Identifier, DOI, currently provided by the ACM by mutual agreement). The database structure also promotes publications, venues, and authors to first-class objects, enabling joins and views on the data, such as *paper—author* and *venue—special_interest_group*.The database currently has 21,107 papers, authored by 19,955 authors. These papers encompass one journal, 17 conferences and hundreds of workshops sponsored by 14 SIG groups. The publication years of these papers range from 1965 to 2012.

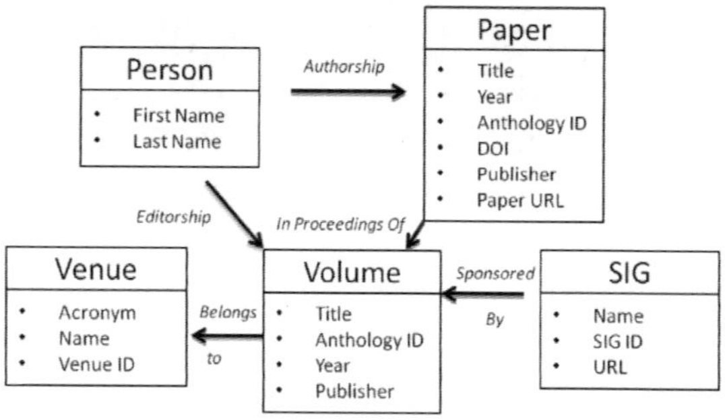

Figure 1: Current database schema for the Anthology.

The database's content is further indexed in inverted search indices using Apache Solr[4]. Solr allows indexing and querying in XML/JSON formats via HTTP requests, powering the frontend website search facility and enabling programmatic search by automated agents in the Anthology's future roadmap. We employ Ruby on Rails (or "Rails", version 3.1), a widely-deployed and mature web development framework, to build the frontend. It follows a Model-View-Controller (MVC) architecture, and favors convention over customization, expediting development and maintenance. Rails provides a closely tied model for basic database interactions, page rendering, web server deployment and provides a platform for integrating plugins for additional functionality. To enable faceted browsing and search, the revamped Anthology integrates the Project Blacklight[5] plugin, which provides the web search interface via our Solr indices. Rails applications can be deployed on many commercial web hosts but not on the current hosting service used by the primary ACL website. We have deployed the new Anthology interface on Heroku, a commercial cloud-based platform that caters to Rails deployment.

3 Frontend Form and Function

Of most interest to Anthology users will be the public website. The remainder of this paper describes

[2]http://dl.acm.org

[3]http://www.informatik.uni-trier.de/~ley/db/

[4]http://lucene.apache.org/solr/

[5]http://projectblacklight.org/, version 3.2

Figure 2: A screenshot of a faceted keyword search, showing additional restrictions on *Author* and *Year* (as a range).

the individual features that have been incorporated in the new interface.

Faceted Browsing: Facets let a paper (or other first-class object, such as authors) be classified along multiple dimensions. Faceted browsing combines both browsing- and search-based navigation: Anthology users can progressively filter the collection in each dimension by selecting a facet and value, and concurrently have the freedom of searching by keyword. It is a prevailing user interface technique in e-commerce sites and catching on in digital libraries.

The current Anthology defines five facets for papers. 'Author', 'Publication Year', 'Venue', 'Attachments' and 'SIG' (Special Interest Group) of the corresponding volume. The 'Year' facet further exposes an interface for date range filtering, while the 'Attachments' allows the selection of papers with software, errata, revisions and/or datasets easily. The website also has a standard search box that supports complex Boolean queries. Figure 2 illustrates some of these functions in a complex query involving both facets and keyword search. This is an improvement over the previous version that employed Google custom search, which can not leverage our structured data to add filtering functionality. Taking back search from Google's custom search also means that our search logs can be provided to our own community for research, that could enable an improved future Anthology.

Programmatic Contributions: The ACL community is uniquely positioned to enhance the Anthology by applying natural language technology on its own publication output. The ACL Anthology Reference Corpus (Bird et al., 2008) previously standardized a version of the Anthology's articles for comparative benchmarking. We take this idea farther by allowing automated agents to post-process information about any publication directly into the publication's corresponding page. An agent can currently provide per-paper supplementary material in an XML format (shown below) to the editor. After suitable validation as non-spam, the editor can ingest the XML content into the Anthology, incorporating it into the paper's webpage. Such functionality could be used to highlight summarization, information extraction and other applications that can process the text of papers and enrich them.

We use the Anthology ID to uniquely identify the associated paper. Currently the system is provisioned to support supplementary data provided as 1) text (as shown in Figure 3), 2) an embedded webpage, and 3) hyperlinks to websites (similar to how attachments are shown).

```
<paper id="P11-1110">
  <content name="keywords", type="text">
    <item>
      discourse, implicit reference, coherence,
      readability
    </item>
  </content>
</paper>
...
```

Figure 3: Excerpt of a programmatic contribution to the Anthology. The excerpt shows a keyword contribution on paper P11-1110.

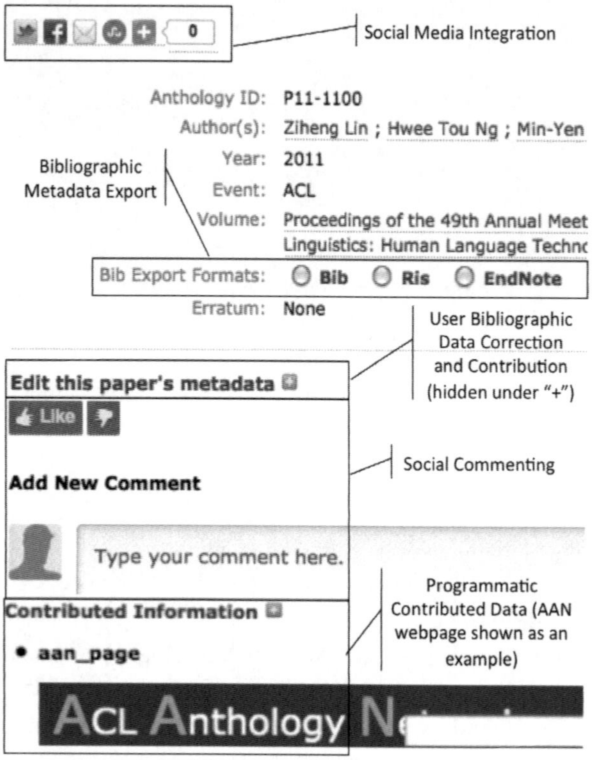

Figure 4: (Compressed) individual publication view with callout highlights of features.

Bibliographic Metadata Export: The previous Anthology exposed bibliographic metadata in BibTeX format, but its production was separate from the canonical XML data. In the revamp, we transform the database field values into the MODS bibliography interchange format. We then integrated the Bibutils[6] software module that exports MODS into four end-user formats: BibTeX, RIS, EndNote and Word. This lessens the effort for users to cite works in the Anthology by matching major bibliography management systems. Our use of Blacklight also enhances this ability, allowing the selection of multiple items to be exported to bibliographic exporting formats or to be shared by email.

User Contributed Data: While social media features are quintessential in today's Web, scholarly digital libraries and academic networks have yet to utilize them productively. One vehicle is to allow the readership to comment on papers and for those comments to become part of the public record. To accomplish this, we integrated a commenting plugin from Disqus[7], which enables users logged into other social media platforms to leave comments.

We also want to tighten the loop between reader feedback and Anthology management. Our revamp allows users to submit corrections and additions to any paper directly through a web form on the individual paper's webpage. Post-publication datasets, corrections to author name's and paper errata can be easily processed in this way. To avoid spam changes, this feature requires the Anthology editor to manually validate the changes. Figure 4 shows the individual publication view, with metadata, bibliographic export, metadata editing, commenting, and user (programmatic) contribution sections.

Author Pages: As a consequence of using Rails, it becomes trivially easy to create pages for other first-class data elements. Currently, we have created webpages per author, as shown in Figure 5. It gives the canonical listing of each author's publications within the Anthology in reverse chronological order and includes a list of the popular co-authors and publication venues. This feature brings the Anthology up to parity with other similar digital libraries. We hope it will spur authors to report publications under different variants of their names so a naming authority for ACL authors can result partially from community effort.

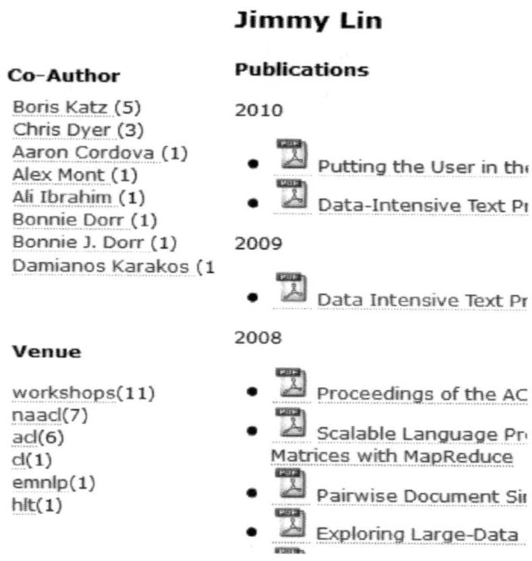

Figure 5: (Compressed) author page with corresponding co-author and venue information.

[6] http://sourceforge.net/p/bibutils/home/Bibutils/

[7] http://www.disqus.com

4 Usage Analysis

The revised Anthology interface is already seeing heavy use. We analyzed the application logs of the new Anthology website over a period of five days to understand the impact and usage of the new features. During this period the website has received 16,930 page requests. This is an increase over the original website, which garnered less than 7,000 page views during the same period. The average response time of the server is 0.73 seconds, while the average load time of a page is measured at 5.6 seconds. This is slow – web usability guidelines suggest load times over 200 milliseconds are suboptimal – but as the website is deployed on the cloud, server response can be easily improved by provisioning additional resources for money. Currently the new Anthology interface is run on a no-cost plan which provides minimal CPU bandwidth to serve the dynamically generated webpages to the readership.

The majority of the requests (11,398) use the new faceting feature; indeed only 30 requests use the traditional search box. The most used facet patterns include "Author, Venue" (51.6%) followed by "Author, Venue, Year" (14.8%). While we believe that it is too early to draw conclusions on user behavior, the overwhelming preference to use facets reveals that faceted browsing is a preferable navigational choice for the bulk of the Anthology users.

3,180 requests reached individual (detailed) publication views, while 2,455 requests accessed author pages. Approximately 62% of the total requests had a visit duration under 10 seconds, but 22% requests last between 11 seconds to 3 minutes, with the remaining 16% sessions being up to 30 minutes in length. The noticeable large ratio of long visits support our belief that the newly-added features encourages more user engagement with the Anthology. Since the website went live, we have received 3 valid requests for metadata changes through the new interface. Up to now, there has not been any use of the social media features, but we believe Anthology users will adopt them in due course.

5 Conclusion and Future Work

S.R. Ranganathan, arguably the father of faceted classification, proposed that "the library is a growing organism" as one of his laws of library science (Ranganathan, 1931). We observe that this is true in the digital context as well.

We will support the legacy ACL Anthology interface until the end of 2012 in parallel with the new interface, gradually phasing in the new interface as the primary one. Our immediate goal is to flesh out the per-author, -venue, -SIG views of the data, and to enable resource discovery via Open Archives Initiative's Protocol for Metadata Harvesting (OAI-PMH) (Lagoze et al., 2002), an open protocol for harvesting metadata by web crawlers. Our medium term outlook hopes to furtherincorporate grassroot ACL resources such as the ACL Anthology Network (Radev et al., 2009) and the ACL Searchbench (Schäfer et al., 2011).

We are most excited by the ability to incorporate programmatic contributions made by NLP software into the Anthology. We hope that the community makes full use of this ability to showcase the importance of our natural language processing on scholarly data and improve its accessibility and relevance to others.

References

Steven Bird, Robert Dale, Bonnie J. Dorr, Bryan Gibson, Mark Joseph, Min-Yen Kan, Dongwon Lee, Brett Powley, Dragomir R. Radev, and Yee Fan Tan. 2008. The ACL Anthology Reference Corpus: A reference dataset for bibliographic research in computational linguistics. In *LREC'08*.

Carl Lagoze, Hebert Van de Sompel, Michael Nelson, and Simeon Warner. 2002. The open archives initiative protocol for metadata harvesting, version 2.0. http://www.openarchives.org/OAI/2.0/ openarchivesprotocol.htm, June.

Dragomir R. Radev, Pradeep Muthukrishnan, and Vahed Qazvinian. 2009. The ACL Anthology Network corpus. In *Proceedings of the 2009 Workshop on Text and Citation Analysis for Scholarly Digital Libraries*, pages 54–61.

S. R. Ranganathan. 1931. *The Five Laws of Library Science*. Madras Library Association (Madras, India) and Edward Goldston (London, UK).

Ulrich Schäfer, Bernd Kiefer, Christian Spurk, Jörg Steffen, and Rui Wang. 2011. The ACL Anthology Searchbench. In *Proceedings of the 49th Association for Computational Linguistics: Human Language Technologies: Systems Demonstrations*, pages 7–13.

Towards an ACL Anthology Corpus with Logical Document Structure

An Overview of the ACL 2012 Contributed Task

Ulrich Schäfer
DFKI Language Technology Lab
Campus D 3 1
D-66123 Saarbrücken, Germany
ulrich.schaefer@dfki.de

Jonathon Read, Stephan Oepen
Department of Informatics
Universitetet i Oslo
0316 Oslo, Norway
{jread|oe}@ifi.uio.no

Abstract

The ACL 2012 Contributed Task is a community effort aiming to provide the full ACL Anthology as a high-quality corpus with rich markup, following the TEI P5 guidelines—a new resource dubbed the ACL Anthology Corpus (AAC). The goal of the task is threefold: (a) to provide a shared resource for experimentation on scientific text; (b) to serve as a basis for advanced search over the ACL Anthology, based on textual content and citations; and, by combining the aforementioned goals, (c) to present a showcase of the benefits of natural language processing to a broader audience. The Contributed Task extends the current Anthology Reference Corpus (ARC) both in size, quality, and by aiming to provide tools that allow the corpus to be automatically extended with new content—be they scanned or born-digital.

1 Introduction—Motivation

The collection of the Association for Computational Linguistics (ACL) Anthology began in 2002, with 3,100 scanned and born-digital[1] PDF papers. Since then, the ACL Anthology has become *the* open access collection[2] of scientific papers in the area of Computational Linguistics and Language Technology. It contains conference and workshop proceedings and the journal *Computational Linguistics* (formerly the *American Journal of Computational Linguistics*). As of Spring 2012, the ACL Anthology comprises approximately 23,000 papers from 46 years.

Bird et al. (2008) started collecting not only the PDF documents, but also providing the textual content of the Anthology as a corpus, the *ACL Anthology Reference Corpus*[3] (ACL-ARC). This text version was generated fully automatically and in different formats (see Section 2.2 below), using off-the-shelf tools and yielding somewhat variable quality.

The main goal was to provide a *reference corpus* with fixed releases that researchers could use and refer to for comparison. In addition, the vision was formulated that manually corrected *ground-truth* subsets could be compiled. This is accomplished so far for citation links from paper to paper inside the Anthology for a controlled subset. The focus thus was laid on bibliographic and bibliometric research and resulted in the ACL Anthology Network (Radev et al., 2009) as a public, manually corrected citation database.

What is currently missing is an easy-to-process XML variant that contains high-quality running text and logical markup from the layout, such as section headings, captions, footnotes, italics etc. In principle this could be derived from LaTeX source files, but unfortunately, these are not available, and furthermore a considerable amount of papers have been typeset with various other word processing software.

Here is where the ACL 2012 Contributed Task starts: The idea is to combine OCR and PDFBox-like born-digital text extraction methods and re-assign font and logical structure information as part of a rich XML format. The method would rely on OCR exclusively only in cases where no born-digital

[1] The term born-digital means natively digital, i.e. prepared electronically using typesetting systems like LaTeX, OpenOffice, and the like—as opposed to digitized (or scanned) documents.

[2] `http://aclweb.org/anthology`

[3] `http://acl-arc.comp.nus.edu.sg`

PDFs are available—in case of the ACL Anthology mostly papers published before the year 2000. Current results and status updates will always be accessible through the following address:

```
http://www.delph-in.net/aac/
```

We note that manually annotating the ACL Anthology is not viable. In a feasibility study we took a set of five eight-page papers. After extracting the text using PDFBox[4] we manually corrected the output and annotated it with basic document structure and cross-references; this took 16 person-hours, which would suggest a rough estimate of some 25 person-years to manually correct and annotate the current ACL Anthology. Furthermore, the ACL Anthology grows substantially every year, requiring a sustained effort.

2 State of Affairs to Date

In the following, we briefly review the current status of the ACL Anthology and some of its derivatives.

2.1 ACL Anthology

Papers in the current Anthology are in PDF format, either as scanned bitmaps or digitally typeset with LaTeX or word processing software. Older scanned papers were often created using type writers, and sometimes even contained hand-drawn graphics.

2.2 Anthology Reference Corpus (ACL-ARC)

In addition to the PDF documents, the ACL-ARC also contains (per page and per paper)

- bitmap files (in the PNG file format)
- plain text in 'normal' reading order
- formatted text (in two columns for most of the papers)
- XML raw layout format containing position information for each word, grouped in lines, with font information, but no running text variant.

The latter three have been generated using OCR software (OmniPage) operating on the bitmap files.

[4]http://pdfbox.apache.org

However, OCR methods tend to introduce character and layout recognition errors, from both scanned and born-digital documents.

The born-digital subset of the ACL-ARC (mostly papers that appeared in 2000 or later) also contains PDFBox plain text output. However, this is not available for approximately 4% of the born-digital PDFs due to unusual font encodings. Note though, that extracting text from PDFs in normal reading order is not a trivial task (Berg et al., 2012), and many errors exist. Furthermore, the plain text is not dehyphenated, necessitating a language model or lexicon-based lookup for post-processing.

2.3 ACL Anthology Network

The ACL Anthology Network (Radev et al., 2009) is based on the ACL-ARC text outputs. It additionally contains manually-corrected citation graphs, author and affiliation data for most of the Anthology (papers until 2009).

2.4 Publications with the ACL Anthology as a Corpus

We did a little survey in the ACL Anthology of papers reporting on having used the ACL Anthology as corpus/dataset. The aim here is to get an overview and distribution of the different NLP research tasks that have been pursued using the ACL Anthology as dataset. There are probably other papers outside the Anthology itself, but these have not been looked at.

The pioneers working with the Anthology as corpus are Ritchie et al. (2006a, 2006b). They did work related to citations which also forms the largest topic cluster of papers applying or using Anthology data.

Later papers on citation analysis, summarization, classification, etc. are Qazvinian et al. (2010), Abu-Jbara & Radev (2011), Qazvinian & Radev (2010), Qazvinian & Radev (2008), Mohammad et al. (2009), Athar (2011), Schäfer & Kasterka (2010), and Dong & Schäfer (2011).

Text summarization research is performed in Qazvinian & Radev (2011) and Agarwal et al. (2011a, 2011b).

The HOO ("Help our own") text correction shared task (Dale & Kilgarriff, 2010; Zesch, 2011; Rozovskaya et al., 2011; Dahlmeier et al., 2011) aims at developing automated tools and techniques that assist authors, e.g. non-native speakers of English, in writing (better) scientific publications.

Classification/Clustering related publications are Muthukrishnan et al. (2011) and Mao et al. (2010).

Keyword extraction and topic models based on Anthology data are addressed in Johri et al. (2011), Johri et al. (2010), Gupta & Manning (2011), Hall et al. (2008), Tu et al. (2010) and Daudaravičius (2012). Reiplinger et al. (2012) use the ACL Anthology to acquire and refine extraction patterns for the identification of glossary sentences.

In this workshop several authors have used the ACL Anthology to analyze the history of computational linguistics. Radev & Abu-Jbara (2012) examine research trends through the citing sentences in the ACL Anthology Network. Anderson et al. (2012) use the ACL Anthology to perform a people-centered analysis of the history of computational linguistics, tracking authors over topical subfields, identifying epochs and analyzing the evolution of subfields. Sim et al. (2012) use a citation analysis to identify the changing factions within the field. Vogel & Jurafsky (2012) use topic models to explore the research topics of men and women in the ACL Anthology Network. Gupta & Rosso (2012) look for evidence of text reuse in the ACL Anthology.

Most of these and related works would benefit from section (heading) information, and partly the approaches already used *ad hoc* solutions to gather this information from the existing plain text versions. Rich text markup (e.g. italics, tables) could also be used for linguistic, multilingual example extraction in the spirit of the ODIN project (Xia & Lewis, 2008; Xia et al., 2009).

3 Target Text Encoding

To select encoding elements we adopt the TEI P5 Guidelines (TEI Consortium, 2012). The TEI encoding scheme was developed with the intention of being applicable to all types of natural language, and facilitating the exchange of textual data among researchers across discipline. The guidelines are implemented in XML; we currently use inline markup, but stand-off annotations have also been applied (Bański & Przepiórkowski, 2009).

We use a subset of the TEI P5 Guidelines as not all elements were deemed necessary. This process was made easier through Roma[5], an online tool that assists in the development of TEI validators. We note that, while we initially use a simplified version, the schemas are readily extensible. For instance, Przepiórkowski (2009) demonstrates how constituent and dependency information can be encoded following the guidelines, in a manner which is similar to other prominent standards.

A TEI corpus is typically encoded as a single XML document, with several `text` elements, which in turn contain `front` (for abstracts), `body` and `back` elements (for acknowledgements and bibliographies). Then, sections are encoded using `div` elements (with `xml:ids`), which contain a heading (`head`) and are divided into paragraphs (`p`). We aim for accountability when translating between formats; for example, the `del` element records deletions (such as dehyphenation at line breaks).

An example of a TEI version of an ACL Anthology paper is depicted in Figure 1 on the next page.

4 An Overview of the Contributed Task

The goal of the ACL 2012 Contributed Task is to provide a high-quality version of the textual content of the ACL Anthology as a corpus. Its rich text XML markup will contain information on logical document structure such as section headings, footnotes, table and figure captions, bibliographic references, italics/emphasized text portions, non-latin scripts, etc.

The initial source are the PDF documents of the Anthology, processed with different text extraction methods and tools that output XML/HTML. The input to the task itself then consists of two XML formats:

- *PaperXML* from the ACL Anthology Searchbench[6] (Schäfer et al., 2011) provided by DFKI Saarbrücken, of all approximately 22,500 papers currently in the Anthology (except ROCLING which are mostly in Chinese). These were obtained by running a commercial OCR program and applying logical markup postprocessing and conversion to XML (Schäfer & Weitz, 2012).

[5]`http://www.tei-c.org/Roma/`

[6]`http://aclasb.dfki.de`

```xml
<?xml version="1.0" encoding="UTF-8"?>
<TEI xmlns="http://www.tei-c.org/ns/1.0"
  xmlns:xsi="http://www.w3.org/2001/XMLSchema-instance"
  xsi:schemaLocation="http://www.tei-c.org/ns/1.0 aclarc.tei.xsd" xml:lang="en">
  <teiHeader>
    <fileDesc>
      <titleStmt>
        <title>Task-oriented Evaluation of Syntactic Parsers and Their Representations</title>
        <author>
          Yusuke Miyao† Rune Sætre† Kenji Sagae† Takuya Matsuzaki† Jun'ichi Tsujii†‡*
          †Department of Computer Science, University of Tokyo, Japan
          ‡School of Computer Science, University of Manchester, UK
          National Center for Text Mining, UK
          {yusuke,rune.saetre,sagae,matuzaki,tsujii}@is.s.u-tokyo.ac.jp
        </author>
      </titleStmt>
      <publicationStmt>
        <publisher>Association for Computational Linguistics</publisher>
        <pubPlace> Columbus, Ohio, USA</pubPlace>
        <date>June 2008</date>
      </publicationStmt>
      <sourceDesc> [...] </sourceDesc>
    </fileDesc>
    <encodingDesc> [...] </encodingDesc>
  </teiHeader>
  <text>
    <front>
      <div type="abs">
        <head>Abstract</head>
        <p> [...]  </p>
      </div>
    </front>
    <body>
      <div xml:id="SE1">
        <head>Introduction</head>
        <p>
          Parsing technologies have improved considerably in
          the past few years, and high-performance syntactic
          parsers are no longer limited to PCFG-based frame<del type="lb">-</del>
          works (<ref target="#BI6">Charniak, 2000</ref>;
          [...]
        </p>
      </div>
    </body>
    <back>
      <div type="ack">
        <head>Acknowledgements</head>
        <p> [...] </p>
      </div>
      <div type="bib">
        <head>References</head>
        <listBibl>
          <bibl xml:id="BI1">
            D. M. Bikel. 2004. Intricacies of Collins' parsing model.
            <hi rend="italic">Computational Linguistics</hi>, 30(4):479–511.
          </bibl>
          [...]
        </listBibl>
        <pb n="54"/>
      </div>
    </back>
  </text>
</TEI>
```

Figure 1: An example of a TEI-compliant version of an ACL Anthology document P08-1006. Some elements are truncated ([...]) for brevity.

- TEI P5 XML generated by PDFExtract. For papers from after 1999, an additional high-quality extraction step took place, applying state-of the art word boundary and layout recognition methods directly to the native, logical PDF structure (Berg et al., 2012). As no character recognition errors occur, this will form the master format for textual content if available.

Because both versions are not perfect, a large, initial part of the Contributed Task requires automatically adding missing or correcting markup, using information from OCR where necessary (e.g. for tables). Hence, for most papers from after 1999 (currently approx. 70% of the papers), the Contributed Task can make use of both representations simultaneously.

The role of *paperXML* in the Contributed Task is to serve as fall-back source (1) for older, scanned papers (mostly published before the year 2000), for which born-digital PDF sources are not available, or (2) for born-digital PDF papers on which the PDFExtract method failed, or (3) for document parts where PDFExtract does not output useful markup such as currently for tables, cf. Section 4.2 below.

A big advantage of PDFExtract is its ability to extract the full Unicode character range without character recognition errors, while the OCR-based extraction methods in our setup are basically limited to Latin1 characters to avoid higher recognition error rates.

We proposed the following eight areas as possible subtasks towards our goal.

4.1 Subtask 1: Footnotes

The first task addresses identification of footnotes, assigning footnote numbers and text, and generating markup for them in TEI P5 style. For example:

```
We first determine lexical heads of nonterminal
nodes by using Bikel's implementation of
Collins' head detection algorithm
<note place="foot" n="9">
 <hi rend="monospace">http://www.cis.upenn.edu/
 ~dbikel/software.html</hi>
</note>
(<ref target="#BI1">Bikel, 2004</ref>;
 <ref target="#BI11">Collins, 1997</ref>).
```

Footnotes are handled to some extent in PDFExtract and *paperXML*, but the results require refinement.

4.2 Subtask 2: Tables

Task 2 identifies figure/table references in running text and links them to their captions. The latter will also have to be distinguished from running text. Furthermore, tables will have to be identified and transformed into HTML style table markup. This is currently not generated by PDFExtract, but the OCR tool used for *paperXML* generation quite reliably recognizes tables and transforms tables into HTML. Thus, a preliminary solution would be to insert missing table content in PDFExtract output from the OCR results. In the long run, implementing table handling in PDFExtract would be desirable.

```
<ref target="#TA3">Table 3</ref> shows the
time for parsing the entire AImed corpus,...
<figure xml:id="TA3">
 <head>Table 3: Parsing time (sec.)</head>
 <!-- TEI table content markup here -->
</figure>
```

4.3 Subtask 3: Bibliographic Markup

The purpose of this task is to identify citations in text and link them to the bibliographic references listed at the end of each paper. In TEI markup, bibliographies are contained in `listBibl` elements. The contents of `listBibl` can range from formatted text to moderately-structured entries (`biblStruct`) and fully-structured entries (`biblFull`). For example:

```
We follow the PPI extraction method of
<ref target="#BI39">Sætre et al. (2007)</ref>,
which is based on SVMs ...
<div type="bib">
 <head>References</head>
 <listBibl>
  <bibl xml:id="BI39">
  R. Sætre, K. Sagae, and J. Tsujii. 2007.
  Syntactic features for protein-protein
  interaction extraction. In
  <hi rend="italic">LBM 2007 short papers</hi>.
  </bibl>
 </listBibl>
</div>
```

A citation extraction and linking tool that is known to deliver good results on ACL Anthology papers (and even comes with CRF models trained on this corpus) is ParsCit (Councill et al., 2008). In this volume, Nhat & Bysani (2012) provide an implementation for this task using ParsCit and discuss possible further improvements.

4.4 Subtask 4: De-hyphenation

Both *paperXML* and PDFExtract output contain soft hyphenation indicators at places where the original paper contained a line break with hyphenation. In *paperXML*, they are represented by the Unicode soft hyphen character (in contrast to normal dashes that also occur). PDFExtract marks hyphenation from the original text using a special element. However, both tools make errors: In some cases, the hyphens are in fact hard hyphens. The idea of this task is to combine both sources and possibly additional information, as in general the OCR program used for *paperXML* more aggressively proposes de-hyphenation than PDFExtract. Hyphenation in names often persists in *paperXML* and therefore remains a problem that will have to be addressed as well. For example:

```
In this paper, we present a comparative
eval<del type="lb">-</del>uation of syntactic
parsers and their output
represen<del type="lb">-</del>tations based on
different frameworks:
```

4.5 Subtask 5: Remove Garbage such as Leftovers from Figures

In both *paperXML* and PDFExtract output, text remains from figures, illustrations and diagrams. This occurs more frequently in *paperXML* than in PDFExtract output because text in bitmap figures undergoes OCR as well. The goal of this subtask is to recognize and remove such text.

Bitmaps in born-digital PDFs are embedded objects for PDFExtract and thus can be detected and encoded within TEI P5 markup and ignored in the text extraction process:

```
<figure xml:id="FI3">
 <graphic url="P08-1006/FI3.png" />
 <head>
  Figure 3: Predicate argument structure
 </head>
</figure>
```

4.6 Subtask 6: Generate TEI P5 Markup for Scanned Papers from *paperXML*

Due to the nature of the extraction process, PDFExtract output is not available for older, scanned papers. These are mostly papers from before 2000, but also e.g. EACL 2003 papers. On the other hand, *paperXML* versions exist for almost all papers of the ACL Anthology, generated from OCR output. They still need to be transformed to TEI P5, e.g. using XSLT. The *paperXML* format and transformation to TEI P5 is discussed in Schäfer & Weitz (2012) in this volume.

4.7 Subtask 7: Add Sentence Splitting Markup

Having a standard for sentence splitting with unique sentence IDs per paper to which everyone can refer to later could be important. The aim of this task is to add sentence segmentation to the target markup. It should be based on an open source tokenizer such as JTok, a customizable open source tool[7] that was also used for the ACL Anthology Searchbench semantic index pre-processing, or the Stanford Tokenizer[8].

```
<p><s>PPI extraction is an NLP task to identify
protein pairs that are mentioned as interacting
in biomedical papers.</s> <s>Because the number
of biomedical papers is growing rapidly, it is
impossible for biomedical researchers to read
all papers relevant to their research; thus,
there is an emerging need for reliable IE
technologies, such as PPI identification.
</s></p>
```

4.8 Subtask 8: Math Formulae

Many papers in the Computational Linguistics area, especially those dealing with statistical natural language processing, contain mathematical formulae. Neither *paperXML* nor PDFExtract currently provide a means to deal with these.

A math formula recognition is a complex task, inserting MathML[9] formula markup from an external tool (formula OCR, e.g. from InftyReader[10]) could be a viable solution.

For example, the following could become the target format of MathML embedded in TEI P5, for $\exists\delta > 0 \ni f(x) < 1$:

```
<mrow>
  <mo> there exists </mo>
  <mrow>
    <mrow>
      <mi> &#916; <!--GREEK SMALL DELTA--></mi>
      <mo> &gt; </mo>
      <mn> 0 </mn>
```

[7] http://heartofgold.opendfki.de/repos/trunk/jtok; LPGL license

[8] http://nlp.stanford.edu/software/tokenizer.shtml; GPL V2 license

[9] http://www.w3.org/TR/MathML/

[10] http://sciaccess.net/en/InftyReader/

```
    </mrow>
    <mo> such that </mo>
    <mrow>
      <mrow>
        <mi> f </mi>
        <mo> &#2061; <!--FUNCTION APPL.--></mo>
        <mrow>
          <mo> ( </mo>
          <mi> x </mi>
          <mo> ) </mo>
        </mrow>
      </mrow>
      <mo> &lt; </mo>
      <mn> 1 </mn>
    </mrow>
  </mrow>
</mrow>
```

An alternative way would be to implement math formula recognition directly in PDFExtract using methods known from math OCR, similar to the page layout recognition approach.

5 Discussion—Outlook

Through the ACL 2012 Contributed Task, we have taken a (small, some might say) step further towards the goal of a high-quality, rich-text version of the ACL Anthology as a corpus—making available both the original text and logical document structure.

Although many of the subtasks sketched above did not find volunteers in this round, the Contributed Task, in our view, is an on-going, long-term community endeavor. Results to date, if nothing else, confirm the general suitability of (a) using TEI P5 markup as a shared target representation and (b) exploiting the complementarity of OCR-based techniques (Schäfer & Weitz, 2012), on the one hand, and direct interpretation of born-digital PDF files (Berg et al., 2012), on the other hand. Combining these approaches has the potential to solve the venerable challenges that stem from inhomogeneous sources in the ACL Anthology—e.g. scanned, older papers and digital newer papers, generated from a broad variety of typesetting tools.

However, as of mid-2012 there still is no ready-to-use, high-quality corpus that could serve as a shared starting point for the range of Anthology-based NLP activities sketched in Section 1 above. In fact, we remain slightly ambivalent about our recommendations for utilizing the current state of affairs and expected next steps—as we would like to avoid much work getting underway with a version of the corpus that we know is unsatisfactory. Further, obviously, versioning and well-defined release cycles will be a prerequisite to making the corpus useful for comparable research, as discussed by Bird et al. (2008).

In a nutshell, we see two possible avenues forward. For the ACL 2012 Contributed Task, we collected various views on the corpus data (as well as some of the source code used in its production) in a unified SVN repository. Following the open-source, crowd-sourcing philosophy, one option would be to make this repository openly available to all interested parties for future development, possibly augmenting it with support infrastructure like, for example, a mailing list and shared wiki.

At the same time, our experience from the past months suggests that it is hard to reach sufficient momentum and critical mass to make substantial progress towards our long-term goals, while contributions are limited to loosely organized volunteer work. A possibility we believe might overcome these limitations would be an attempt at formalizing work in this spirit further, for example through a funded project (with endorsement and maybe financial support from organizations like the ACL, ICCL, AFNLP, ELRA, or LDC).

A potential, but not seriously contemplated 'business model' for the ACL Anthology Corpus could be that only groups providing also improved versions of the corpus would get access to it. This would contradict the community spirit and other demands, viz. that all code should be made publicly available (as open source) that is used to produce the rich-text XML for new papers added to the Anthology. To decide on the way forward, we will solicit comments and expressions of interest during ACL 2012, including of course from the R50 workshop audience and participants in the Contributed Task. Current results and status updates will always be accessible through the following address:

http://www.delph-in.net/aac/

The ACL publication process for conferences and workshops already today supports automated collection of metadata and uniform layout/branding. For future high-quality collections of papers in the area of Computational Linguistics, the ACL could think about providing extended macro packages for conferences and journals that generate rich text and document structure preserving (TEI P5) XML versions as a side effect, in addition to PDF generation. Technically, it should be possible in both LaTeX and (for sure) in word processors such as OpenOffice or MS Word. It would help reducing errors induced by the tedious PDF-to-XML extraction this Contributed Task dealt with.

Finally, we do think that it will well be possible to apply the Contributed Task ideas and machinery to scientific publications in other areas, including the envisaged NLP research and existing NLP applications for search, terminology extraction, summarization, citation analysis, and more.

6 Acknowledgments

The authors would like to thank the ACL, the workshop organizer Rafael Banchs, the task contributors for their pioneering work, and the NUS group for their support. We are indebted to Rebecca Dridan for helpful feedback on this work.

The work of the first author has been funded by the German Federal Ministry of Education and Research, projects TAKE (FKZ 01IW08003) and Deependance (FKZ 01IW11003). The second and third authors are supported by the Norwegian Research Council through the VerdIKT programme.

References

Abu-Jbara, A., & Radev, D. (2011). Coherent citation-based summarization of scientific papers. In *Proceedings of the 49th annual meeting of the association for computational linguistics: Human language techologies* (pp. 500–509). Portland, OR.

Agarwal, N., Reddy, R. S., Gvr, K., & Rosé, C. P. (2011a). Scisumm: A multi-document summarization system for scientific articles. In *Proceedings of the ACL-HLT 2011 system demonstrations* (pp. 115–120). Portland, OR.

Agarwal, N., Reddy, R. S., Gvr, K., & Rosé, C. P. (2011b). Towards multi-document summarization of scientific articles: Making interesting comparisons with SciSumm. In *Proceedings of the workshop on automatic summarization for different genres, media, and languages* (pp. 8–15). Portland, OR.

Anderson, A., McFarland, D., & Jurafsky, D. (2012). Towards a computational history of the ACL:1980–2008. In *Proceedings of the ACL-2012 main conference workshop: Rediscovering 50 years of discoveries.* Jeju, Republic of Korea.

Athar, A. (2011). Sentiment analysis of citations using sentence structure-based features. In *Proceedings of the ACL 2011 student session* (pp. 81–87). Portland, OR.

Bański, P., & Przepiórkowski, A. (2009). Stand-off TEI annotation: the case of the National Corpus of Polish. In *Proceedings of the third linguistic annotation workshop* (pp. 64–67). Suntec, Singapore.

Berg, Ø. R., Oepen, S., & Read, J. (2012). Towards high-quality text stream extraction from PDF. Technical background to the ACL 2012 Contributed Task. In *Proceedings of the ACL-2012 main conference workshop on Rediscovering 50 Years of Discoveries.* Jeju, Republic of Korea.

Bird, S., Dale, R., Dorr, B., Gibson, B., Joseph, M., Kan, M.-Y., Lee, D., Powley, B., Radev, D., & Tan, Y. F. (2008). The ACL Anthology Reference Corpus: A reference dataset for bibliographic research in computational linguistics. In *Proceedings of the sixth international conference on language resources and evaluation (LREC-08).* Marrakech, Morocco.

Councill, I. G., Giles, C. L., & Kan, M.-Y. (2008). ParsCit: An open-source CRF reference string parsing package. In *Proceedings of LREC-2008* (pp. 661–667). Marrakesh, Morocco.

Dahlmeier, D., Ng, H. T., & Tran, T. P. (2011). NUS at the HOO 2011 pilot shared task. In *Proceedings of the generation challenges session at the 13th european workshop on natural language generation* (pp. 257–259). Nancy, France.

Dale, R., & Kilgarriff, A. (2010). Helping Our Own: Text massaging for computational linguistics as a new shared task. In *Proceedings of the 6th international natural language generation conference.* Trim, Co. Meath, Ireland.

Daudaravičius, V. (2012). Applying collocation segmentation to the ACL Anthology Reference Corpus. In *Proceedings of the ACL-2012 main conference workshop: Rediscovering 50 years of discoveries.* Jeju, Republic of Korea.

Dong, C., & Schäfer, U. (2011). Ensemble-style self-training on citation classification. In *Proceedings of 5th international joint conference on natural language processing* (pp. 623–631). Chiang Mai, Thailand.

Gupta, P., & Rosso, P. (2012). Text reuse with ACL: (upward) trends. In *Proceedings of the ACL-2012 main conference workshop: Rediscovering 50 years of discoveries.* Jeju, Republic of Korea.

Gupta, S., & Manning, C. (2011). Analyzing the dynamics of research by extracting key aspects of scientific papers. In *Proceedings of 5th international joint conference on natural language processing* (pp. 1–9). Chiang Mai, Thailand.

Hall, D., Jurafsky, D., & Manning, C. D. (2008). Studying the history of ideas using topic models. In *Proceedings of the 2008 conference on empirical methods in natural language processing* (pp. 363–371). Honolulu, Hawaii.

Johri, N., Ramage, D., McFarland, D., & Jurafsky, D. (2011). A study of academic collaborations in computational linguistics using a latent mixture of authors model. In *Proceedings of the 5th ACL-HLT workshop on language technology for cultural heritage, social sciences, and humanities* (pp. 124–132). Portland, OR.

Johri, N., Roth, D., & Tu, Y. (2010). Experts' retrieval with multiword-enhanced author topic model. In *Proceedings of the NAACL HLT 2010 workshop on semantic search* (pp. 10–18). Los Angeles, California.

Mao, Y., Balasubramanian, K., & Lebanon, G. (2010). Dimensionality reduction for text using domain knowledge. In *COLING 2010: Posters* (pp. 801–809). Beijing, China.

Mohammad, S., Dorr, B., Egan, M., Hassan, A., Muthukrishan, P., Qazvinian, V., Radev, D., & Zajic, D. (2009). Using citations to generate surveys of scientific paradigms. In *Proceedings of human language technologies: The 2009 annual conference of the north american chapter of the association for computational linguistics* (pp. 584–592). Boulder, Colorado.

Muthukrishnan, P., Radev, D., & Mei, Q. (2011). Simultaneous similarity learning and feature-weight learning for document clustering. In *Proceedings of textgraphs-6: Graph-based methods for natural language processing* (pp. 42–50). Portland, OR.

Nhat, H. D. H., & Bysani, P. (2012). Linking citations to their bibliographic references. In *Proceedings of the ACL-2012 main conference workshop: Rediscovering 50 years of discoveries.* Jeju, Republic of Korea.

Przepiórkowski, A. (2009). TEI P5 as an XML standard for treebank encoding. In *Proceedings of the eighth international workshop on treebanks and linguistic theories* (pp. 149–160). Milano, Italy.

Qazvinian, V., & Radev, D. R. (2008). Scientific paper summarization using citation summary networks. In *Proceedings of the 22nd international conference on computational linguistics (COLING 2008)* (pp. 689–696). Manchester, UK.

Qazvinian, V., & Radev, D. R. (2010). Identifying non-explicit citing sentences for citation-based summarization. In *Proceedings of the 48th annual meeting of the association for computational linguistics* (pp. 555–564). Uppsala, Sweden.

Qazvinian, V., & Radev, D. R. (2011). Learning from collective human behavior to introduce diversity in lexical choice. In *Proceedings of the 49th annual meeting of the association for computational linguistics: Human language techologies* (pp. 1098–1108). Portland, OR.

Qazvinian, V., Radev, D. R., & Ozgur, A. (2010). Citation summarization through keyphrase extraction. In *Proceedings of the 23rd international conference on computational linguistics (COLING 2010)* (pp. 895–903). Beijing, China.

Radev, D., & Abu-Jbara, A. (2012). Rediscovering ACL discoveries through the lens of ACL Anthology Network citing sentences. In *Proceedings of the ACL-2012 main conference workshop: Rediscovering 50 years of discoveries.* Jeju, Republic of Korea.

Radev, D., Muthukrishnan, P., & Qazvinian, V. (2009). The ACL Anthology Network corpus. In *Proceedings of the 2009 workshop on text and citation analysis for scholarly digital libraries.* Morristown, NJ, USA.

Radev, D. R., Muthukrishnan, P., & Qazvinian, V. (2009). The ACL Anthology Network. In *Proceedings of the 2009 workshop on text and citation analysis for scholarly digital libraries* (pp. 54–61). Suntec City, Singapore.

Reiplinger, M., Schäfer, U., & Wolska, M. (2012). Extracting glossary sentences from scholarly articles: A comparative evaluation of pattern bootstrapping and deep analysis. In *Proceedings of the ACL-2012 main conference workshop: Rediscovering 50 years of discoveries.* Jeju, Republic of Korea.

Ritchie, A., Teufel, S., & Robertson, S. (2006a). Creating a test collection for citation-based IR experiments. In *Proceedings of the human language technology conference of the NAACL, main conference* (pp. 391–398). New York City.

Ritchie, A., Teufel, S., & Robertson, S. (2006b). How to find better index terms through citations. In *Proceedings of the workshop on how can computational linguistics improve information retrieval?* (pp. 25–32). Sydney, Australia.

Rozovskaya, A., Sammons, M., Gioja, J., & Roth, D. (2011). University of illinois system in HOO text correction shared task. In *Proceedings of the generation challenges session at the 13th european workshop on natural language generation* (pp. 263–266). Nancy, France.

Schäfer, U., & Kasterka, U. (2010). Scientific authoring support: A tool to navigate in typed citation graphs. In *Proceedings of the NAACL HLT 2010 workshop on computational linguistics and writing: Writing processes and authoring aids* (pp. 7–14). Los Angeles, CA.

Schäfer, U., Kiefer, B., Spurk, C., Steffen, J., & Wang, R. (2011). The ACL Anthology Searchbench. In *Proceedings of the ACL-HLT 2011 system demonstrations* (pp. 7–13). Portland, OR.

Schäfer, U., & Weitz, B. (2012). Combining OCR outputs for logical document structure markup. Technical background to the ACL 2012 Contributed Task. In *Proceedings of the ACL-2012 main conference workshop on Rediscovering 50 Years of Discoveries.* Jeju, Republic of Korea.

Sim, Y., Smith, N. A., & Smith, D. A. (2012). Discovering factions in the computational linguistics community. In *Proceedings of the ACL-2012 main conference workshop: Rediscovering 50 years of discoveries.* Jeju, Republic of Korea.

TEI Consortium. (2012, February). *TEI P5: Guidelines for electronic text encoding and interchange.* (http://www.tei-c.org/Guidelines/P5)

Tu, Y., Johri, N., Roth, D., & Hockenmaier, J. (2010). Citation author topic model in expert search. In *COLING 2010: Posters* (pp. 1265–1273). Beijing, China.

Vogel, A., & Jurafsky, D. (2012). He said, she said: Gender in the ACL anthology. In *Proceedings of the ACL-2012 main conference workshop: Rediscovering 50 years of discoveries.* Jeju, Republic of Korea.

Xia, F., Lewis, W., & Poon, H. (2009). Language ID in the context of harvesting language data off the web. In *Proceedings of the 12th conference of the european chapter of the ACL (EACL 2009)* (pp. 870–878). Athens, Greece.

Xia, F., & Lewis, W. D. (2008). Repurposing theoretical linguistic data for tool development and search. In *Proceedings of the third international joint conference on natural language processing: Volume-i* (pp. 529–536). Hyderabad, India.

Zesch, T. (2011). Helping Our Own 2011: UKP lab system description. In *Proceedings of the generation challenges session at the 13th european workshop on natural language generation* (pp. 260–262). Nancy, France.

Towards High-Quality Text Stream Extraction from PDF

Technical Background to the ACL 2012 Contributed Task

Øyvind Raddum Berg, Stephan Oepen, and Jonathon Read
Department of Informatics, Universitetet i Oslo
{oyvinrb|oe|jread}@ifi.uio.no

Abstract

Extracting textual content and document structure from PDF presents a surprisingly (depressingly, to some, in fact) difficult challenge, owing to the purely display-oriented design of the PDF document standard. While a variety of lower-level PDF extraction toolkits exist, none fully support the recovery of original text (in reading order) and relevant structural elements, even for so-called born-digital PDFs, i.e. those prepared electronically using typesetting systems like LaTeX, OpenOffice, and the like. This short paper summarizes a new tool for high-quality extraction of text and structure from PDFs, combining state-of-the-art PDF parsing, font interpretation, layout analysis, and TEI-compliant output of text and logical document markup.[†]

1 Introduction—Motivation

To view a collection of scholarly articles like the ACL Anthology as a structured knowledge base substantially transcends a naïve notion of a *corpus* as a mere collection of running text. Research literature is the result of careful editing and typesetting and, thus, is organized around its complex internal structure. Relevant structural elements can comprise both *geometric* (e.g. pages, columns, blocks, or tables) and *logical* units (e.g. titles, abstracts, headings, paragraphs, or citations)—where (ideally) geometric and logical document structure play hand in hand to a degree that can make it hard to draw clear dividing lines in some cases (e.g. in itemized or numbered lists).

To date, the dominant standard for electronic document archival is *Portable Document Format* (PDF), originally created as a proprietary format by Adobe Systems Incorporated in the early 1990s and subsequently made an open ISO standard (which was officially adopted in 2008 and embraced by Adobe through a public license that grants royalty-free usage). PDF is something of a composite standard, unifying at least three basic technologies:

1. A subset of the PostScript page 'programming' language, dropping constructs like loops and branches, but including all graphical operations to draw layout elements, text, and images.

2. A font embedding system which allows a document to 'carry along' a broad variety of fonts (in various formats), as may be needed to ensure display just as the document was designed.

3. A structured storage system, which organizes various data objects—for example images and fonts—inside a PDF document.

All data objects in a PDF file are represented in a visually-oriented way, as a sequence of operators which—when interpreted by a PDF renderer—will draw the document on a page canvas. This is a natural approach considering the design roots of PDF as a PostScript successor and its original central role in desktop publishing applications; but the implications of such visually-centered design are unfortunate for the task of recovering textual content and logical document structure.

Interpretation of PDF operators will provide one with all the individual characters, as well as their formatting and position on the page. However, they generally do not convey information about higher level text units such as tokens, lines, or columns—information about boundaries between such units is only available implicitly through whitespace, i.e. the

[†]We are indebted to Rebecca Dridan, Ulrich Schäfer, and the ACL workshop reviewers for helpful feedback on this work.

mere absence of textual or graphical objects. Furthermore, data fragments comprising content text on a page may consist of individual characters, parts of a word, whole lines, or any combination thereof—as dictated by font properties and kerning requirements. Complicating text extraction from PDF further, there are no rules governing the order in which content is encoded in the document. For example, to produce a page with a two-column layout, the page could be drawn by first drawing the first lines of the left and right columns, then the second lines, etc. Obtaining text in logical reading order, however, obviously requires that the text in the left column be processed before the one on the right, so a naïve approach to text extraction based on the sequencing of objects in the PDF file might produce undesirable results.

Since the standard is now open and free for anyone to use, we are fortunate to have several mature, open-source libraries to handle low-level parsing and manipulation of objects in PDF documents. For this project, we build on Apache PDFBox[1], for its maturity, relatively active support, and interface flexibility. Originally as an MSc project in Computer Science (Berg, 2011), we have developed a parameterizable toolkit for high-quality text and structure extraction from born-digital PDFs, which we dub PDFExtract.[2] In this application, we seek to approximate this structure by using all the visual clues and information we have available.

The data presented in a PDF file consists of streams of objects; by placing hardly any significance on the order of elements within these streams, and more on the visual result obtained by (virtually) 'rendering' PDF operations, the task of text and structure extraction is shifted slightly—from what traditionally amounts to stream-processing, and towards a point of view related to *computer vision*.

This view, in fact, essentially corresponds to the same problem tackled by OCR software, though without the need to perform actual character recognition. Some of the key elements of PDFExtract, thus, build on related OCR techniques and adapt and extend these to the PDF processing task. The process of 'understanding' a PDF document in this context is called document layout analysis, a task which is commonly treated as two sequential subprocesses. First, a page image is subjected to *geometric* layout analysis; the result of this first stage then serves as input for a subsequent step of *logical* layout analysis and content extraction. The following sections briefly review core aspects of the design and implementation of PDFExtract, ranging from low-level whitespace detection (§ 2), over geometric and logical layout analysis (§ 3 and § 5, respectively), to aspects of font handling (§ 4).

2 Whitespace Detection

As a prerequisite to all subsequent analysis, segment boundaries between tokens, lines, columns, and other blocks of content need to be made explicit. Such boundaries are predominantly represented through whitespace, which is not overtly represented among the data objects in PDF files. The approach to whitespace detection and page segmentation in PDFExtract is an extension of the framework proposed by Breuel (2002) (originally in the context of OCR).

The first step here is to find a cover of the background whitespace of a document in terms of maximal empty rectangles. This is accomplished in a top-down procedure, using a whole page as its starting point, and working in a way abstractly analogous to quicksort or branch and bound algorithms. Whitespace rectangles are identified in order of decreasing 'quality' (as determined by size, shape, position, and relations to actual page content), which means that the result will in general be globally optimal—in the sense that no other (equal-sized) sequence of covering rectangles would yield a larger total quality sum.

Figure 1 illustrates the main idea of the algorithm, which starts from a bound (initially the page at large) and a set of non-empty rectangles, called *obstacles*. If the set is empty, it means that the bound is a maximal rectangle with respect to other obstacles (surrounding the bound). If, as in Figure 1, there are obstacles, the bound needs to be further subdivided. To this end, we choose one obstacle as a *pivot*, which ideally is centered somewhere around the middle of the bound. As no maximal rectangle can contain obstacles, in particular not the pivot, there are four possibilities for the solution of the maximal whitespace

[1]See `http://pdfbox.apache.org/` for details.

[2]See `http://github.com/elacin/PDFExtract/`.

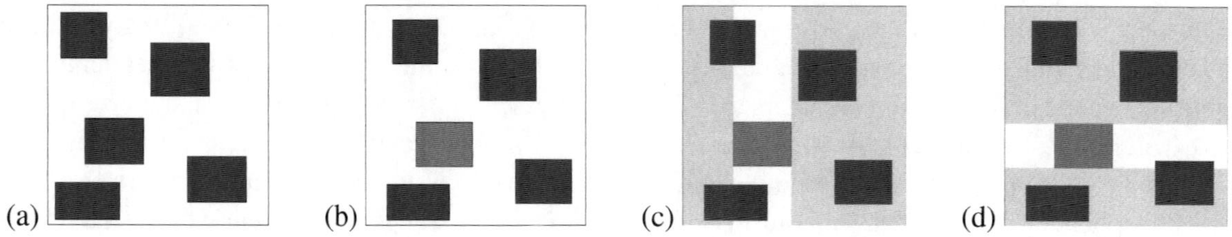

Figure 1: Schematic example of *one iteration* of the whitespace covering algorithm. In (a) we see some obstacles (in blue) contained within a bounding rectangle; in (b) one of them is chosen as as pivot (in red); and (c) and (d) show how the original bound is divided into four smaller rectangles (in grey) around the pivot.

rectangle problem—one for each side of the pivot. The areas of these four sub-bounds are computed, a list of intersecting obstacles is computed for each of them, and they are processed in turn.

As originally proposed by Breuel (2002), the basic procedure proved applicable to born-digital PDFs, though leaving room for improvements both in terms of the quality of results and run-time performance. Some deficiencies that were observed in processing documents from the ACL Anthology (and other samples of scholarly literature) are exemplified in Figure 2, relating to smallish, 'stray' whitespace rectangles in the middle of otherwise contiguous segments (top row in Figure 2), challenges related to relative differences in line spacing (middle), and spurious vertical boundaries introduced by so-called *rivers*, i.e. accidental alignment of horizontal spacing across lines (bottom). Besides adjustments to the rectangle 'quality' function, the problems were addressed by (a) allowing a small degree

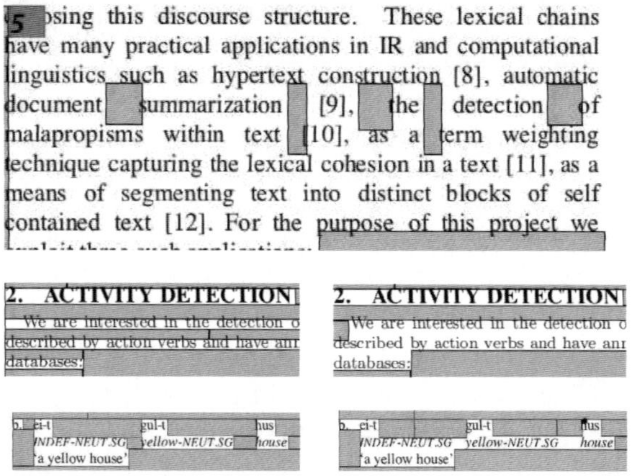

Figure 2: Select challenges to whitespace covering approach: stray whitespace inbetween groups of text (top); inter- vs. intra-paragraph spacing (middle); and 'rivers' leading to spurious vertical boundaries (bottom).

of overlap between whitespace rectangles and obstacles, (b) a strong preference for contiguous areas of whitespace (thus making the procedure work from the page borders inwards), (c) variable lower bounds on the height and width of whitespace rectangles, computed dynamically from font properties of surrounding text, and (d) a small number of specialized heuristic rules, to block unwanted whitespace rectangles in select configurations. Berg (2011) provides full details for these adaptations, as well as for algorithmic optimizations and parameterization that enable run-time throughputs of tens of pages per cpu second.

3 Determining Page Layout

The high-level goal in analyzing page layout is to produce a hierarchical representation of a page in terms of *blocks* of homogenous content, thus making explicit relevant spatial relationship between them. In the realm of OCR, this task is often referred to as *geometric layout analysis* (see, for example, (Cattoni et al., 1998)), whereas the term *(de)boxing* has at times been used in the context of text stream extraction from PDFs. In the following paragraphs, we will focus on column boundary detection, but PDFExtract essentially applies the same general techniques to the identification of other relevant inter-segment boundaries.

While whitespace rectangles are essential to column boundary identification, there is of course no guarantee for the existence of *one* rectangle which were equivalent to a whole column boundary. First, as a natural consequence of the whitespace detection procedure, horizontal rectangles can 'interrupt' candidate colum boundaries. Second, there may well be typographic imperfections causing gaps in the identified whitespace (as exemplified in the top of Fig-

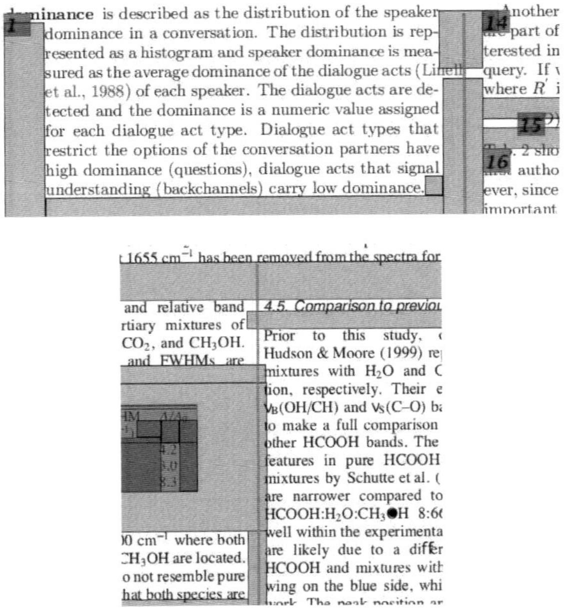

Figure 3: Select challenges to column identification: text elements protruding into the margin (top) and gaps in whitespace rectangle coverage (often owed to processing bounds imposed for premium performance).

ure 3), or it can be the case that geometric constraints or computational limits imposed on the whitespace cover algorithm result in 'missing' whitespace rectangles (in the bottom of Figure 3). Whereas the original design of Breuel (2002) makes no provisions for these cases, PDFExtract adapts a revised, three-step approach to column detection, viz. (a) extracting an initial set of candidate boundaries; (b) heuristically expanding column boundary candidates vertically; and (c) combining logically equivalent boundaries and filtering unwarranted ones. Here, both steps (a) and (b) assume geometric constraints on the aspect ratio of candidate column boundaries, as well as on the existence and relative proportions of surrounding non-whitespace content. Again, please see Berg (2011) for further background on these steps.

With column boundaries in place, PDFExtract proceeds to the identification of *blocks* of content (which may correspond to, for example, logical paragraphs, headings, displayed equations, tables, or graphical elements). This step, essentially, is realized through a recursive 'flooding' function, forming connected blocks from adjacent, non-whitespace PDF data objects where there are no intervening whitespace rectangles. Regions that (by content or font properties) can be identified as (parts of) mathematical equations receive special attention at this stage, allowing limited amounts of horizontally separating whitespace to be ignored for block formation. In a similar spirit, line segmentation (i.e. grouping of vertically aligned data objects) is performed block-wise—sorting content within each block by Y-coordinates and determining baselines and inter-line spacing in a single downwards pass.

The final key component in geometric layout analysis is the recovery of reading order (recalling that PDFs do not provide reliable sequencing information for data objects). PDFExtract adapts one of the two techniques suggested by Breuel (2003), viz. topological sorting of lines (which can include single-line blocks, where no block-internal line segmentation was detected) based on (a) relations of hierarchical nesting and (b) relative geometric positions. PDFExtract was tested against a set of some 100 diverse PDF documents (from different sources of scholarly literature, a range of distinct PDF generators, quite variable layout, and multiple languages), and its topological content sorting (detailed further in Berg, 2011) was found to give very satisfactory results in terms of reading order recovery.

4 Font Handling and Word Segmentation

Many of the steps of geometric layout analysis outlined above depend on accurate coordinate information for glyphs, which turned out an unforeseen low-level challenge in our approach of building PDFExtract on top of Apache PDFBox. Figure 4 (on the left) shows a problematic example of 'raw' glyph placement information. Several factors contribute to incorrect glyph positioning, including the sheer variety of font types supported in PDFs, missing information about non-standard, embedded fonts, and design limitations and bugs in PDFBox. To work around common issues, PDFExtract includes a couple of patches to PDFBox internals as well as specialized code for different types of font embedding in PDF to perform boundary box computation, position offsetting, and and mapping to Unicode code points. The (much improved though not quite perfect) result of these adjustments, when applied to our running example, is depicted in the middle of Figure 4.

With the ultimate goal of creating a high-quality

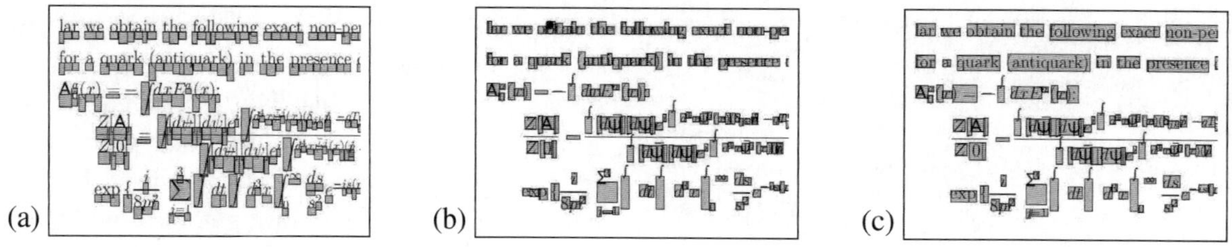

Figure 4: Examples of font-related challenges (before and after correction) and word segmentation.

(structured) text corpus from ACL Anthology documents, *word segmentation* naturally is a mission-critical component of PDFExtract. Seeing that inter-word whitespace is more often than not *omitted* from PDF data objects, word segmentation—much like other sub-tasks in geometric layout analysis—operates in terms of display positions. Determining whether the distance between two adjacent glyphs represents a word-separating whitespace or not, might sound simple—but in practice it proved difficult to devise a generic solution that performs well across differences in fonts and sizes (and corresponding variation in kerning, i.e. intra-word spacing), deals with both high-quality and poor typography, and is somewhat robust to remaining inaccuracies in glyph positions . PDFExtract arrived at a novel algorithm that approximates character text spacing (as could be set by the PDF T_c operator) by averaging a selection of the smaller character distances within a line. The resulting average character spacing is subsequently used to *normalize* horizontal distances, i.e. subtract line-specific character spacing from every distance on that line—to ideally center character distances around zero, while leaving word distances larger (they will also be relatively much larger than before in comparison). The identification of word boundaries itself, accordingly, becomes straightforward, comparing normalized distances to a percentage of the local font size. The results of this process are shown for our example in the right of Figure 4.

5 (Preliminary) Logical Layout Analysis

In our view, thorough geometric layout analysis is an important prequisite of logical layout analysis. Hence, the emphasis of Berg (2011) was with respect to the geometric analysis. However, what follows is an overview of the preliminary procedure in PDFExtract to determine logical document structure from geometric layout and typographic information.

The process begins by collating a set of text *styles* (i.e. unique combinations of font type and size). Then, various heuristics govern the assignment of styles to logical roles:

Body text Choose whichever style occurs most frequently (in terms of the number of characters).

Title Choose the header-like block on the first page that has the largest font size.

Abstract If one of the first pages has a single-line block with a style which is bigger or bolder than body text, and contains the word abstract, it is chosen as an abstract header. All body text until the next heading is the abstract text.

Footnote Search for blocks on the lower part of the page that are smaller than body text; check that they start with a number or other footnote-indicating symbol.

Sections Identify section header styles by compiling a list of styles that are either larger than or have some emphasis on the body text style, and have instances with evidence of section numbering (e.g. *1.1*, *(1a)*). Infer the nesting level of each section header style from its order of occurrence in the document; a section heading will always appear earlier than a subsection heading, for instance.

Having identified the different components in the document, these are used to create a logical hierarchical representation following the TEI P5 Guidelines (TEI Consortium, 2012) as introduced by Schäfer et al. (2012). Title, abstract, floaters, and figures are separated from the main text. The body of the document is then collated into a tree of section elements, with headers and body text. Body text is collected by combining consecutive text blocks that have identical styles, before inferring paragraphs on the basis of indented initial lines. Dehyphenation is tackled using a combination of a lexicon and a set of orthographic rules.

6 Discussion—Outlook

PDFExtract provides a fresh and open-source take on the problem of high-quality content and structure extraction from born-digital PDFs. Unlike existing initiatives (e.g. the basic `TextExtraction` class of PDFBox or the pdftotext command line utility from the Poppler library[3]), PDFExtract discards sequencing information available in the so-called PDF text stream, but instead applies and adapts techniques from OCR—notably a whitespace covering algorithm, column, block, and line detection, recovery of reading order based on line-oriented topological sort, and improved word segmentation taking advantage of specialized PDF font interpretation. While very comprehensive in terms of its geometric layout analysis, PDFExtract to date only make available a limited range of logical layout analysis functionality (and output into TEI-compliant markup), albeit also in this respect more so than pre-existing PDF text stream extraction approaches.

For the ACL 2012 Contributed Task on *Rediscovering 50 Years of Discoveries* (Schäfer et al., 2012), PDFExtract outputs for the born-digital subset of the ACL Anthology are a component of the 'starter package' offered to participants, in the hope that content and structure derived from OCR techniques (Schäfer & Weitz, 2012) and those extracted directly from embedded content in the PDFs will complement each other. As discussed in more detail by Schäfer et al. (2012), the two approaches have in part non-overlapping strengths and weaknesses, such that aligning content elements that correspond to each other across the two universes could yield a multi-dimensional, ideally both more complete and more accurate perspective. PDFExtract is a recent development and remains subject to refinement and extension. Beyond a limited quantitative and qualitative evaluation review by Berg (2011), the exact quality levels of text and document structure that it makes available (as well as relevant factors of variation, across different types of documents in the ACL Anthology) remains to be determined empirically.

We make available the full package, accompanied by some technical documentation (Berg, 2011), as well as a sample of gold-standard TEI-compliant target outputs) in the hope that it may serve as the basis for future work towards the ACL Anthology Corpus—both at our own sites (i.e. the University of Oslo and DFKI Saarbrücken) and collaborating partners. We would enthusiastically welcome additional collaborators in this enterprise and will seek to provide any reasonable assistance required for the deployment and extension of PDFExtract.

[3] See `http://poppler.freedesktop.org/`.

References

Berg, Ø. R. (2011). *High precision text extraction from PDF documents.* MSc Thesis, University of Oslo, Department of Informatics, Oslo, Norway.

Breuel, T. (2002). Two geometric algorithms for layout analysis. In *Proceedings of the 5th workshop on Document Analysis Systems* (pp. 687–692). Princeton, USA.

Breuel, T. (2003). Layout analysis based on text line segment hypotheses. In *Third international workshop on Document Layout Interpretation and its Applications.* Edinburgh, Scotland.

Cattoni, R., Coianiz, T., & Messelodi, S. (1998). *Geometric layout analysis techniques for document image understanding. A review* (ITC-irst Technical Report TR#9703-09). Trento, Italy.

Schäfer, U., Read, J., & Oepen, S. (2012). Towards an ACL Anthology corpus with logical document structure. An overview of the ACL 2012 contributed task. In *Proceedings of the ACL-2012 main conference workshop on Rediscovering 50 Years of Discoveries.* Jeju, Republic of Korea.

Schäfer, U., & Weitz, B. (2012). Combining OCR outputs for logical document structure markup. Technical background to the ACL 2012 Contributed Task. In *Proceedings of the ACL-2012 main conference workshop on Rediscovering 50 Years of Discoveries.* Jeju, Republic of Korea.

TEI Consortium. (2012, February). *TEI P5: Guidelines for electronic text encoding and interchange.* (http://www.tei-c.org/Guidelines/P5)

Combining OCR Outputs for Logical Document Structure Markup

Technical Background to the ACL 2012 Contributed Task

Ulrich Schäfer **Benjamin Weitz**
DFKI Language Technology Lab
Campus D 3 1, D-66123 Saarbrücken, Germany
{ulrich.schaefer|benjamin.weitz}@dfki.de

Abstract

We describe how *paperXML*, a logical document structure markup for scholarly articles, is generated on the basis of OCR tool outputs. *PaperXML* has been initially developed for the ACL Anthology Searchbench. The main purpose was to robustly provide uniform access to sentences in ACL Anthology papers from the past 46 years, ranging from scanned, typewriter-written conference and workshop proceedings papers, up to recent high-quality typeset, born-digital journal articles, with varying layouts. *PaperXML* markup includes information on page and paragraph breaks, section headings, footnotes, tables, captions, boldface and italics character styles as well as bibliographic and publication metadata. The role of *paperXML* in the ACL Contributed Task *Rediscovering 50 Years of Discoveries* is to serve as fall-back source (1) for older, scanned papers (mostly published before the year 2000), for which born-digital PDF sources are not available, (2) for born-digital PDF papers on which the PDFExtract method failed, (3) for document parts where PDFExtract does not output useful markup such as currently for tables. We sketch transformation of *paperXML* into the ACL Contributed Task's TEI P5 XML.

1 Introduction

Work on the ACL Anthology Searchbench started in 2009. The goal was to provide combined sentence-semantic, full-text and bibliographic search in the complete ACL Anthology (Schäfer et al., 2011), and a graphical citation browser with citation sentence context information (Weitz & Schäfer, 2012). Since the ACL-HLT 2011 conference, the Searchbench is available as a free, public service[1].

A fixed subset of the Anthology, the *ACL Anthology Reference Corpus*[2] (ACL-ARC), contains various representations of the papers such as PDF, bitmap and text files. The latter were generated with PDFBox[3] and OCR (Omnipage[4]), applied to the PDF files or bitmap versions thereof. Its static nature as infrequently released reference corpus and low character recognition quality especially of older, badly scanned papers, made us to look for alternatives. For quick, automatic updates of the Searchbench index, a robust method for getting the text from old and new incoming PDF files was needed.

After a thorough comparison of different PDF-to-text extraction tools, a decision was made to process every PDF paper in the Anthology with ABBYY PDF Transformer[5], for various reasons. It ran stably and delivered good character recognition rates on both scanned, typewriter-typeset proceeding papers as well as on born-digital PDF of various sources, even on papers where PDFbox failed to extract (usable) text. Reading order recovery, table recognition and output rendering (HTML) was impressive and de-hyphenation for English text worked reasonably well. All in all, ABBYY did not deliver perfect results, but at that time was the best and quickest solution to get most of the millions of sentences from the papers of 46 years.

The role of this OCR-based approach in the ACL

[1] http://aclasb.dfki.de
[2] http://acl-arc.comp.nus.edu.sg
[3] http://pdfbox.apache.org
[4] http://www.nuance.com/omnipage
[5] http://www.abbyy.com

Contributed Task *Rediscovering 50 Years of Discoveries* (Schäfer et al., 2012) is to serve as fall-back source when the more precise PDFExtract method (Berg et al., 2012) is not applicable.

2 Target Format

The focus of the Searchbench text extraction process was to retrieve NLP-parsable sentences from scientific papers. Hence distinguishing running text from section headings, figure and table captions or footnotes was an important intermediate task.

PaperXML is a simple logical document markup structure we specifically designed for scientific papers. It features tags for section headings (with special treatment of abstract and references), footnotes, figure and table captions. The full DTD is listed in the Appendix. A sample document automatically generated by our extraction tool is displayed in Figure 2 on the next page. In *paperXML*, figures are ignored, but table layouts and character style information such as boldface or italics are preserved.

3 Algorithm

Volk et al. (2010) used two different OCR products (the above mentioned Omnipage and ABBYY) and tried to improve the overall recognition accuracy on scanned text by merging their outputs. This approach adds the challenge of having to decide which version to trust in case of discrepancy. Unlike them, we use a single OCR tool, ABBYY, but with two different output variants, *layout* and *float*, that in parts contain complementary information. As no direct XML output mode exists, we rely on HTML output that can also be used to render PDF text extraction results in a Web browser.

3.1 Core rich text and document structure extraction

Our algorithm uses the *layout* variant as primary source. *Layout* tries to render the extracted text as closely as possible to the original layout. It preserves page breaks and the two-column formatting that most ACL Anthology papers (except the CL Journal and some older proceedings) share.

In the *float* variant, page and line breaks as well as multiple column layout are removed in favour of a running text in reading order which is indispensable for our purposes. However, some important layout-specific information such as page breaks is not available in the *float* format. Both variants preserve table layouts and character style information such as boldface or italics. Reading order in both variants may differ. A special code part ensures that nothing is lost when aligning the variants.

We implemented a Python[6] module that reads both HTML variants and generates a consolidated XML condensate, *paperXML*. It interprets textual content, font and position information to identify the logical structure of a scientific paper.

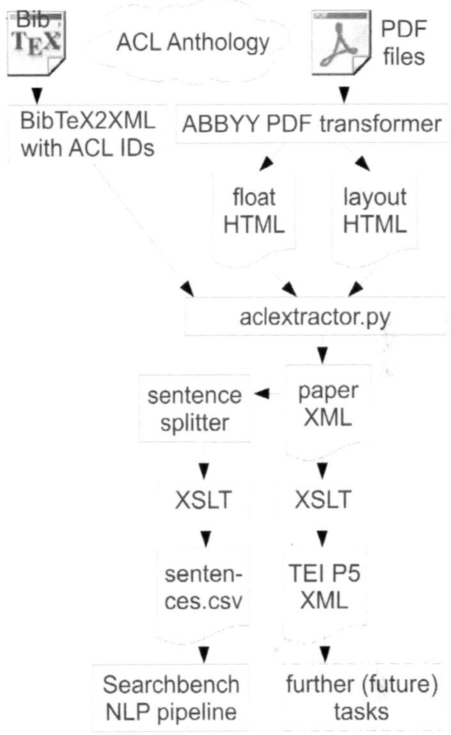

Figure 1: PDF-to-*paperXML* workflow

Figure 1 depicts the overall workflow. In addition to the two HTML variants, the code also reads BibTeX metadata in XML format of each paper. A rather large part in the document header of the generated *paperXML* addresses frontpage and bibliographic metadata. Section 3.2 explains why and how this information is extracted and processed.

Using XSLT[7], *paperXML* is then transformed into a tab-separated text file that basically contains one sentence per line plus additional sentence-related

[6]http://www.python.org

[7]http://www.w3.org/TR/xslt

```
<?xml version="1.0" encoding="UTF-8"?>
<article>
 <header>
  <firstpageheader>
   <page local="1" global="46"/>
   <title>Task-oriented Evaluation of Syntactic Parsers and Their Representations</title>
   <pubinfo>Proceedings ofACL-08: HLT,pages 46-54, Columbus, Ohio, USA, June 2008. ©2008 Association [...]</pubinfo>
   <author surname="Miyao" givenname="Yusuke">
    <org name="University of Tokyo" country="Japan" city="Tokyo"/>
   </author>
    [...]
  </firstpageheader>
  <frontmatter>
   <p><b>Task-oriented Evaluation of Syntactic Parsers and Their Representations</b></p>
   <p><b>Yusuke Miyao<footnote anchor="1"/>"  Rune Saetre<footnote anchor="1"/>"  Kenji Sagae
     <footnote anchor="1"/>"  Takuya Matsuzaki<footnote anchor="1"/>"  Jun'ichi Tsujii<footnote anchor="1"/>"** </b>
     ^Department of Computer Science, University of Tokyo, Japan * School of Computer Science, University of Manchester,
     UK *National Center for Text Mining, UK</p>
   <p>{yusuke,rune.saetre,sagae,matuzaki,tsujii}@is.s.u-tokyo.ac.jp</p>
  </frontmatter>
  <abstract>This paper presents a comparative evaluation of several state-of-the-art English parsers [...]</abstract>
 </header>
 <body>
  <section number="1" title="Introduction">
   <p>Parsing technologies have improved considerably in the past few years, and high-performance syntactic parsers are
     no longer limited to PCFG-based frameworks (Charniak, 2000; [...]</p>
  </section>
  <section number="2" title="Syntactic Parsers and Their Representations">
   <p>This paper focuses on eight representative parsers that are classified into three parsing frameworks:
    <i>dependency parsing, phrase structure parsing, </i>and <i>deep parsing.</i> [...] </p>
   <subsection number="2.1" title="Dependency parsing">
    <p>Because the shared tasks of CoNLL-2006 and CoNLL-2007 focused [...] </p>
    <p><b>mst </b>McDonald and Pereira (2006)'s dependency parser,<footnote anchor="1"/> based on the Eisner
     algorithm for projective dependency parsing (Eisner, 1996) with the second-order factorization.</p>
    <footnote label="1">http://sourceforge.net/projects/mstparser</footnote>
    <figure caption="Figure 1: CoNLL-X dependency tree"/>
   </subsection>
  [...]
   <subsection number="4.2" title="Comparison of accuracy improvements">
    <p>Tables 1 and 2 show the accuracy [...] </p>
    [...]
    <p>While the accuracy level of PPI extraction is the similar for the different parsers, parsing speed differs significantly.
     <page local="7" global="52"/> The dependency parsers are much faster than the other parsers, [...] </p>
    <table caption="Table 1: Accuracy on the PPI task with WSJ-trained
     parsers (precision/recall/f-score)" class="main" frame="box" rules="all" border="1" regular="False">
     <tr class="row"> [...]
    </table>
  <section title="Acknowledgments">
   <p>This work was partially supported by Grant-in-Aid for Specially Promoted Research (MEXT, Japan) [...]</p>
  </section>
  <references>
   <p>D. M. Bikel. 2004. Intricacies of Collins' parsing model. <i>Computational Linguistics, </i>30(4):479-511.</p>
   <p>T. Briscoe and J. Carroll. 2006. Evaluating the accuracy of an unlexicalized statistical parser on the PARC [...]</p>
    [...]
  </references>
 </body>
</article>
```


Figure 2: An example of an automatically generated *paperXML* version of the ACL Anthology document P08-1006. Parts are truncated ([. . .]) and some elements are imbalanced for brevity.

characteristics such as type (paragraph text, heading, footnote, caption etc.) page and offset. This output format is used to feed NLP components such as taggers, parsers or term extraction for the Searchbench's index generation. On the right hand side of the diagram, we sketch a potentional transformation of *paperXML* into TEI P5 for the Constributed Task. It will be discussed in Section 4.

The extraction algorithm initially computes the main font of a paper based on the number of characters with the same style. Based on this, heuristics allow to infer styles for headings, footnotes etc. While headings typically are typeset in boldface in recent publications, old publications styles e.g. use uppercase letters with or without boldface.

On the basis of this information, special section headings such as `abstract`, and `references` are inferred. Similarly, formatting properties in combination with regular expressions and Levenshtein distance (Levenshtein, 1966) are used to identify `footnotes`, `figure` and `table captions` etc. and generate corresponding markup.

A special `doubt` element is inserted for text fragments that do not look like normal, running text.

3.2 Bibliographic metadata and author affiliations

Conference or publication information can often be found on the first page footer or header or (in case of the CL journal) on every page. Our code recognizes and moves it to dedicated XML elements. The aim is not to interrupt running text by such 'noise'.

Publication authors, title and conference information as well as page number and PDF URL is commonly named bibliographic metadata. Because this information was partly missing in the ACL Anthology, special care was taken to extract it from the papers. In the *paperXML* generation code, author affiliations from the title page are mapped to author names using gazetteers, position information, heuristics etc. as part of the *paperXML* generation process. This experimental approach is imperfect, leads to errors and would definitely require manual correction. A solution would be to use manually corrected author affiliation information from the ACL Anthology Reference Corpus (Bird et al., 2008). This information, however, is not immediately available for recent proceedings or journal articles. Therefore, we developed a tool with a graphical user interface that assists quick, manual correction of author affiliation information inferred from previous publications of the same author in the Anthology by means of the ACL ARC data.

Independently from the *paperXML* extraction process, bibliographic metadata for each paper in the ACL Anthology has been extracted from BIBTEX files and, where BIBTEX was missing, the Anthology index web pages. We semi-automatically corrected encoding errors and generated easy-to-convert BIBTEXML[8] files for each paper. Using the page number information extracted during the *paperXML* generation process, our code enriches BIBTEXML files with page number ranges where missing in the ACL Anthology's metadata. This is of course only possible for papers that contain page numbers in the header or footer. The resulting BIBTEXML metadata are available at DFKI's public SubVersioN repository[9] along with the affiliation correction tool.

4 Transformation to TEI P5

The ACL Contributed Task *Rediscovering 50 Years of Discoveries* (Schäfer et al., 2012) proposes to use TEI P5[10] as an open standard for document structure markup. The overall structure of *paperXML* is largely isomorphic to TEI P5, with minor differences such as in the position of page break markup. In *paperXML*, page break markup is inserted after the sentence that starts before the page break, while in TEI P5, it appears exactly where it was in the original text, even within a hyphenated word.

The Python code that generates *paperXML* could be modified to make its output conforming to TEI. Alternatively, transformation of *paperXML* into the TEI format could be performed using XSLT. Table 1 summarizes mapping of important markup elements. Details of the element and attribute structure differ, which makes a real mapping more complicated than it may seem from the table.

[8] `http://bibtexml.sourceforge.net`

[9] `http://aclbib.opendfki.de`

[10] `http://www.tei-c.org/Guidelines/P5`

TEI element	*paperXML* element
TEI	article
teiHeader	header
author (unstructured)	author (structured)
title	title
div type="abs"	abstract
front	header/abstract
body	body
back	(no correspondance)
div type="ack"	section title= "Acknowledgments"
div type="bib"	references
p	p
head	section title="..."
hi rend="italic"	i
hi rend="bold"	b
hi rend="underline"	u
del type="lb"	- (Unicode soft hyphen)
pb n="52"	page local="7" global="52"
table	table
row	tr
cell	td

Table 1: Element and attribute mapping (incomplete) between *paperXML* and TEI P5

5 Summary and Outlook

We have described a pragmatic and robust solution for generating logical document markup from scholarly papers in PDF format. It is meant as an OCR-based fall-back solution in the ACL Contributed Task *Rediscovering 50 Years of Discoveries* (Schäfer et al., 2012) when the more precise PDFExtract method (Berg et al., 2012) is not applicable because it can only handle born-digital PDF documents. Moreover, the approach can serve as fall-back solution where PDFExtract fails or does not produce markup (e.g. currently tables). Our solution has been shown to work even on typewriter-typeset, scanned papers from the 60ies. Correctness of the produced markup is limited by heuristics that are necessary to select at markup and layout borders, reconstruct reading order, etc. Levenshtein distance is used at several places in order to cope with variants such as those induced by character recognition errors. The approach is implemented to produce XML documents conforming to the *paperXML* DTD that in turn could be transformed to TEI P5 using XSLT.

Acknowledgments

This work has been funded by the German Federal Ministry of Education and Research, projects TAKE (FKZ 01IW08003) and Deependance (FKZ 01IW11003).

References

Berg, Ø. R., Oepen, S., & Read, J. (2012). Towards high-quality text stream extraction from PDF. Technical background to the ACL 2012 Contributed Task. In *Proceedings of the ACL-2012 main conference workshop on Rediscovering 50 Years of Discoveries.* Jeju, Republic of Korea.

Bird, S., Dale, R., Dorr, B., Gibson, B., Joseph, M., Kan, M.-Y., Lee, D., Powley, B., Radev, D., & Tan, Y. F. (2008). The ACL Anthology Reference Corpus: A reference dataset for bibliographic research in computational linguistics. In *Proceedings of the sixth international conference on language resources and evaluation (LREC-08).* Marrakech, Morocco.

Levenshtein, V. I. (1966). Binary codes capable of correcting deletions, insertions, and reversals. *Soviet Physics Doklady*, *10*(8), 707—710.

Schäfer, U., Kiefer, B., Spurk, C., Steffen, J., & Wang, R. (2011). The ACL Anthology Searchbench. In *Proceedings of the ACL-HLT 2011 system demonstrations* (pp. 7–13). Portland, OR.

Schäfer, U., Read, J., & Oepen, S. (2012). Towards an ACL Anthology corpus with logical document structure. An overview of the ACL 2012 contributed task. In *Proceedings of the ACL-2012 main conference workshop on Rediscovering 50 Years of Discoveries.* Jeju, Republic of Korea.

Volk, M., Marek, T., & Sennrich, R. (2010). Reducing OCR errors by combining two OCR systems. In *ECAI-2010 workshop on language technology for cultural heritage, social sciences, and humanities* (pp. 61–65). Lisbon, Portugal.

Weitz, B., & Schäfer, U. (2012). A graphical citation browser for the ACL Anthology. In *Proceedings of the eighth international conference on language resources and evaluation LREC-2012* (pp. 1718–1722). Istanbul, Turkey: ELRA.

Appendix: *paperXML* DTD

```
<!-- paperXML DTD second version as of
     2009-10-16 Ulrich.Schaefer@dfki.de -->

<!ELEMENT article (header, body) >

<!ELEMENT header (file?, pdfmetadata?,
          ocrmetadata?, firstpageheader,
          frontmatter?, abstract) >

<!ELEMENT pdfmetadata (meta)* >

<!ELEMENT ocrmetadata (meta)* >

<!ELEMENT meta EMPTY >
<!ATTLIST meta name    CDATA #REQUIRED
               content CDATA #REQUIRED >

<!ELEMENT firstpageheader (page, title,
          subtitle?, pubinfo?, author*) >

<!ELEMENT frontmatter (p)* >

<!ELEMENT title (#PCDATA) >

<!ELEMENT subtitle (#PCDATA) >

<!ELEMENT pubinfo (#PCDATA) >

<!ELEMENT author (#PCDATA | org)* >
<!ATTLIST author surname    CDATA #IMPLIED
                 middlename CDATA #IMPLIED
                 givenname  CDATA #IMPLIED
                 address    CDATA #IMPLIED
                 email      CDATA #IMPLIED
                 homepage   CDATA #IMPLIED >

<!ELEMENT org EMPTY >
<!ATTLIST org name    CDATA #IMPLIED
              country CDATA #IMPLIED
              city    CDATA #IMPLIED >

<!ELEMENT abstract (#PCDATA | b | i | u |
                   footnote)* >

<!ELEMENT body (section*, references?,
          appendix*) >

<!ELEMENT section (subsection | p | footnote |
          table | figure | page | doubt)* >
<!ATTLIST section number CDATA #IMPLIED
                  title  CDATA #REQUIRED >

<!ELEMENT subsection (subsubsection | p | table|
         footnote | table | figure | doubt)* >
<!ATTLIST subsection number CDATA #IMPLIED
                     title  CDATA #REQUIRED >

<!ELEMENT subsubsection (p | footnote | table |
          figure | page | doubt)* >
<!ATTLIST subsubsection number CDATA #IMPLIED
                        title  CDATA #REQUIRED >

<!ELEMENT references (p | footnote | page |
          doubt)* >

<!ELEMENT appendix (p | footnote | table |
          figure | page | doubt)* >
<!ATTLIST appendix number CDATA #IMPLIED
                   title  CDATA #REQUIRED >

<!ELEMENT p (#PCDATA | page | b | i | u |
          footnote)* >

<!ELEMENT page EMPTY >
<!ATTLIST page local  CDATA #REQUIRED
               global CDATA #IMPLIED >

<!-- boldface -->
<!ELEMENT b (#PCDATA | i | u | footnote)* >

<!-- italics -->
<!ELEMENT i (#PCDATA | b | u | footnote)* >

<!-- underlined -->
<!ELEMENT u (#PCDATA | i | b | footnote)* >

<!ELEMENT footnote (#PCDATA) >
<!ATTLIST footnote label  NMTOKEN #IMPLIED
                   anchor NMTOKEN #IMPLIED >

<!-- text that is probably not sentential -->
<!ELEMENT doubt (#PCDATA) >
<!ATTLIST doubt alpha     CDATA #REQUIRED
                length    CDATA #REQUIRED
                tooSmall  CDATA #REQUIRED
                monospace CDATA #REQUIRED >

<!ELEMENT figure (#PCDATA | p)* >
<!ATTLIST figure caption CDATA #IMPLIED >

<!-- rest is HTML-like table markup -->
<!ELEMENT table (tr)* >
<!ATTLIST table caption CDATA #IMPLIED
                class   CDATA #IMPLIED
                frame   CDATA #IMPLIED
                rules   CDATA #IMPLIED
                border  CDATA #IMPLIED
                regular CDATA #IMPLIED >

<!ELEMENT tr (td)* >
<!ATTLIST tr class CDATA #IMPLIED >

<!ELEMENT td (p)* >
<!ATTLIST td class   CDATA #IMPLIED
             rowspan CDATA #IMPLIED
             colspan CDATA #IMPLIED >
```

Linking Citations to their Bibliographic references

Huy Do Hoang Nhat
Web IR / NLP Group (WING)
National University of Singapore
huydo@comp.nus.edu.sg

Praveen Bysani
Web IR / NLP Group (WING)
National University of Singapore
bpraveen@comp.nus.edu.sg

Abstract

In this paper we describe our participation in the contributed task at ACL Special workshop 2012. We contribute to the goal of enriching the textual content of ACL Anthology by identifying the citation contexts in a paper and linking them to their corresponding references in the bibliography section. We use Parscit, to process the Bibliography of each paper. Pattern matching heuristics are then used to connect the citations with their references. Furthermore, we prepared a small evaluation dataset, to test the efficiency of our method. We achieved 95% precision and 80% recall on this dataset.

1 Introduction

ACL Anthology represents the enduring effort to digitally archive all the publications related to CL and NLP, over the years. Recent work by (Bird et al., 2008) to standardize the corpus in ACL Anthology, makes it more than just a digital repository of research results. The corpus has metadata information such as 'title', 'author (s)', 'publication venue' and 'year' about each paper along with their extracted text content. However it lacks vital information about a scientific article such as position of footnote (s), table (s) and figure captions, bibliographic references, italics/emphasized text portions, non-latin scripts, etc.

We would like to acknowledge funding support in part by the Global Asia Institute under grant no. GAI-CP/20091116 and from the National Research Foundations grant no. R-252-000-325-279.

The special workshop at ACL 2012, celebrates 50 years of ACL legacy by gathering contributions about the history, evolution and future of computational linguistics. Apart from the technical programme, the workshop also hosts a contributed task to enrich the current state of Anthology corpus. A rich-text format of the corpus will serve as a source of study for research applications like citation analysis, summarization, argumentative zoning among many others.

We contribute to this effort of enriching the Anthology, by providing a means to link citations in an article to their corresponding bibliographic references. Robert Dale [1] defines *citation*, as a text string in the document body that points to a *reference* at the end of the document. Several citations may co-refer to a single reference string. As an example consider the following sentence,

> Few approaches to parsing have tried to handle disfluent utterances (notable exceptions are *Core & Schubert, 1999; Hindle, 1983; Nakatani & Hirschberg, 1994).*

The portion of texts in *italics* are the citations and we intend to annotate each citation with an unique identifier of their bibliographic reference.

```
<ref target="BI10">Hindle, 1983</ref>
```

Such annotations are useful for navigating between research articles and creating citation networks among them. These networks can be used to understand the bibliometric analysis of a corpus.

[1] http://web.science.mq.edu.au/ rdale/

2 Design

The task organizers distribute the entire Anthology in two different XML formats, 'paperXML' that is obtained from Optical Character Recognition (OCR) software and 'TEI P5 XML' that is generated by PDFExtract (ϕyvind Raddum Berg, 2011). We chose to process the PDFExtract format as it has no character recognition errors. Since the expected output should also follow 'TEI P5' guidelines, the latter input simplifies the process of target XML generation. The task of linking citations to references primarily consists of three modules.

1. Processing the 'Bibliography' section of a paper using Parscit.
2. Formatting the Parscit output to TEI P5 guidelines and merging it with the input XML.
3. Generating an identifier and citation marker for each reference and annotating the text.

Figure 1 illustrates the overall design of our work. Below we describe in detail about the modules used to accomplish this task.

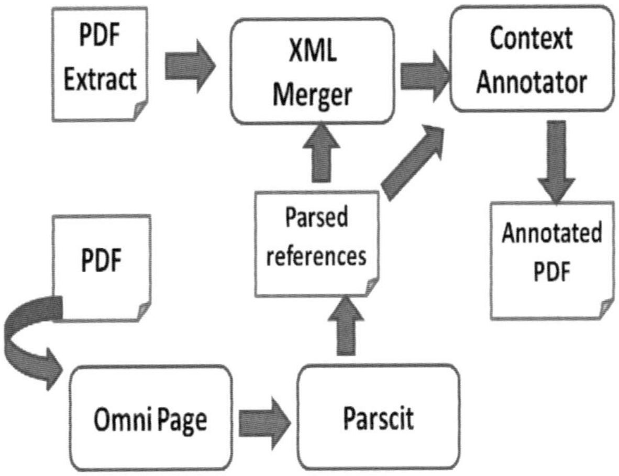

Figure 1: Overall design for linking citation text to references

Bibliography Parser: Parscit (Councill et al., 2008) is a freely available, open-source implementation of a reference string parsing package. It formulates this task as a sequence labelling problem that is common to a large set of NLP tasks including POS tagging and chunking. Parscit uses a conditional random field formalism to learn a supervised model and apply it on unseen data. During training, each reference is represented using different classes of features such as n-gram, token identity, punctuation and other numeric properties. Parscit can label each reference with 13 classes that correspond to common fields used in bibliographic reference management software. Unlike heuristic methods, Parscit's supervised learning model can handle different standards followed by different communities and inadvertent manual errors in the Bibliography. Prior to processing, Parscit segments the Bibliography section from the rest of the paper using SectLabel (Luong et al., 2010), its extension for logical document structure discovery.

Parscit works either with plain text or the Omnipage output of a paper. Omnipage [2] is a state of the art OCR engine that provides detailed information about the layout of a document. Omnipage also handles older, scanned papers. It gives the logical index of every line in terms of page, column, paragraph, and line number. The layout information is used by Parscit to remove noise such as page numbers and footnotes between references and properly divide them. Following is the Omnipage output for the word "Rahul Agarwal" in the original pdf,

```
<ln l="558" t="266" r="695" b="284"
  bold=true  superscript="none"
  fontSize="1250" fontFamily="roman">
 <wd l="558" t="266" r="609" b="284">
   Rahul </wd> <space/>
 <wd l="619" t="266" r="695" b="283">
   Agarwal </wd>
</ln>
```

The 'l' (left), 'r' (right), 't' (top), 'b' (bottom) attributes gives the exact location of an element in a page. Further, features such as 'bold', 'underlined', 'superscript/ subscript' and 'fontFamily' contribute towards an accurate identification and parsing of references. For example, the change from one font family to another usually serves as a separator between two different fields like 'author' and 'title' of the paper. As PDFExtract currently does not provide such information, we processed the original 'pdf' file using Omnipage and then finally parsed it using Parscit. Below is the XML output from Parscit for a single reference,

[2] www.nuance.com/omnipage/

```
<citation valid="true">
<authors>
 <author>R Agarwal</author>
 <author>L Boggess</author>
</authors>
<title>A simple but useful approach
to conjunct identification.</title>
<date>1992</date>
<marker>Agarwal, Boggess, 1992
</marker>  </citation>
```

We used Parscit to segment the Bibliography section into individual references. Additionally we use the author, title, publication year information together with the original marker of each reference to generate citation markers that are used to find the context of each reference (explained later). During this process, we generated the Omnipage output for the present Anthology that consists of 21,107 publications. As the ACL ARC has Omnipage outputs only till 2007, our contribution will help to update the corpus.

XML Merger: The original XML output from Parscit doesn't conform with the TEI P5 guidelines. The 'XML Merger' module formats the Parscit output into a 'listBibl' element and merges it with the PDFExtract. The 'listBibl' element contains a list of 'biblStruct' elements, in which bibliographic sub-elements of each reference appear in a specified order. Each reference is also assigned a 'unique id' within the paper to link them with their citation texts. The Bibliography section in the PDFExtract is replaced with the TEI compatible Parscit output such as below,

```
<listBibl>
 <bibl xml:id="BI2">
  <monogr>
  <author>R Agarwal</author>
  <author>L Boggess</author>
  <title>A simple but useful approach
   to conjunct identification.</title>
  <imprint>
   <date>1992</date>
  </imprint>
  </monogr>
 </bibl>
```

To ensure a proper insertion, we search for labels such as "References", "Bibliography", "References and Notes", or common variations of those strings. In the case of having more than one match, the context of first reference is used to resolve the ambiguity. The match is considered as the starting point of the Bibliography section, and the terminal reference string from the Parscit output is used to mark the end of it. After validating the matched portion based on the position of its starting and ending markers, it is replaced with the formatted 'listBibl' element.

Context Annotator: The final step is to bridge the links between references and citation strings in the merged XML. Several morphologically different markers are generated for each reference based on the 'author' and 'publication year' information provided by Parscit. These markers are used to find the corresponding citation string in the merged XML. The markers may vary depending upon the number of authors in a reference or the bibliography style of the paper. Sample markers for a reference with multiple authors are listed below,

```
Author1, Author2, Author3, Year
Author1 et.al, Year
Author1 and Author2, Year
```

Although Parscit provide the citation markers for each reference, the recall is very low. We extended these citation markers to make them more robust and thus improve the overall recall. Below are the extensions we made to the default markers.

1. Additional marker to allow square brackets and round brackets in the parentheses. Such markers help to identify citations such as (Author, Year), [Author, Year], (Author, [year])

2. Parscit markers only identify the citations with the 4-digit format of the year. We modified it to recognize both 4-digit and 2-digit format of the year. *e.g. Lin, 1996 and Lin, 96*

3. Parscit doesn't differentiate between identical reference strings with same author and year information. We resolved it by including the version number of the reference in the marker. *e.g. Lin, 2004a and Lin, 2004b*

4. Heuristics are added to accommodate the default citation texts as specified in the reference strings. For example in the reference string,

[Appelt85] Appelt, D. 1985 Planning English Referring Expressions. Artificial Intelligence 26: 1-33.

[Appelt85] is identified as the citation marker. Each marker is represented using a regular expression. These regular expressions are applied on the text from merged XML. The matches are annotated with the unique id of its corresponding reference such as '<ref target= BI10>'

3 Challenges

The accuracy of Parscit is a bottle-neck for the performance of this task. The false negatives produced by Parscit leads to erroneous linkage between citation texts and reference ids. In certain cases Parscit fails to identify portions of Bibliography section and skips them while processing. This results in an incorrect parsing and thus faulty linkage. Apart from Parscit, we faced problems due to the character mismatching between Omnipage and PDFExtract outputs of a paper. For example the string 'Pulman' is recognized as Pullan by Omnipage and as Pulman by PDFExtract. The citation markers generated from Parscit output in this case fails to identify the context in the PDFExtract.

4 Evaluation

As there is no dataset to test the efficiency of our method, we prepared a small dataset for evaluation purposes. We manually sampled 20 papers from the Anthology, making sure that all the publication venues are included. The citation strings in each paper are manually listed out along with the corresponding reference id. For citation styles where no Author and Year information is present, we used the contextual words to identify the citation text. The citation strings are listed in the same order as they appear in the paper. Below we provide an extract of the dataset, consisting of papers with three different citation styles,

```
P92-1006   proposed [13]      BI13
T87-1018   Mann&Thompson83    BI6
W00-0100   Krymolowski 1998   BI9
```

The first column is the Anthology id of the paper, second column is the citation string from the paper and third column is the unique id of the reference. We measure the performance in terms of precision and recall of the recognized citations. There are a total of 330 citation strings in the dataset. Our method identified 280 strings as citations, out of which 266 are correct. Hence the precision is 0.95 (266/280) and the recall is 0.801 (266/330). The low recall is due to the incorrect recognition of author and year strings by Parscit which lead to erroneous marker generation. The precision is affected due to the flaws in Parscit while differentiating citations with naked numbers.

In future we plan to devise more flexible markers which can handle spelling mistakes, using edit distance metric. Partial matches and sub-sequence matches need to be incorporated to support long distance citations. Parscit can further be improved to accurately parse and identify the reference strings.

Acknowledgements

We would like to thank Dr. Min-Yen Kan at National University of Singapore for his valuable support and guidance during this work.

References

Steven Bird, Robert Dale, Bonnie J. Dorr, Bryan Gibson, Mark T. Joseph, Min yen Kan, Dongwon Lee, Brett Powley, Dragomir R. Radev, and Yee Fan Tan. 2008. The acl anthology reference corpus: A reference dataset for bibliographic research in computational linguistics.

Isaac G. Councill, C. Lee Giles, and Min yen Kan. 2008. Parscit: An open-source crf reference string parsing package. In *International Language Resources and Evaluation*. European Language Resources Association.

Minh-Thang Luong, Thuy-Dung Nguyen, and Min-Yen Kan. 2010. Logical structure recovery in scholarly articles with rich document features. *International Journal of Digital Library Systems*, 1(4):1–23.

ϕyvind Raddum Berg. 2011. High precision text extraction from PDF documents.

Author Index

Association for Computational Linguistics
209 N. Eighth Street
Stroudsburg, Pennsylvania 18360

CURRAN ASSOCIATES INC
proceedings.com

Workshop on Linguistic Distances 2006

Held in conjunction with COLING/ACL 2006

Sydney, Australia
23 July 2006

ISBN: 978-1-61738-507-0